THE RIG-VEDIC AND POST-RIG-VEDIC POLITY

(1500 BCE - 500 BCE)

R.U. S. PRASAD, Ph.D

VERNON PRESS

Dedicated to my son Shantanu

For his human qualities

---

www.vernonpress.com

In the Americas:
Vernon Press
1000 N West Street,
Suite 1200, Wilmington,
Delaware 19801
United States

In the rest of the world
Vernon Press
C/Sancti Espiritu 17,
Malaga, 29006
Spain

Library of Congress Control Number: 2015934785

ISBN 978-1-62273-036-0

Table of Contents

Acknowledgements 7

Foreword 11

Abbreviations 13

Preface 15

Chapter I Introduction 19

- Vedic Age (1500 BCE- 500 BCE) 19
- Dating of the Ṛgveda 31
- Timeline of the later Vedic Texts 34
- Composition of the Ṛgveda and other Vedic texts - Possible locations 35

Chapter II Sources of Study and Methodology 39

Chapter III Development of Vedic Canon and Polity 43

Chapter IV Vedic Concepts of Nationalism and Sovereignty 53

Chapter V Vedic Rāṣṭra 59

Chapter VI Important Ṛgvedic Tribes 65

- a) Anus 68
- b) Druhyus 69
- c) Pūrus: 70
- d) Turvaśas 71
- e) Yadus 72
- f) Other Ṛgvedic Tribes 73

Chapter VII Vedic Grid 83

Chapter VIII The Post-Ṛgvedic Tribes 87

Chapter IX Political System and Institutions during the Rig-Vedic and Post Rig-Vedic Periods 93

a) Institution of Kingship 97

b) Origin of Kingship 99

c) Selection or Election of a King 103

d) Deposition of a King 104

e) The King's Consecration 105

f) The King's Duties 106

g) Subsidiary Political Institutions and Administrative Apparatus 107

Chapter X Ṛgvedic and Post Ṛgvedic Social Practices 117

a) Social Characteristics 117

b) Status of Women 120

c) Varṇa System 123

Chapter XI Vedic Values and Religious Practices 127

a) Concept of Ṛta 127

b) Cult of Sacrifice 128

Chapter XII Tribal Kingdoms 133

a) The Kuru-Pañcālas Ascendancy 133

b) Kosala-Videha Realm 138

Chapter XIII Features of the Post Ṛgvedic Period 139

Chapter XIV Second Urbanization 143

Chapter XV Summary and Conclusions 147

Appendix I 155

a) Vedic Aryans- Migrants or Indigenous 155

b) Vedic Aryans and the Harappan Culture 157

Appendix II 163

1) The Ṛgveda (RV) 164

2) The Yajur-Veda (YV) 167

3) The Sāma-Veda (SV) 168

4) The Atharva-Veda (AV) 168

5) The Brāhmaṇas 173

6) The Āraṇyakas 175

7) The Upaniṣads 175

8) The Sūtras (Approx. 500-200 B.C.) 179

Bibliography 183

Glossary 195

Index 201

List of Tables

Table I: Anus 69

Table II: Druyhus 70

TableIII: Pūrus 71

Table IV: Turvaśas 72

Table V: Yadus 72

Table VI: Other Ṛgvedic Tribes 73

Table VII: Summary of Post Ṛgvedic Tribes 87

Table VIII: The Vedas 170

List of Maps

Map 1: Rig-Vedic Tribes - Geographical Location 83

Map 2: Rig-Vedic Tribes/ Kings or Chieftains/Priestly Families 84

Map 3: Name of Rig-Vedic Tribes/Books of Rig-Veda 85

Map 4: Post Rig-Vedic Tribes 91

Acknowledgements

Through the ages, the Vedas have been regarded to contain the quintessence of India's wisdom, philosophical speculation and spiritual practices. What makes the Vedic texts unique among the ancient scriptures is their multi-dimensional and all-encompassing approach in dealing with matters falling in spiritual and material domain. Max Müller describes the Vedas as an 'oasis in the vast desert of ancient Asiatic history' where ' we come across a stratum of ancient thought, of ancient feelings, hopes, joys and fears of ancient religion'.

Having been brought up in traditional Indian value system, where we studied religious scriptures at home even when we pursued formal and more Western –oriented education in school/college environment, the enigma of the Vedas invariably appeared as something beyond comprehension. The latent desire to understand the various aspects of the Vedas and what they postulate, provided the necessary stimulus to go deeper into the subject.

It was a pursuit of this passion which initially brought me in touch with Professor S.K. Shukla of the Department of Special Sanskrit Studies, Jawaharlal Nehru University, Delhi. I acknowledge with gratitude his help in refreshing my knowledge of Sanskrit and providing me his perspective on the subject as also access to books in the Sanskrit library. I, however, plunged into the research work with much greater vigor after I joined as an Associate in the Department of South Asian Studies, Harvard University.

I would like to record my deep sense of gratitude to Professor Michael Witzel, Wales Professor of Sanskrit and Director Graduate Studies, Department of South Asian Studies, Harvard University who guided me in numerous ways to navigate through this complex subject. His support at each stage of the work has been invaluable which he extended unhesitatingly despite his extremely busy schedule and other important commitments. But for his encouragement and active help at all stages, including going through the manuscript several times, it would not have been possible to write this book.

I also record my sense of gratitude to Professor Hermann Kulke (em), Kiel University, Germany, Professor Patrick Olivelle, ex-Professor of Sanskrit and Indian Religions, University of Texas at Austin, Professor

Noboru Karashima (em) University of Tokyo, and Professor Edwin Bryant, Rutgers State University of New Jersey, for sparing their valuable time to go through the manuscript and for their comments. Professor Kulke's suggestions helped me considerably in improving the manuscript. I have also benefitted from interaction with various other scholars particularly, Prof Francis X. Clooney, Parkman Professor of Divinity and Professor of Comparative Theology and Director of the Center for the Study of World Religions, Harvard, Princeton's Professor Richard Fox Young, Timby Chair, History of Religions and Professor D.N Jha Ex-Head of the Department of History, Delhi University. I also acknowledge with gratitude the support and encouragement I received from Professor P. Patil, Chairperson, Department of South Asian Studies, Harvard University.

My thanks are also due to Ms Jane Gray, former Administrator and her successor Ms Cheryl, Department of South Asian Studies, for providing me the requisite facilities which helped me in the completion of my research project. I have no words to express my thanks to the staff of Widener, Tozzer, Law School and Kennedy School libraries of Harvard University for providing reading and borrowing facilities of primary and secondary literature and allied material connected with the subject of my research. I acknowledge with gratitude the contributions of Rosario Batana and Monica Ternero, Vernon Press for ensuring publication of this book in a very short time.

In writing this book I also received help from the works of numerous other scholars which find duly referenced in this book. I would like to gratefully acknowledge the benefit and assistance I derived from these works, particularly in formulating my approach to the subject. My gratitude is also due to reviewers whose comments have been very helpful in shaping this work.

I am dedicating this book to my son Shantanu who has been a pillar of strength and support to me all through. His wife Rima also contributed by providing logistic support. I am thankful to my two sons-in law, Kumar Sanjeev and Kunal for sharing their perspective with me on the subject. I also acknowledge my two daughters, Vandana for being a source of encouragement and Shivi, for helping me in various ways in giving a final shape to this work. Last but not the least, the support of my wife Kanchan has been the most crucial in all stages of this work, from the beginning to its completion without which it would not have been possible to take the work to its logical conclusion.

Foreword

This remarkable book, entitled *Rig-Vedic and Post-Vedic Polity,* deals with the oldest Indian polities that we can ascertain in the extant texts, that is the Vedas. For the first time in this context, Dr. R.U.S. Prasad (carrying out post-doctoral research as an Associate of the Dept. of South Asian Studies) makes use of a robust framework of time and place, without which any study on the Vedic period gets lost in the vast spaces of Northern India and over period of many uncharted centuries.

He clearly defines the five linguistic and textual layers of Vedic texts, from the Rigveda down to the Upanishads and early Vedic Sutras, and he attributes these texts to certain areas, ranging from eastern Afghanistan to the borders of Bengal and Orissa.

Based on this framework, his study unravels various historical developments that took place in a certain area at a certain time and their spread to neighboring areas. A typical example is the emergence of Kuru dominance with its Vedic orthopraxy and its subsequent spread eastwards to the Panchalas and beyond.

This approach helps enormously in demarcating the change from the tribal, pastoral society of the Rigveda to the emergence of the first large confederacy, that of the Kuru-Pancalas. It also allows to delineate its further impact on the eastern areas (Kosala, Videha in northern Bihar) which were induced by Sanskritization sponsored by the local nobility and rulers, and which led to the adoption of the Kuru model.

R.U.S. Prasad clearly brings out the role that the alliance between Ksatriyas and Brahmins (brahmakshatra) played in establishing and perpetuating the Kuru model that has dominated the other two classes (the Vaishya and Shudra varna) ever since, in fact until today.

In this context, he also deals with the incipient system of specialized occupations that finally lead to the early-post-Vedic caste system, and he highlights the role of women during the Vedic and in the newly emerging post-Vedic, Hindu society.

I congratulate him for this innovative book and expect that it will be well received.

Michael Witzel

Wales Professor of Sanskrit &
Director of Graduate Studies,
Department of South Asian Studies
Harvard University

Abbreviations

AB	Aitareya -Brāhmaṇa
ĀDS	Āpastamba- Dharmasūtra
AV	Atharva-Veda
AA	Aitareya Āraṇyaka
BD	Baudhāyana- Dharmasūtra
BSS	Baudhāyana - Śrautasūtra
BAU	Bṛhadāraṇyaka-Upaniṣad
CU	Chāndogya- Upaniṣad
GD	Gautama-Dharmasūtra
GB	Gopatha- Brāhmaṇa
JAOS	Journal of American Oriental Society
JB	Jaiminīya- Brāhmaṇa
JRAS	Journal of the Royal Asiatic Society
KU	Kauśitakī- Upaniṣad
KB	Kauśitakī-Brāhmaṇa
KS	Kaṭhaka- Saṃhitā
KSS	Kātyāyana-Śrautasūtra
MS	Maitrāyaṇī Saṃhitā
PB	Pañcaviṃśa-Brāhmaṇa
PS	Paippalāda Saṃhitā (composed in Eastern Punjab and Haryana in Kuru land under the Kuru kings.
RV	Ṛgveda (or Rig-Veda)
SB	Śatapatha Brāhmaṇa
SGS	Śāṅkhāyana Gṛhyasūtra
SS	Śrauta Sūtra

SV	Sāma-Veda
TB	Taittirīya Brāhmaṇa
TA	Taittirīya Āraṇyaka
TS	Taittirīya- Saṃhitā
VD	Vasiṣtha- Dharmasūtra
VS	Vājasaneyi-Saṃhitā
YV	Yajur-Veda

Preface

A study of Vedic polity is a daunting task. We are looking at a period centuries before Common Era, without any recorded history or chronology, or vestige of archaeological findings. The only material that is available to us is in political and religious literature. These limitations render the task of a proper analysis and assessment of evidence difficult.

After Sayana, one of the early commentators on the Vedas, who flourished in the 14th century A.D., there was a gap in the study of Vedic literature. Some efforts were made in this direction during the 18th century. However, it was not until the early 19th century that we come across any serious attempt to unravel India's ancient past – particularly the nature of polity, institutions, and social life that flourished during the Vedic period.

The 19th and the early 20th centuries witnessed a surge of interest from western scholars in ancient Indian literature and a body of scholarly writings emerged covering particularly, the Vedic texts. Among them, Henry Thomas Colebrooke was perhaps the first to introduce the Vedas to the western world through his Paper on the Vedas contributed to the Asiatic Researches in 1805[1]. It was only a matter of time for others to follow suit. Although the list is long, some of the notable treatises that need to be mentioned include Rudolph Roth's "*Zur Litteratur und Geschichte des Weda*" or "On the Literature and History of the Veda" that was published in 1840; Theodor Aufrecht's "*The hymns of the Rgveda*" Max Müller's "*A History of Ancient Sanskrit Literature*;" A.A. Macdonell's "*A History of Sanskrit Literature and Hymns from the Rgveda*;" John Muir's "*Original Sanskrit Texts on the Origin and History of the People of India, their Religion and Institutions*;" Maurice Bloomfield's "*Hymns of Atharva-Veda*;" Hermann Oldenberg's Vedic Hymns translated (Sacred Books of the East, Vol. 46, part II); Hermann Grassmann's "*Rgveda*;" Alfred Ludwig's "*Der Rigveda oder die heiligen Hymnen der Brahmana*;" R.T. H. Griffith's "*The Hymns of the Rigveda*;" K.F. Geldner's "*Der Rgveda*;" W.D. Whitney's "*Atharva-Veda Samhita*;" A.B. Keith's "*The Veda of the Black Yajus School*;" and A.B. Keith and A. A. Macdonell's "*Vedic Index of Names and Subjects.*"

[1] Asiatic Researches, Vol.8, Cal, 1805; pp.369-474

These seminal works provide a brilliant exposition and understanding of the Vedic and later Vedic texts but their focus was more on the literary and religious aspects of the Indian mind. Upinder Singh[2] an eminent historian has succinctly observed that "a major contribution of these scholars lay in their efforts to collect, edit and translate ancient Indian texts" and " the Brahmanical perspective of ancient Sanskrit texts was often uncritically taken as reflecting the Indian past". Looking at the Vedic texts from a purely religious lens and disguising political features as a part of religious practice did not do full justice to the political content of these texts. Instead, they merely strengthened the impression that the Indian polity during the Vedic period was devoid of political features. The great Indian savants such as Bal Gangadhar Tilak, Maharshi Dayanand and R.G. Bhandarkar, who aroused political consciousness and national awareness in the country through their writings, also encouraged people to appreciate the relevance of ancient texts, particularly the Vedas, for uplifting the tenor of economic, social and political life. Following up on their writings successive generations of Indian scholars, such as P.V. Kane, R.N. Dandekar, V.S. Ghate, S.P. Pandita, R.C. Datta, N.C. Bandyopadhaya, R.C. Mozumdar, K.P.Jayaswal, A.S. Altekar, U.N. Ghoshal, Beni Prasad, R.S. Sharma,V.P. Varma and H.N. Sinha, Romila Thapar to name a few who, in their writings, attempted to deal with the historiography of ancient India in a balanced perspective and some of them also tried to isolate various facets of polity from the overwhelming religious character of the Vedic texts. As Upinder Singh has further observed that the "Indian scholars of the late 19th and the first half of the 20th centuries [...] were responsible for meticulously weaving together data from texts, inscriptions, coins and other material remains to amplify the contours of the ancient Indian past". Recent writings of some western scholars such as John Spellman (Political theory of Ancient India), Wilhelm Rau (Staat und Gessellschaft), Hartmut Scharfe (The State in Indian Tradition), Michael Witzel, J.B.S. Kuiper, Edwin Bryant, Walter S. Fairservis, J.C. Heesterman, Rainer Stuhrmann, Christopher Minkowski, James Santucci , Harry Falk, Patrick Olivelle, Hermann Kulke, Theodore Nicolas Proferes, Jarrod L. Whitaker etc. display a more intensive and balanced approach towards evaluating different aspects of Vedic literature.

---

[2] Upinder Singh, A History of Ancient and Early Medieval India-From the Stone Age to the 12th Century, Pearson Education, a Division of Dorling Kindersley (India) Pvt. Ltd., Delhi, 2009, p. 7-8

However, most of the early books on the subject focused more on examination and interpretation of religious practices and the metaphysical side of the Indian mind. The later works have tried to correct the imbalance by isolating political aspects from the essentially religious character of these texts. In the chain of such works, this book attempts to provide a focused treatment of the Ṛgvedic and post Ṛgvedic polity and deals with the relevant and connected issues in a holistic manner.

The book is about the Vedic Aryans, the various stages involved in their progression from the Ṛgvedic period to the post Ṛgvedic period and how this progression was reflected in their polity, and social, religious and cultural life. The book is also about the interaction between the distinct way of life pursued by the Vedic Aryans and the indigenous people with whom they came in contact and how this interaction initiated a process of acculturation between the two societies.

The Vedic civilization has carved out a niche for itself as we traverse through various phases of Indian history from the ancient to the medieval and further to the modern periods. Its importance lies not so much in the number of battles a chieftain/king fought and won, or in the territories that they acquired, but in the ideas, systems and values that they developed and the institutions that they created.

The book critically examines the nature of Vedic polity, the functionalities of its various institutions, and the Vedic social and religious practices. That includes the institution of kingship, government machinery, role of various entities including Purohita, the Sabhā and the Samiti, position of women, the institution of Varṇa and progression of Brahmins and Kṣatriyas in the social hierarchy and features of tribal kingdoms, such as Kuru-Pañcālas and Kosala-Videhas. It outlines in historical perspective the various stages involved in the development of Vedic canon and polity and how the two processes have gone along together in successive stages. What emerges from this study is a vibrant civilization nurtured by the Vedic Aryans on the Indian subcontinent, which also sowed the seeds of institutions that flowered in the later periods.

Further, the available details of each of the tribes (around 50 odd tribes) including the location of their habitat, their time line, the names of their chieftains and their linkage with priestly clans have been provided. Such details along with linkages in a consolidated form at one place are generally not available. Construction of a Vedic grid and its graphic representation is a unique feature of the book. The grid focuses on the relative order of Ṛgvedic hymns, representing the collections of various priestly clans, relationship of the various tribes and priestly clans to the books of Ṛgveda, geographical features of tribal settlements and linking the same with a chronological grid of poets and chieftains identified from the hymns. The Vedic grid is designed to bring greater clarity and evoke a better understanding of the Vedic polity.

Besides, a discussion on the various facets of the Ṛgvedic and post Ṛgvedic polity, including a separate treatment of the Vedic concepts of nationalism, sovereignty and 'Raṣṭra' (or nation), the book also focuses on the Second Urbanization that occurred between the sixth and the fourth centuries B.C.E, along the Ganges valley. Additionally, the book (Appendix I) briefly references the discussions on Aryan migration and the relationship of the Vedic Aryans with the Harappan culture. Further, a brief outline of Vedic literature, including their subject-matter and the relative importance of deities, judged from the number of times they are invoked in the Vedic hymns in a tabular form, have also been provided in Appendix II.

The book tracks the experiences of Vedic Aryans from primitive times when they struggled to find food and shelter, through intermediate phases as they built the contours of civilized living before finally emerging as a developed civilization in various aspects. These phases are not unique to Vedic Aryans but all the great civilizations have passed through such stages.

An attempt has been made in the book to show with due corroboration that the tribal polity was not deficient in political content contrary to the view held by some scholars to depict Vedic Aryans as apolitical and inward looking. Taking a cue from the previous scholarship and recent writings on the subject and literary evidence available through Vedic and allied literature, the book attempts to provide an insight into the level of attainments of Vedic Aryans in a variety of spheres, evolving from the tribal pastoral stage to a developed stage and bequeathing the Vedic corpus, a legacy of perennial value for mankind

It is not for me to indicate the extent to which I have succeeded in this endeavour. In this matter, the readers would be in the best position to make their assessment.

Chapter I
Introduction

"The Vedas, I feel convinced, will occupy scholars for centuries to come, and we take and maintain forever, its position as the most ancient of books in the library of mankind".

- Friedrich Max Müller

Vedic Age (1500 BCE- 500 BCE)

The story of Vedic India begins with the demise of mature Harappan phase around 1900 BCE and ingress of Aryans in successive batches around 1500 BCE into the northwestern region of the Indian sub-continent. The collapse of the mature Harappan phase was triggered most likely by ecological or tectonic reasons. The Harappan civilization was urban centric with well laid out urban settlements and a high level of cultural organization. The disintegration of the urban phase, scholars believe, occurred in a progressive manner and involved an eastward drift of population to regions corresponding to modern Saurashtra, Haryana and Delhi where some elements of the Harappan culture still survived. The settlements in these regions, however, do not provide any conclusive evidence for survival of any critical feature of the Harappan culture, such as, international trade, seals, drainage system etc. In fact, the post-urban phase witnessed a return to, what Allchin calls, the material culture 'closer to that of the pre-urban stage.'[3] The demise of this civilization also had another important fall-out. With the disappearance of the semblance of economic and political unity, which the mature Harappan phase represented, a power vacuum was created in the region to the northwest of India. This presented an opportunity for incursions by the pastoralist Vedic tribes who ventured into the region around 1500 BCE. Later they moved to areas along the river Yamuna and even the Ganges as can be inferred from the later vedic texts. The network of Vedic tribes was thus established in the entire region which would correspond to the area of the Greater Panjab up to Delhi and the upper Ganges as well as adjacent areas in Afghanistan.

---

[3] The Archaeology of Early Historic South Asia- the emergence of city and states: Allchin F.R., Cambridge University Press, 1995. P.38

The question of the origin of the Vedic Aryans is a hotly debated issue among the scholars and it continues to be so. This issue has been discussed in detail in Appendix I of the book. There is, no meeting point between the nationalist discourse which regards the Vedic Aryans as indigenous people, and the protagonists of migration theory who hold that the Vedic Aryans came from outside. There is, however, a broad consensus among the scholars which favours their migration from the Central Asian region. The movement of Vedic Aryans from this region, it is believed, was actuated by their desire to escape from harsh living conditions they faced and a search for a more hospitable terrain to elk out a living. This seems plausible since even Alexander[4] during his campaign had to encounter the rigours of inhospitable terrain of the Central Asian region and serious logistical crisis, when he led his troops early in the spring of 329 BCE, north across the Hindukush into Bactria. This was the first of many such disasters he encountered due to "exceptionally harsh weather and rugged terrain of the area". Initially, the Vedic tribes were confined to areas surrounding Afghan mountains as the older books of the Ṛgveda (Books 4 and 6) seem to suggest. This region, where they initially settled had semi-arid climate and suffered from paucity of rain. This did not present to them as an ideal location for their settlement and soon they moved eastwards in search of arable land and better pastures along the lower Himalayan foothills. Finally, they found the vast expanse of the Sapta-Sindhu[5] region which covers the northwestern plank of the Indian sub-continent as suitable for their settlement. The region was endowed with availability of water on a regular basis and a salubrious climate which the Aryans found very attractive for pursuing their pastoral profession in an unhindered manner. The climatic factors and the availability of water seem to have been a crucial and determining element in the movement of the Indo-Aryan speaking tribes in successive stages. Discussing the

---

[4] The geographical situation of Central Asia as described in *The LandMark Arrian (The Campaigns of Alexander)* Ed. James Romm , Pantheon Books, New York, 2010 (A new translation by Pamela Mensch).

[5] The standard list of rivers included under the expression Sapta-Sindhu fluctuates.It is common to identify this expression with seven rivers, namely, Kubhā(Kabul), Sindhu(the Indus), Vitastā (Jhelum), Asiknī(Chenab), Paruṣṇī (Ravi), Vipāś (Beas) and Śutudrī (Sutlej). These rivers along with rivers Sarasvati and Gomal (Gomati) find mention in the Book X hymn 75 of the Rig-Veda but the river Vipāś (Beas) is missing here.

importance of water availability, Harry Falk[6] has attributed this as a factor in the movement of the Indo-Aryan tribes from the Central Asian region "fed by the melting snows for a short time in spring with changing quantities from year to year" to the region along the Sapta-Sindhu fed by perennial rivers drawing water from the melting Himalayan snow. The availability of regular water supply haunted the Aryans again when they moved towards east in the Madhyadesa region (Uttar Pradesh and surrounding areas), where they had to face the uncertainties of monsoon rains. The mythology regarding Indra's (Warrior god) victory over the cosmic serpent Vṛtra resulting in liberation of waters, underscores the importance of water availability for Vedic Aryans for meeting their economic needs as also performance of rituals. This event also led to personification of Indra as a god of the rains.

The other credible reason for the movement of the Indo-Aryans from the Central Asian region could have been the demise of the urban civilization that flourished in the Indus Valley and the abandonment of settlements in the Indus and Sarasvati[7] regions. The course of infiltration towards the north-west region initially and from there to fertile plains eastwards was, perhaps, actuated by the search for better pastures and arable land that was more conducive to the production of crops such as, rice and millet.

However, on coming to the north-west region of India, the Aryan tribes encountered antagonism from both man and nature. First, they had to struggle to secure their existence from the original inhabitants who offered resistance; secondly, they had to devise formulae for overcoming the vagaries of nature. To meet the first challenge, required better leadership, formidable (perceived as *manly*) warriors and more effective resources.

The use of horses and light-spoked wheel chariots which they had brought, helped them to outmanouvre their opponents when faced with

---

6 "The Purpose of Rig-Vedic Ritual": H.Falk in *Inside the Texts Beyond the Texts,* Harvard Oriental Series, Opera Minora Vol.II, Cambridge 1997.

7 Sarasvati is believed to have been a mighty river during the Vedic period and finds mention several times in the Ṛgveda. This river is believed to have originated from the Shivalik hills in the Panjab (India) and ran its full course parallel to the Indus river before emptying itself in the Rann of Kutch. Recent researches associate this river with a palaeo channel, a dried up river bed and links it with the Harappan sites prior to the demise of the Harappan civilization around 1900 BCE.

such resistance. The Ṛgveda mentions about such resistance in the stone forts of the local leader Śambara[8] in the mountainous area of the Northwest. The Vedic tribes ensured their success through effective use of these resources. They also turned to deities to obtain success in such encounters. The Ṛgvedic hymns abound in invocations to Indra, perceived as a warrior god, seeking his benediction for success in battle and to shower his blessings on the clan. Whitaker[9] while discussing the importance of masculine gods in the Ṛgvedic hymns, also refers to poet-priests insistence on men to keep Indra on their side in the eventuality of a war and "that this relationship can be achieved only through ritual performances". To meet the second challenge of escaping the vagaries of nature, they invoked different deities found in the Vedic hymns, such as Varuṇa (lord of cosmic law), Agni (Fire god), Marut (a group of deities symbolizing storm, thunder, lightning, wind and rain), Uṣas (the goddess of Dawn) and Prithvi (the earth) etc., who personified nature in its various forms. The Vedic Aryans did not worship animal figures unlike the Harappans.

The process of migration into the new found territory was, however, not entirely disruptive. Such skirmishes with the indigenous tribes did not halt the progress of Indo-Aryan culture. The long duration of the Ṛgvedic period, as many scholars contend, drawing support from the various Ṛgvedic hymns, could not have passed without close interaction at different levels between the Aryan and non-Aryan tribes. This interaction was mostly but not always one of acrimony and constant strife but also had a peaceful dividend reflected in the initiation of "multiple processes of cultural, social and linguistic acculturation" on mutual basis between the two. While, on the one hand, this led to the adaptation by the local tribes to the salient features of Aryan culture, such as Vedic Sanskrit, Vedic gods, pastoralism and social structure, on the other, some non-Aryan words also entered Ṛgvedic lexicon, such as, names of low level deities piśāca, Cūmuri, and names of poets like Kāṇva and Kavaṣa.

[8] According to Macdonell and Keith in Vedic Index Vol.II, the name Sambara finds mention in various books of Rig-veda (Bk.i. 51,6; 54,4; 59,6; I0I,2; I03,8; Bk.ii. I2,II; Bk.iv.26,3; 30,I4;Bk.vi.I8,8;26,5; Bk.vii.I8,20; 99,5. He is reckoned as an enemy of Indra. He is supposed to have had a number of forts, variously mentioned in the Rig-veda with Divodasa as his great enemy who won victories over him with Indra's aid. Sambara was believed to be an aboriginal enemy, living in the mountains

[9] Strong Arms and Drinking Strength, Whitaker, J.L., OUP, 2011, P. 18

The culmination of these processes resulted in "Aryanization" of local population and "Indianization" of the immigrating Indo-Aryans. This is clearly reflected in the researches of Kuiper who has established how the language of the Aryan tribes was brought "into harmony with the languages of the indigenous families, in particular Dravidian and Munda".[10] Kuiper[11] has also carried out a detailed analysis of words of foreign origin in the Ṛgvedic lexemes and concluded that they constitute approximately 4 percent. This figure, he maintains, represents a much slower process of Aryanization as compared to western societies where the process of acculturation is much faster. This is primarily because the local population did not have to adjust to the new environment ushered in by the Aryans as they were already 'firmly rooted in their dwelling places and probably were in the majority'.

On the political plane too, there are instances of Aryan kings with non-Aryan names, such as Balbutha and Bṛbu.[12] This was something similar to what happened later to Alexander's empire after his demise which broke up into Hellenistic kingdoms each with its own dynasty.[13] While Alexander's campaigns ensured spread of Greek culture, "the Hellenistic kingdoms revealed a two way effects of accommodation and assimilation".

It is generally acknowledged that the Indo-Aryan speaking people who came to India sometime in the second millennium BCE, composed the Vedic texts which not only contain rituals and their explanation but also philosophical speculation. They are also regarded as the first reference point of political thought and institutions in ancient India. The Vedic literature which were compiled in different time span, show how the Indian thought process underwent a change in successive phases and what impact it had on political and social institutions and the way of life of Vedic Aryans. The Vedic corpus bequeathed by the Vedic Aryans stands out as their monumental gift to mankind.

---

10 The genesis of a Linguistic Area, Kuiper, F.B.J, Text of the Collitz lecture delivered at the summer meeting of the Linguistic Society of America at Ann Arbor, July 30, 1965.

11 Aryans in the Rgveda, F.B.J. Kuiper, Rodopi B.V., Amsterdam-Atlanta, GA 1991, Printed in The Netherlands

12 Electronic Journal of Vedic Studies, Vol.2, 1966

13 Arrian Alexander the Great, The Anabasis and the Indica, Trans. by Martin Hammond, Oxford World's Classics,2013, P.Xii

After the Indus civilization, the influx of these Vedic tribes is regarded as the next important development in shaping early Indian civilization. The Vedic age, in fact, is identified with the timeline of the composition of Vedic texts, beginning with the composition of the Ṛgveda, the oldest and the most venerated Vedic text for which the maximally possible time frame is reckoned between 1400-1000 BCE. This period is characterized as the Rgvedic phase.

The time frame for the composition of the later Vedic texts, namely, the Yajur-Veda, the Sāma-Veda, the Atharva-Veda , the Brāhmaṇas, the Āraṇyakas ending with the Upaniṣads is suggested as the early part of the first millennium BCE which is identified with the post Ṛgvedic phase. To the list of the later Vedic texts, the Dharmasūtras, the earliest law books, written circa 500 BCE-200 BCE could also be added in the category of post Ṛgvedic texts and identified with the post Ṛgvedic phase. These Dharmasūtras deal with taxation, property, family matters and issues having a bearing on political institutions and social life of the time. These taken together constitute the Vedic corpus. Thus the Vedic corpus encompasses various phases of socio-political development, ranging from the Ṛgvedic to Atharva-Vedic times and that of the other Mantra collections (post Ṛgvedic) of the Yajur-Veda, the Sāma-Veda and the Ṛgveda Khilas and the period of the early Krishna Yajur-Veda prose.

These texts mirror the social, religious and philosophical speculation of the Indian mind, and present a curious blend of religion with politics where the practice of *Ṛta* (cosmic law later morphed into Dharma) – as the highest harmonizing principle – regulates the political and social order. The contents of Vedic literature cover a vast ground with the hymns of the Ṛgveda, usually addressed to the Vedic gods, providing a brilliant exposition of the personified power of nature; the Yajur-Veda representing liturgical formulas and growing complexity in ritualistic practice; the Sāma-Veda, borrowing heavily from the Ṛgveda as is the case with the other Vedas, with verses to be chanted at Soma sacrifice and the Atharva-Veda, containing charms and spells as also blessings and curses, as well as theosophic matters.

The other strand of the Vedic literature, consists of the Brāhmaṇas, the Āraṇyakas, the Upaniṣads and the earlier Sūtras. The Brāhmaṇas provide explanation of rituals to be practiced during sacrificial ceremonies; the Āraṇyakas, also called 'Forest Books' and being mystical in their contents, were supposed to be communicated by the teacher to the disciples in the solitude of the forest. The Upaniṣads, characterized by philosophical speculation, represented the evolved mindset of Vedic Aryans. As Brian Black[14] puts it "the Upanishadic orientation towards the self marks a significant transformation in relation to previous Vedic literature, which primarily focuses on the description and meaning of ritual actions." The earlier Sūtras represented the first attempt towards systematizing Brahmanic rituals and provided the guidelines for conduct of daily life.

The predominantly religious character of Vedic literature, and high philosophical content of the Upaniṣads led some scholars to view the persona of Vedic Aryans as a group of inward looking people with natural inclination towards metaphysics and self-introspection. Max Müller[15], a great German scholar and Indologist, who produced monumental works covering different aspects of the Vedic literature, also extolled the metaphysical side of the Indian mind and described the Hindus as "a nation of philosophers". On the face of it, such observations seem to be credible since the tenor of social, religious and political life of Vedic Aryans was guided by the cardinal principle of Ṛta (Cosmic and social law). This gravitated their thinking towards natural philosophy and introspection. Geographical factors also influenced the psyche of Vedic Aryans in no small measure. This draws support from the geographical location of India, being bounded by the sea on three sides with the great Himalayan range casting its shadow from the north. It was in the Sapta-Sindhu region that the Ṛgvedic texts were composed during the early second millennium BCE. The references of names, places, rivers, events etc. occurring in this text unmistakably belong to this region and not the places significant in the Harappan context.

The two phases of the Vedic period, namely, the Ṛgvedic Saṃhitā period and the Mantra period (during which the Post-Ṛgvedic texts were composed) differ from each other in many respects. Geographically, the Ṛgvedic period flourished in the north and north-west regions including the Sapta-Sindhu areas whereas during the post-Ṛgvedic period, the scene of activities shifted to the Ganga-Yamuna belt, Madhyadesha (Central region) and further towards east and the south. Politically, the early phase was dominated by some major and many smaller Vedic tribes; the Ṛgvedic

---

14 The Character of the Self in Ancient India, Brian Black, State University of New York Press, 2007. P.1

15 F.Max Muller, A History of Ancient Sanskrit Literature, Vol.1, P.30-31, second revised edition, 1860, Williams and Norgate, 20 South Frederick Street, Edinburgh

period is essentially a story of two major tribes, the Pūrus and later the Bharatas, covering a span of some five or six generations of their kings, characterized by intermittent strife. This period was interspersed with the presence of only a few of the other prominent tribes during the early Ṛgvedic period. These were the Yadus-Turvaśas; Anus-Druhyus and later joined by the Pūrus.

The Vedic polity in the earlier phase was both tribal and pastoral in character. Romila Thapar[16], an eminent historian, prefers to describe the tribal phase of the Ṛgvedic polity as "lineage society" as this term represented "the centrality of lineage in all its aspects... particularly in relation to power and access to resources [...]". During the early Vedic period, the tribal chief or the ruling elite derived legitimacy through lineage and this factor was considered vital for differentiation between the ruling elite and the people outside the elite group. It was not a homogenous entity but consisted of several tribal groupings with different identities, inhabiting different locations. Names of various clans find mention in the Ṛgveda, some representing Indo-Aryan speaking stock while others belonging to indigenous stream. The broad social division consisted of the Vedic tribes and the non-Vedic people. These two categories were differentiated on grounds of colour of their skin or as Romila Thapar[17] describes it as adherence to 'different cultural forms'. The governance structure was fairly simple and so was the ritual practice excepting Soma ritual which became fairly complex even in the Ṛgvedic period. The lowest unit in the structure of the Ṛgvedic polity was the family (Kula), following patriarchical norms with grāma (equivalent to a village) as the next higher tier, followed by a group of clans. The Vedic Jana was the highest social unit which represented the whole tribe. The role of protector devolved upon that individual in the tribe who was considered the most capable of protecting the interest of his tribe. Such an individual donned the mantle of chief of the tribe. A question has sometimes been raised whether an institution of spies had existed during the early Vedic period. In the Ṛgvedic, the word *spas*, denoting a spy, occurs 14 times. For example, the sun or the stars are taken to be the spy of the gods; however, it needs to be clarified that an organized spy system had not yet emerged during the Vedic period. The need for the same, perhaps, did not arise for

---

[16] From Lineage to State, Romila Thapar, OUP, New Delhi, 1990, P.18

[17] The Penguin History of Early India-From the Origins to AD 1300, Romila Thapar,2002, P.112

administering small tribal communities. For the Vedic period, Scharfe[18] also maintains that "the rulers of small tribal communities had sufficient opportunities to run informal checks on their employees and subjects as also to gather information on their neighbors. Even covert operations hardly needed an organizational set up."

The post-Ṛgvedic phase witnessed a consolidation of tribes under the umbrella of two major groups of tribes, namely, the Kuru-Pañcāla and the Kosala-Videha. There was perceptible social stratification of society into four classes with the Brahmins and Kṣatriyas emerging strong against the Vaiśyas and Śūdras who were relegated to the last two tiers of society. Perceptible changes also occurred in ritual practices, which had now become much more complex. Similarly, the governance structure no longer remained a simple framework but assumed a more elaborate character in order to meet the requirement of additional manpower arising from changes in the structure of the polity and diversification of economic activities. The spy system which was non-existent during the Ṛgvedic period, however, appeared much later during the Mauryan times. The Mauryan kings maintained a network of spy system which covered all parts of empire. These spies secretly fed information to the king about officials, ministers and people. The occupational structure of the society also underwent a change with agriculture and crafts becoming an important feature of economic activities.

Indeed the coming of the Vedic tribes in the Sapta-Sindhu region (qualified by seven rivers, namely, Kubhā (Kabul), Sindhu (the Indus), Vitastā (Jhelum), Asiknī (Chenab), Paruṣṇī (Ravi), Vipāś (Beas)[19] and Śutudrī (Sutlej) and their later movement towards further east and south east was an event of great political and social significance. It was not just a conquest process through use of horses or light spoked wheel chariots but, perhaps, a beginning of acculturation process both in political and socio-cultural terms to which both the Vedic Aryans and the indigenous tribes contributed in successive phases.

The foregoing serves as a brief account of developments that followed the arrival of the Vedic Aryans in the Indian sub-continent up to the

---

[18] *The State in Indian Tradition,* Hartmut Scharfe, E.J. Brill, Leiden, The Netherlands, 1989, P. 160

[19] The name of Vipāś is missing in the list of names of rivers which find a mention in Book X, hymn 75 of the Rig-Veda. The list, however, includes the rivers Sarasvati and Gomal (Gomati).

redaction of their monumental texts beginning with the Ṛgveda to the earlier Sūtras , the time-line spanning 1500 BCE- 400 BCE . However, the composition of these texts and the matter they contain have been variously interpreted by scholars, with those following a western line of investigation and others who veer round the nationalist discourse holding diametrically opposite views on the subject. One also comes across different views depending upon the time-line of the scholars. The 19th and early 20th centuries Western scholars mostly viewed these texts from a religious lens, with Frederick von Max Muller describing indulgence in metaphysics and philosophical speculation as the special forte of Vedic Aryans. The scholars of their ilk, perhaps, missed to uncover or highlight non-theological content situated in these texts. The nationalistic stream of scholars while eulogizing India's past, also ferreted out evidence from the Vedic hymns to substantiate their claim of linkages between some aspects of Vedic political institutions with institutions such as the state and other representative bodies that we know in the modern context. No doubt, one does come across in the Ṛgvedic hymns and other vedic texts, mention of various terms like Rajan (King), the Sabhā (a clan assembly, later evolved into an elite body) and the Samiti (folk assembly, also used, according to some scholars, for consultation on important matters), Purohita (the priest) and other subsidiary entities in the administrative apparatus, but these have to be appreciated keeping the context in view. How far such a view-point could be sustained in the modern context, is open to question. Between the two opposing viewpoints, perhaps, the truth lies somewhere in between.

We, however, cannot ignore the fact these institutions of the Vedic period bore seeds of political institutions which flowered later towards the end of the post Ṛgvedic period and assumed a definite shape when we come to the age of the Mauryas and the Guptas. A distinct trend and a new approach is now seen among the Western and Indian scholars to go beyond purely religious aspects of the Vedic texts and provide new interpretation to what is embedded in these texts. For example, Theodore Proferes[20], comes up with a new interpretation to the three-fold hierarchy of fires practiced by Vedic Aryans and relates it to the Vedic view of sovereignty (his views are discussed later in the book while dealing with Vedic concept of sovereignty). Drifting away from the nationalist

[20] Vedic Ideals of Sovereignty and the Poetics of Power, Theodore N. Proferes, American Oriental Series, Vol.90,New Haven, Connecticut, 2007. P.23-25

discourse, R.S. Sharma[21], an eminent historian underscores the importance of "social and economic processes" in the development of polity in ancient India. Others of his ilk discuss the importance of discovery of iron around 1000 BCE and breakdown of kin structure during the post Ṛgvedic phase in the context of their impact on the nature of Vedic polity. This is not to suggest that ritualism that pervades the Vedic period and is the centre-piece of Vedic texts ceased to be a factor. Far from it, the stranglehold of ritualism, in fact grew as we traverse from the Ṛgvedic to post Ṛgvedic period and continued to exercise great influence on Vedic polity in all its aspects. The ritualistic practices, particularly after an extensive Srauta reform, became very complex during the post Ṛgvedic phase and since the priestly class being well-versed with these rituals, were the only people possessing the ability to execute them, there was an exponential increase in their importance and authority. The king also perceived that it was only through the medium of the priests he could perform such rituals to connect with the god and receive his benediction for strengthening his position. This confluence of interest prepared the ground for the development of a close nexus between the Brahmins (priestly class) and the king. The performance of complex rituals posited the king as the chief sacrificer and provided him with an occasion to assert his authority among the people. The priestly class also saw in this an opportunity to ensure and consolidate their elevated status in the society. This strong alliance between the king and the priestly class came to be euphemistically described as "Brahma-Kṣatra" which did not go unchallenged towards the end of the post Ṛgvedic phase. The continued brahminical dominance and complex ritualistic practices evoked sharp reaction from society during this phase and the emergence of two rational schools of thought, Buddhism and Jainism is seen as a reaction against the brahminical dominance and evil aspects of ritualistic practices.

Indian culture and civilization continue to be tied to the umbilical cord of the values and philosophy enunciated in the Vedic texts. This continuity is evident in language, literature, social and religious practices. The recitation of Vedic hymns on religious and social occasions continue to be in vogue till the present day. Indeed the evolution of Indian thought process from the stage of worship of nature deities as seen during the Rig-Vedic period to philosophical speculation involving a spirit of inquiry, a search for truth and self-realization as embedded in the Upaniṣads, is

---

[21] Aspects of Political Ideas and Institutions in Ancient India, R.S. Sharma, Motilal Banarsidass Publishers, Delhi, Reprint 2009. P.414

unparalleled in the history of human civilizations. This has imparted vitality to the Indian civilization and accounts for the continuity of its core values and traditions despite a long period of trials and tribulations and that of alien rule it has been subjected to. It remains a country where the ancient sages divined the Vedas and composed the Upaniṣads and disseminated the spirit of inner peace, truth and eternal bliss. Putting across in the context of Indian civilization, Dr S. Radhakrishnan[22], an eminent philosopher says that "the civilization which is inspired by the spiritual insight of our sages is marked by a certain moral integrity, a fundamental loyalty, a fine balance of human desires and social demands, and it is these that are responsible for its vitality and continuity."

While the continuity with the past culture in many aspects denotes the vitality of the Indian civilization, the linkages with the past seems to have been lost in the case of some of the other ancient civilizations, such as the Egyptian and the Mesopotamian. The Egyptian civilization flourished on the banks of river Nile some five thousand years ago. It has to its credit unique achievements under the successive rule of Pharaohs in the spheres of art, architecture, culture, language, mathematics and astronomy. The civilization, however, decayed after the end of the rule of the last of the Pharaoh in 343 BCE, following defeat at the hands of the Persians, and later under the Greek, Roman and Arab occupation. What survives now are the monuments and the relics that serve as a reminder of the glorious past of this great civilization. The Mesopotamian civilization flourished in the valley between the Tigris and Euphrates rivers. Around 3000 BCE, the Sumerians, Akkadians, Babylonians and Assyrians inhabited the region of ancient Mesopotamia. The invention of the first writing by the Sumerians was the high point of this civilization. Various factors including the chaotic situation in the aftermath of the fall of the last Sumerian dynasty around 2000 BCE, are attributed for the decline of this civilization. In the case of this civilization also the link with the past no longer survives.

---

[22] Dr S. Radhakrishnan, *The Cultural Heritage of India*, Vol.I, P.xxiii, The Rama Krishna Mission, Institute of Culture, Kolkata, First ed. 1937.

Dating of the Ṛgveda

Various attempts have been made by scholars to date the Ṛgveda on different parameters. Some scholars, like Arnold[23] use metrical tests; others, including Ludwig[24] and Jacobi[25], prefer astronomical factors; still others rely on discoveries at Boghaz-Koi (where names identical to Ṛgvedic gods, namely, Indra, Varuṇa, Mitra and Nāsatya [Aśvin]) have been found in Mitanni records of 14th century BCE. Hence, it seems plausible to assume the Mitannian records as predating the Ṛgveda. The names of these gods are just one item among many others (royal names, horse colours etc. etc.) that are Indo-Aryan. This finds support from Prof. Michael Witzel, who holds that "the dates of Mitanni and Kassite documents point to mid-2nd millennium BCE" and that "their form is clearly pre-Ṛgvedic". This, according to him, is a clear pointer to the fact that the composition of the Ṛgveda would have taken place after 1600/1500 BCE and the bulk of Ṛgvedic hymns is likely to have been composed between c.1250- 1100 BCE. This position holds good unless there is a change in the date of 'first smelted iron' or unless new discoveries in Bactria, Sīstān, the Hindukush and Gandhara throw some new light on the movement of Indo-Aryan speakers.[26]

Perhaps, if we juxtapose the time frame of composition of bulk of the Ṛgvedic, with the time frame of 5-6 generations of kings and of contemporary poets of the Pūru-Bharata tribes, it will be reasonable to conclude that the beginning of the Ṛgvedic period is somewhere around 1500 BCE. and if we take into account 1000 BCE as the possible date for

---

23 Professor Edwin Arnold is credited with the research connected with determination of different stages in the composition of the Ṛgveda and he does so by dividing the text into five layers using the metrical test. Keith, however, finds this criterion as "unsound" as it depends "on a purely hypothetical reconstruction of the metrical history of the hymns..." (Keith, *The Religion and Philosophy of the Veda*, Pt.I, P.3).

24 Ludwig has deduced 11th centur BCE as the date for Ṛgveda on the basis of two eclipses mentioned in that text. Reference, Keith's The Religion and Philosophy of the Veda, Pt.I, P.4

25 Prof. Jacobi has expressed the view that the Ṛgveda dates back to 3rd century BCE. Reference, Keith's The Religion and Philosophy of the Veda, Pt.I, P.4

26 "Mitanni Indo-Aryan Mazda and the date of the Ṛgveda", Michael Witzel, in *The Complex Heritage of Early India-Essays in Memory of R.S. Sharma*, Edited by D.N. Jha, Manohar Publishers, 2014

the introduction of iron in the north-west region on the basis of recently available archaeological inputs and also the fact there is no mention of iron in the Ṛgvedic texts, the end of the Ṛgvedic period could be placed at 1000 BCE. The fact that iron does not figure in the Ṛgveda and only appears in the post Ṛgvedic texts, it follows that the composition and completion of the Ṛgvedic texts would have taken place before c. 1000 BCE. This is also because the language of the Ṛgveda is slightly later than the language of the Mitanni records[27] and the Rgvedic period is believed to be much later than the common Indo-Iranian period (around 2000 BCE). Max Müller has assumed that the Ṛgvedic hymns were composed between 1200 and 1000 years before the Christian era and the later Saṃhitās between 1000 and 800 years before the Christian era. Max Müller's views on dating of the Ṛgveda are merely based on the model which allows 200 years for each of the four stages for composition of Vedic texts. There is also a view that the composition of the Ṛgveda took place during 1400-1000 BCE while the other Vedas were composed around 1000 BCE.

The maximally possible time frame of 1400-1000 BCE for the Ṛgvedic period explains the redaction of the Ṛgveda in two stages – first, relating to the period of kings of the Pūru-Bharata tribes, and the second, the period of the Kurus when the Book X was added to the corpus. The political and social life evolved considerably during the second stage. In the first phase, the Aryan tribes on coming mostly from the Central Asian region, settled down in the Sapta-Sindhu region. The Pūrus and the Bharatas were the dominant tribes in this region. The most notable incident during this period was the Bharata victory under Sudās over the "Ten Kings alliance." (RV VII, Hymn 18). Despite the evidence brought out as above, the issue regarding dating of the Ṛgveda, is still far from being resolved. The refrain of nationalist discourse, however, has been to link the drying up of the Vedic river Sarasvatī around 1900 BCE due to "a major seismic activity in the Himalayan region"[28] with the abandonment of population of mature Harappan phase at Kalibangan (located on the left bank of the river Ghaggar, in Hanumangarh district of Rajasthan, India) around the same time. This, according to them is a clear indication that the Ṛgveda, in

[27] Michael Witzel's article Mitanni Indo-Aryan Mazdā and the date of the RV in R.S. Sharma Memorial Volume, 2014.

[28] Vedic River Sarasvati and Hindu Civilization, Ed. S. Kalyanaraman, PP.104-05, Aryan Books International, New Delhi, 2008.

which the Vedic river Sarasvati finds mention several times, was composed earlier than 1900 BCE and that the Aryans were an indigenous people rather than migrants. It has also been stated that the poets of the Rig-Veda, in which the Sarasvati river and Vedic seers find mention in several hymns, could not have been in the Sarasvati region if we subscribe to the generally accepted position on the dating of the Rig-Veda.

This view seems to erase the distinction between the mature Harappan phase and the beginning of the Ṛgvedic phase which, perhaps, it is difficult to establish conclusively at this stage. In support of the current position regarding the dating of the Rig-Veda, it has been pointed out that the important traits of the mature Harappan phase are not to be found during the Ṛgvedic period. For example, the Harappan polity had an urban character while pastoralism characterized the Ṛgvedic phase. There is hardly much credible evidence of horses being used in Harappa while the animal is a key feature of the Ṛgvedic rituals and was also used in skirmishes against the indigenous tribes.

The possibility of migration of Vedic Aryans from Central Asian region after the demise of the mature Harappan phase, also finds some corroboration at the linguistic level. An intimate relationship is seen between languages spoken in Central Asia (BMAC)[29] and that of the Punjab region. Lubotsky[30], while examining the structure of the Indo-Iranian substratum, has observed that "the phonological and morphological features of Indo-Iranian loan words are strikingly similar to those which are characteristic of Sanskrit loan words" and this indicates that the substratum of Indo-Iranian and Indo-Aryans represent the same language. The occurrence of such loan words in the Ṛgveda is also a pointer to possible immigration of the Aryans from the Central Asian

---

29 Bactria-Margiana Archaeological Complex

30 A. Lubotsky ,The Indo-Iranian Substratum, Early Contacts between Uralic and Indo-European linguistic and Archaeological Considerations; Paper presented at University of Helsinki, 8-10,January, 1999.

region which also helps in dating the Ṛgveda. Witzel[31] has also drawn attention towards a large body of loan words in the oldest Indian and Iranian texts to substantiate the use of the pre-Indo-Iranian languages by people inhabiting the region of BMAC (Bactria-Margiana Archaeological Complex). Edwin Bryant[32], however, questions the basis of "evidence of a linguistic substratum in Indo-Aryan" as a determining element for the origin of Indo-Aryan.

The above discussions clearly bring out the divide that exists among the scholars as regards the dating of the Ṛgveda. Currently, the broadly accepted view is to relate the composition of the Ṛgveda to a period after the arrival of the Aryans (or Indo-Aryans as some scholars prefer to use this terminology) in the Sapta-Sindhu region following the demise of the mature Harappan phase. This position can undergo a change, as Witzel maintains, if any fresh archaeological inputs become available or some credible evidence emerges which may change the currently accepted date of around 1000 BCE for the introduction of iron in the north-west region.

Timeline of the later Vedic Texts

The timeline of the later Vedic texts, such as, Yajur, Sama and Atharva Vedas which were compiled in Haryana and Western Uttar Pradesh, is generally taken to be the early part of the first millennium BCE. The Brāhmaṇas, Āraṇyakas, and the Upaniṣads which also form another strand of the later Vedic texts, were also compiled in Western Uttar Pradesh, during the first half of the first millennium BCE. However, some of them, such as Śatapatha Brāhmaṇa and Bṛhad Āraṇyaka Upaniṣad were compiled during this period in eastern Uttar Pradesh/Bihar. To the list of

[31] Witzel.M, Linguistic Evidence for Cultural Exchange in Prehistoric Western Central Asia. Philadelphia: Sino-Platonic Papers 129, Dec. 2003 http://www.sino-platonic.org/complete/spp129_prehistoric_central_asia_ linguistics.pdf (accessed on 20 March, 2013, In this paper, Witzel has referred to a large number of loan words pertaining to agriculture, flora and fauna and rituals in the oldest Indian and Iranian texts which were part of the languages spoken in the areas covered by the Bactria-Margiana Archaeological Complex (BMAC). These pre-Indo-Iranian languages later found their way into Iran and Northern India. See also Witzel, M. "Early Sources for South Asian Substrate Languages", Mother Tongue, Special Issue, Oct. 1999.

[32] Aryan and Non-Aryan in South Asia, Ed. J. Bronkhorst and M.M Despande, Manohar, 2012,P.80

the later Vedic texts, the earlier Dharmasūtras, the earliest law books, written circa 500-200 BCE could also be added since they deal with issues having a bearing on political institutions and social life of the time and also with taxation, property, family matters. These along with early Vedic texts taken together constitute the Vedic corpus.

Composition of the Ṛgveda and other Vedic texts - Possible locations

There are divergent views as regards the place where the Ṛgvedic poems were composed. E.W. Hopkins has discussed the imagery aspect in his writing "Punjab and the Rgveda"[33] and discounted the possibility of the Punjab plains being one such region. Keith[34] also maintains that keeping in view the stress on natural features by the Vedic poets in the Ṛgveda, it is highly unlikely that the Panjab could have been the region where the bulk of hymns were composed. He has further observed that on this basis, the home of Vedic Aryans could be attributed to the kurukṣetra region between the rivers Sarasvatī and Dṛsadvati (modern Chitang). There is also a contrary view which holds that the Ṛgvedic hymns were composed in the areas watered by the Sapta-Sindhu. According to this view, the Sapta-Sindhu area lies close to the mountains and is endowed with the necessary elements/imagery which the hymns of the Ṛgveda reflect.

---

[33] The Puñjâb and the Rgveda Author(s): Edward Washburn Hopkins Reviewed work(s): Source: Journal of the American Oriental Society, Vol. 19 (1898), pp. 19-28., American Oriental Society, URL: http://www.jstor.org/stable/592471 (accessed on 11th February, 2012). Discounting the Punjab as a possible place for composition of such hymns, Hopkins has observed "If the first home of the Aryans in India can be determined at all by the conditions, topographical and meteorological, described in their early hymns, then decidedly the Punjab was not that home. For here there are neither mountains to be seen nor monsoon storms to burst, yet storm and mountain belong to the very marrow of the Rgveda..." Continuing, he adds "The country divinely meted out by the rivers Sarasouti and Ghuggar, and lying between them, is where the (Rig, etc.) Veda arose, and hence is called brahmdvarta or 'home of the Veda' in the tradition of the learned."

[34] The Religion and Philosophy of the Veda, Pt.I, A.B Keith P.3

The rivers mentioned in the text also offer clues in this respect[35]. The major rivers mentioned in the Ṛgveda include Krumu, Gomal, Kubha (Kabul river)in Eastern Afghanistan and Sarayu (i.e., Haroiiu of the Herat area), a river in western Afghanistan on road to Persia, and the Sapta-Sindhu that cover the North and North-Western regions of India up to the Eastern part of Afghanistan. This goes to show that the early Aryans and their work flourished during the Ṛgvedic period in the regions lying between Yamuna and Sutlej rivers along the upper course of the river Sarasvatī.

Besides the above, geographical locations of the seers and their families to whom authorship of the books of the Ṛgveda is attributed also help in localization of the Ṛgvedic text. The geographical area of the family of priests and their affiliation with certain tribes are discernible in the Ṛgvedic hymns. For example, the Gṛtsamāda clan to whom the composition of Book II of the Ṛgveda is attributed, finds mention in hymns 4.9; 19.8; 39.8 and 41.18 of this book and the affiliation of this school with Bharata tribe seems to be clear from hymn 7.5 of this book. The geographical area of the habitat of this clan seems to be north-western and the Punjab regions. The imagery associated with this area is reflected in Book II. Demolition of Śambara's hundred ancient forts which were known to be located in the mountainous area of the northwest, finds mention in hymn 14.6 of this book. Similarly, the authorship of book III of the Ṛgveda is attributed to Viśvāmitra clan who lived in the Punjab and the Sarasvatī regions; Book IV toVāmadeva clan with habitat in the North-west and the Punjab; Book V to Atri clan, with habitat in the North-west, the Punjab region and along theYamuna; Book VI to Bhāradvāja clan associated with geographical area covered by North-west, the Punjab, the Sarasvatī and the Ganges; Book VII toVasiṣtha clan, associated with geographical area in the Punjab, Sarasvatī and Yamuna regions; and Book VIII to Kāṇva and Āṅgirasa clans associated with geographical area in the North-west and the Punjab region. Association of the seers with the regions mentioned above clearly show that the composition of the Ṛgvedic texts occurred in the Sapta-Sindhu region.

---

[35] One of the possible ways for approximating the habitat of Vedic tribes is by turning to the rivers occurring in Vedic texts, with which they are connected. It should, however, be borne in mind, that these rivers as Macdonell and keith maintain "traversed the alluvial plains of the north [...] were, therefore, [...] liable to constant fluctuations in their channels." (Vedic Index, Vol. I P.XV)

As for the later Vedic texts, there exists a consensus, as discussed earlier, regarding the location of places they were composed. The Brāhmaṇas, Āraṇyakas, and the Upaniṣads which come under the category of the later Vedic texts, were compiled in Western Uttar Pradesh, during the first half of the first millennium BCE. But, some of them, such as the Śatapatha Brāhmaṇa and the Bṛhad Āraṇyaka Upaniṣad were compiled during this period in eastern Uttar Pradesh/Bihar. As regards the locale of composition of Yajurvedic Saṃhitās (Maitrāyaṇī, Kaṭha, Kapiṣthala-kaṭha and the Taittirīya and Vājasaneyi Saṃhitās), the various references to mountains, river flows, climatic conditions help in identification of areas where they were composed. For example, the reference to mountain (the Himalayas) in Maitrāyaṇī Saṃhitā (MS 3.14.11) and the mention of the Kurus (4.2.6) point to areas situated in the Himalayan foothills and the Western Uttar Pradesh[36]. The similarity seen in the contents of Maitrāyanī and the Kaṭha Saṃhitā also shows that these two schools must have flourished in areas close to each other. Most poems of the Atharva-Veda, are Atharva-Vedic and not Ṛgvedic but also borrows to some extent from the Ṛgveda. Its hymns are metrical, which makes it similar to the Ṛgveda in form. Judging from the probability of the existence of Mantra time (Post Ṛgvedic) collections of the typical Atharva-Vedic hymns and also proto-Atharva-Veda form of such hymns (found in the Ṛgveda Book X), it can be surmised that the composition of the Atharva-Vedic texts occurred during the Kuru period and its PS (Paippalada Saṃhitā) was composed in the Kuru territory. This establishes the fact that it was a post-Ṛgvedic text.

---

36 Michael Witzel's Paper On the Localisation of Vedic Texts and Schools, in India and the Ancient World, Gilbert Pollet (ed.), Departement Orientalistiek, Leuven, 1987, P.178-179.

Chapter II
Sources of Study and Methodology

Sources of Study

A major handicap in reconstructing the polity of the Vedic period is the absence of systematic account of ancestral history or sufficient supporting evidence in the form of epigraphic and archaeological records and monuments. In order to overcome this handicap, recapturing the nature of Vedic polity has to involve a close examination of the Vedas and the associated literature as well as archaeological evidences that have emerged lately, besides taking into account the geographical factors that aid in this research. The Vedas, also known as Śruti (i.e. that which is heard directly by the seers), represent a mass of literature, comprising the four Vedas and other texts, such as the Brāhmaṇas, Āraṇyakas and Upaniṣads associated with the *Samhitas*. The Vedas have two main parts, the Saṃhitās and the Brāhmaṇas. The Saṃhitās consist of Mantras or hymns which are metrical hymns recited for prayers while the Brāhmaṇas consist of discussions for practice of these hymns and deliberations on rituals. Some of the Brāhmaṇas may include the treatises called the Āraṇyakas and the Upaniṣads, otherwise they are separate texts. The Āraṇyakas do not expound esoteric significance of the hymns but they are just like the Brāhmaṇas except that they consist of discussions on the Śrauta rituals in the wilderness. Likewise the Upaniṣads too, do not expound esoteric significance of the hymns but discuss the natural philosophy and pathway to achieving liberation through introspection of inner-self.

Following the Upaniṣads, the second category of sacred texts traditionally called 'Smriti' implying what is remembered was composed and they form the secondary sources for this study. These sacred texts include the Sūtras (Śrauta, Grhya, Dharma) and the later Dharmaśāstras (like Manu Smriti), and even the Itihasa (Mahabharata), etc. The Sūtras, such as Śrauta-sūtra, Gṛhyasūtras and Dharmasūtras, constitute an important source of information on late Vedic Brahmanic customs and rituals. These concise rules are designed to fulfil practical needs of people in both religious and temporal matters. These texts also throw light on the institution of kingship and social aspects of the polity besides laws relating to property, taxation etc. The Dharmaśāstras such as

Manu Smṛti, Narada Smṛti and Yajñavalkya Smṛti deal with host of matters, such as, customs, beliefs, life stages (from birth to death), standards of behaviour in society, Rājadharma, laws regarding taxation, inheritance, and the protection of property and person, etc. The epics and the Pūraṇas, as well as various scholarly writings on the subject, also provide an insight into rāja-dharma and other political institutions, their theoretical background, and deal with royal functions and related matters. Further, the chronicles of various foreign travellers and writings in Sanskrit, Pali, and Jain and Buddhist literature also throw light on political, legal and administrative institutions of the times.

Considerable assistance was derived from the secondary sources also in writing this book. Most of these books cover extensive ground on different aspects of the Vedic period. Such books and their authors are duly referenced and also appear in the bibliography section of the book. The list can be long but the notable ones include R.S. Sharma's Aspects of Political Ideas and Institutions in Ancient India, N.C. Bandyopadhyaya's and K.P. Jayaswal's on Hindu Polity, John Spellman's Political Theory of Ancient India, Dr. V.P. Varma's Studies in Hindu Political Thought and its Metaphysical Foundations, Michael Witzel's edited book Inside the Texts Beyond the Texts, Mamata Choudhury's Tribes of Ancient India, Wilhelm Rau's Staat Und GesellSchaft In Alten Indien, U.N. Ghoshal's History of Indian Political Ideas, and Theodore Proferes's Vedic Ideals of Sovereignty.

The inputs available from the primary and the secondary sources have, however, been used, keeping in view the scope of the present study which covers the period beginning from the Ṛgveda up to the earlier Dharmasūtras.

Methodology

We have already discussed the time line relating to the composition of various Vedic texts. To recapitulate the position in this respect, it can be stated that there is broad consensus among the scholars that the composition of the Ṛgveda may have taken place during 1400-1000 B.C while the other Vedas may have been composed around 1000 B.C. , i.e., during the post-Ṛgvedic period. Max Muller[37] classifies the hymns into

[37] Muir, J. Original Sanskrit Texts on the Origin and History of the People of India, their Religion and Institutions, Vol. I, Second edition, Oriental Press, Amsterdam. 1967

two categories – the older and the recent hymns. He places the older hymns between 1200 BCE and 1000 BCE and the recent hymns between 1000 BCE and 800 BCE Regardless of the exact timeframe in which the texts were composed, it is generally accepted that the four Vedas, the Brāhmaṇas, the Āraṇyakas, the Upaniṣads and the earliest Sūtras were composed over a period of time broadly covering the span of the Vedic Age (1500-500 BCE). These texts reflect the nature of the Vedic polity – including its distinctive features such as language, habitat, social, religious and political practices – as they existed during the Vedic period.

The first phase would relate to the Ṛgvedic period and the corresponding geographical area would be North-West and the Punjab regions where the Aryans initially settled down. The second phase would relate to the composition of post-Ṛig-vedic texts after they moved away from the Panjab and the Sapta-Sindhu regions and came over to the Ganga-Yamuna belt, Madhyadesha (Central region) and further towards east and the south. The scene of activities in the post-Ṛgvedic phase shifted to the land of the Kurus and the Pañcālas in the Western UttarPradesh/Madhyadesha. Hence, this study has been designed in two parts, for the sake of clarity and convenience, with the first phase covering the Ṛgvedic period and the second phase the post-Ṛgvedic period up to the earliest Sūtras. Further, the two periods in some cases have been dealt with in an integrated manner wherever it was felt necessary to do so.

Chapter III

Development of Vedic Canon and Polity

A study of Vedic polity cannot be divorced from the course of development of Vedic canon since it is closely related to the various stages of the evolvement of the polity. Virtually the evolvement of Vedic canon and the polity has gone along side by side. Unlike other religious texts which may have come into being as a single text or collection of sacred books at some particular time, the time taken in the composition of the Vedas would cover many centuries, spanning the entire Vedic period. The Rig-Veda reflects the nature of polity that existed during the early Vedic period; likewise, the later Vedic texts depict the changes that occurred in the polity during the post Rig-Vedic phase.

The sacred texts consist of two categories: the 'Sruti' which are traditionally supposed to have been directly heard by inspired seers, but have actually been composed orally by poets and transmitted to various schools, each representing Brahmin priestly clans of a particular area and tribe. In this category would fall the four Veda-Samhitas, Rig, Yajus, Sama and Atharva and other texts, such as the Brāhmaṇas, Āraṇyakas and Upaniṣads associated with the Samhitas. The second category of sacred texts is traditionally called 'Smriti' implying what is remembered and includes the Sutras (Srauta, Grhya, Dharma) and the later Dharmaśāstras (like Manu), and even the Itihasa (Mahabharata), etc.

The Ṛgveda[38] is reckoned as the most venerated and the oldest Vedic text and its redaction occurred in two stages. The first stage corresponded to the period of the kings of the Pūru-Bharata tribes during which the bulk of the hymns was composed. The most notable incident during this period was the Bharata victory under the king Sudās over the "Ten Kings

[38] The Ṛgveda contains a total of 1028 mantras (hymns), divided into ten separate books. The authorship or compiler of each is ascribed to some important ancient seers/priestly clans.

alliance." led by the Pūru tribe[39]. The second stage spilled over to the early post Rig-Vedic period which coincided with the rule of the Kuru tribe[40] in the eastern region during which the last book of the Rig-Veda, namely, Book X was added to the corpus. The compilation of the post Rig-Vedic texts, occurred in a sequential order, following introduction of iron in the north west around 1000 BCE, and broadly covered a time span of c1000BCE-400BCE. The first stage of the Post Ṛgvedic texts included the Sāma-Veda, Yajur-Veda (hymns only), and Atharva-Veda Saṃhitā. The next stage included the compilation of the Brāhmaṇa style prose text of the Black Yajur-Veda[41] only. This was followed by compilation of early Brāhmaṇa texts like Aitareya Brāhmaṇa, Śatapatha Brāhmaṇa, Jaiminīya Brāhmaṇa and later Aitareya Brāhmaṇa, etc. This stage also included the composition of all Āraṇyakas and the early Upaniṣads, such as Bṛhad Āraṇyaka Upaniṣad, Chāndogya Upaniṣad, Jaiminīya Upaniṣad Brāhmaṇa and even the first Śrautasūtras (Baudhāyana and Vādhūla). The last stage included the compilation of late Vedic texts such as, middle Upaniṣads and other Sūtras.

This is how the Vedas and other ancient texts of the Vedic and the post-Ṛgvedic periods were schematically composed and developed. The Vedic canon, thus, includes the four Vedas – Ṛgveda, Yajur-Veda, Sāma-Veda,

[39] RV VII, Hymn 18. As per Puranic tradition, Pūru was one of the five sons of Yayati whom he installed as his successor of the kingdom he ruled, on the banks of the river Sarasvati. Five of Yayati's sons including Pūru were members of the confederacy along with a few other tribes and fought on the banks of the river Parusni against King Sūdas, who was in the genealogical line of the Tritsu king Divodāsa, but were defeated. This is known as the "Battle of Ten Kings" and finds mention in the RV Book VII, hymns 18,33, and 83. God Indra impressed with the libation and exhortations of Vasiṣtha helped Sudās defeat the confederacy of ten tribes.King Sudas was connected with the priestly clan of Vasistha. Bharata is also the name of the tribe which figure prominently in the Rig-Veda as well as in the later Vedic literature, such as Satapatha Brahmana and the Taittiriya Aranyaka. They are believed to be connected with the priestly clan of Visvamitra, a prominent seer during the Rig-Vedic period.

[40] The Kuru tribe is prominent in the Brahmana literature which is a later Vedic text. This tribe is invariably mentioned together with another tribe, namely, the Pañcālas. The territory associated with this tribe is Kurukshetra which evolved as a seat of Brahminical culture during the post Rig-Vedic period.

[41] The Black Yajur-Veda is one of the two divisions of Yajur-Veda and provides both the mantras and prose explanation of sacrificial rites

and Atharva-Veda and treatises called the Brāhmaṇas, Āraṇyakas and the Upaniṣads.

Next, while the four Veda saṃhitās are separated from each other by a certain time span, and one would expect them to be distinct from each other, but this is not so. A sort of continuity is seen among the four Vedas irrespective of distance of time traversed in their respective composition. These compositions stand out as religious lyrics, in praise of the deities and describing ways in which the blessings of different deities could be obtained as also a bunch of charms and rituals for wish fulfillment in different pursuits. They also reflect in some measure the political, socio-religious and economic aspects of the Vedic polity.

The Sāma-Vedic Saṃhitā, like the Ṛgvedic Saṃhitā consists only of metrical hymns and follows the Ṛgvedic Saṃhitā very closely. It is held as a book of chants to be sung during the course of sacrifice and this collection is important from the perspective of canon formation. The Yajur-Vedic Saṃhitā is a text of sacrificial prayers. Like the Sāma-Vedic Saṃhitā, it also borrows to some extent from the hymns of the Ṛgvedic Saṃhitā, its hymns also follow the order in which they were practiced during the sacrificial rituals. As regards the Atharva Veda, even though the influence of the Ṛgvedic text is writ large in its poems, it is different from the other Vedas in subject-matter as it deals with charms and spells and skills to overcome diseases and evil forces. Keith [42]observes that "the Atharva-Veda reflects the practices of the lower side of religious life, and is closer to the common people than the highly hieratic atmosphere of much of the Rgveda…".

The discussions in the preceding chapters reflected on the structure of Vedic texts, the locale of their composition, their relationship with the priestly clans and the Vedic tribes in broad detail. Now we will examine the Ṛgvedic text and the remaining three Vedas, their Brāhmaṇas, Āraṇyakas and the early Upaniṣads in that order to determine the extent to which they reflect the nature of the polity that existed during the Ṛgvedic and post Rig-Vedic phases respectively.

The Vedic corpus reflects discussions on a wide- ranging issues including those having a bearing on political and social institutions that prevailed during the two respective periods. This can be inferred from the terms like Rājan(Noble or a king), Gotra (clan), Vṛata(People),

---

[42] The Religion and Philosophy of the Veda and Upanishads, Part I, A.B. Keith, Motilal Banarsidass Publishers, Delhi, 2007, P.2.

Grāma(Tribal unit or village),Grāmaṇī (Village headman), Jana (a body of men claiming birth from a common ancestor), Viś (a unit of military organization or tribal settlement), Vidhata,[43] Rathakāras (Chariot maker), Senani (commander), the Sabhā(clan assembly, later became an elite body), the Samiti (folk assembly), that occur in the Vedic texts, particularly, the Ṛgveda. The term "Rāṣṭra" (nation) also appears in the Vedic texts several times; there is, however, no exact equivalent term in the English language which can truly explain its meaning. Hence, the term Rāṣṭra cannot be equated with the term 'nation' or 'state' as understood in modern context. This term finds mention 11 times in the Ṛgveda, 71 times in the Śukla Yajur-Veda (White Yajur-Veda)[44] and 59 times in the Atharva-Veda. Further, the Brāhmaṇas, particularly, the Aitareya and the Śatapatha and the Dharmasūtras also depict the political and social aspects of the Vedic polity.

From the Ṛgvedic hymns we can infer that it was a fractured polity, consisting of a number of scattered and mobile tribes, hardly settled in any fixed location, and always yearning for new territories and fresh pastures. The mobile nature of the Indo-Aryans is also evident from their religious practice. The practice of Soma cult and fire rituals, which pervade the Ṛgveda, did not take place in any fixed temples but they had to lay out fire altars on every such occasion. This was a time when hotṛ priest played a crucial role in performing the Ṛgvedic rituals. These rituals provided an occasion to seek benediction of gods and the priests became a medium for performing such rituals. The Ṛgvedic rituals[45] excepting rituals connected with Soma sacrifice, were simple in form and the performance of such rituals was also intended to provide the practitioners a kind of insurance cover against forces inimical to them. The society during this period was witnessing a struggle between the pre-Aryan population and the Indo-Aryans for supremacy and the Vedic hymns do

---

43 . Vedic Index Vol. II (pp.296-297) refers to various interpretations of this word given by the scholars. Roth describes Vidhata as a body which gives orders as also an assembly for secular or religious ends.

44 One of the two divisions of the Yajur-Veda .White Yajur-Veda is mainly concerned with sacrificial formulae but does not explain their application in the rituals.

45 The Rig-Vedic rituals clearly visible only include various forms of fire rituals, three pressing of Soma which was a one day affair and Asvamedha, which may have been an embryonic form of the royal consecration. These rituals were fairly simple and became complex later during the the post Rig-Vedic phase.

mention the names of tribal chiefs on either side and provide some details of important battles they fought. The Aryans were ultimately victorious on such occasions through use of better resources and thereafter, in order to stabilize the progress they had registered, started the process of acculturation of pre-Aryan population which later also involved assimilation of some features of the pre Aryan culture in the Aryan milieu. Although social divisions during this period were not based on caste lines, the famous Puruṣa hymn of Book X.90[46] of the Ṛgveda does provide a hint on the lines the society was evolving. This hymn seems to be a precursor of social division on Varṇa (class) lines that was to appear later during the post Rig-Vedic period. At political level too, the hymns of the Ṛgveda provide some information about the direction in which the polity was evolving. The Ṛgvedic polity did have some basic political institutions referred to earlier, apart from the institution of *rājan* (which denoted tribal leader in the context of the Ṛgvedic polity) such as, the Sabhā and the Samiti, Charioteer, Grāmaṇī, Senani, etc., discussed in detail later in the book. It is, however, not clear whether there was any clear mandate on holders of such positions to limit themselves to the performance of only assigned functions or their role was not clearly demarcated as one would expect in a primitive polity. The Ṛgvedic polity was purely tribal in nature with weak administrative apparatus. The Vedic tribes' major occupation was cattle-rearing and they shared common social and political beliefs and identity. The settlements of the Ṛgvedic tribes came to acquire the nomenclature of *viś* and the inhabitants of these settlements were known as *Viśaḥ*. In many instances, the *viśaḥ* were named after the name of the tribe or the locality of their habitat. For example, there is a reference to

---

46 This celebrated hymn, according Muir.J (Original Sanskrit Texts on the Origin and History of the People of India, their religions and Institutions, Vol.I, P.7) mentions about the four-fold origin of the Hindu race. It has been subject to various interpretations. Some scholars have interpreted this hymn to denote the origin of four castes, namely, the Brahmans, kshatriyas, vais´yas and the su¯dra´s. The English translation of hymns 90.11 and 90.12 of book X of the Rig-Veda runs as follows: "When (the gods) divided Purusha, into how many parts they cut him up? What was his mouth? What arms (had he)? What (two objects) are (said to have been) his thighs and feet? The Brahman was his mouth; the Rajanya (here it, perhaps, refers to a Kshatriya) was made his arms; the being (called) the Vaishyas, he was his thighs; the Sudra sprang from his feet". "Purusha" is said to represent the 'cosmic being'.

Asiknī *viśaḥ*[47] and *viś* of Tṛtsu[48] in the Rig-Veda (RV VII.5.3 and RV VII 33.6). Other levels of political entities which find mention in the Ṛgveda is 'Jana', which perhaps reflect a higher level in the polity. For example, RV, III, 53.12, refers to the Bharatas forming a Jana and the description of 'Five tribes' as "Pañca-Janāḥ" which finds mention in almost every book of the Ṛgveda. The bond of kinship was strong among the people in the *viś* and they followed a patrilineal system. The political and social life evolved considerably during the second stage.

The post Ṛgvedic phase which started around 1000 BCE witnessed a transformation in the nature of the polity with little kingdoms emerging in the place of a couple of major and scattered tribal outfits which had characterized the early Vedic period. Significant developments occurred during this period at political and socio-religious levels. The depiction of political and social condition during this period is found all over the Brāhmaṇas (Post Rig-Vedic texts). At the political level, we discern a trend towards the polity acquiring the features of an emerging state with fixed settlements and replacing the 'wagon of trains' that had characterized the mobile nature of the habitat of the Ṛgvedic tribes. Further, the merger of tribes under the Kuru leadership led to its emergence as a super tribe with a larger territorial domain which also accommodated non-Aryan tribes. The polity thus acquired a more inclusive character and resulted in the weakening of the kinship bond which had characterized the early Vedic polity. The post Ṛgvedic phase also witnessed the polity acquiring a bigger role in the management of its expanded sphere of activities in areas such as, security, enhancement of productive resources through engagement in agriculture, crafts and a motley of other economic activities. There are also hints which suggest the beginning of a trend towards democratization of the polity which, of course, found full expression during the post Vedic period. R.S. Sharma[49] was referring, perhaps, to this trend discernible in Aitareya Brāhmaṇa (AB VIII.14) which in his view contains "the first and nearest attempt at the classification of the types of government or

[47] Asikini is the Rig-Vedic name of the modern river Chenab and flows in the north west region of India and is one of the seven rivers which together go by the nomenclature of Sapta-Sindhu

[48] According to Geldner (in Vedische Studien), Trtsu refers to the name of a king who helped Sudas in the 'Battle of ten kings'.

[49] Aspects of Political Ideas and Institutions in Ancient India, R.S. Sharma, Motilal Banarsidass,2009,P.129

chieftainship [...] where the terms *svarājya* and *vairājya* are used in the sense of power structures which did not have one-man rule". At the social level, the inclusion of non-Aryan tribes in the polity also signaled a beginning of the process of acculturation to which both the Aryan and non-Aryan tribes contributed. This is evident from changes that occurred at religious and linguistic levels. Further, we also notice a beginning of institutionalization of the Varṇa system where differentiation in the social order, based on functions became more pronounced. This is reflected in the higher status accorded to the Brahmins and kṣatriyas as compared to the vaiṣyas and the sūdras in the society. Thus, the stratification of society into four Varṇas further strengthened the position of the Brahmins and the Kṣatriyas. The Brāhmaṇa period saw the emergence of a strong coalition of the Brahman and Kṣatriya which was arraigned against the Śūdra and dāsa. This coalition is also described as brahma-kṣatra alliance and draws support from scholars, such as, David Carpenter, Barbara Holdrege and Brian Smith. According to them, the Brāhmaṇas view the 'Vedas primarily as a form of ritual and cosmological speech that guarantees social status...'.[50] . While the Brāhmaṇas' view of the Vedas as a form of ritual speech seems to be correct, it also needs to be stated that the Brāhmaṇas deal with cosmology but more in the margin. The Vedic ritual influences the cosmos and the society. Since only the Brahmins know about it in detail, they underline their social status, while in reality they were subject to kṣatriya dominance and were employed by them perhaps, just like today's purohitas.

This qualitative change in the social order during the post Ṛgvedic phase is nowhere seen as more pronounced than in the religious practices. The transformation of the Rig-Vedic rituals into Srauta rituals[51] occurred towards the end of the Rig-Vedic period but the actual Srauta reform happened under the Kuru kings. Discussion of the new Srauta rituals led to reform in ritualistic practices which became more complex and had their impact on the further development of the Vedic Canon. The transformation of the Ṛgvedic ritual into Śrauta ritual during the post-Ṛgvedic period saw division of priestly functions among the four

---

50 Authority, Anxiety and Canon, Essays in Vedic Interpretation, Edited by Laurie L. Patton, State University of New York Press, Albany, 1994.

51 The term 'Srauta' is derived from 'sruti'. Hence, Srauta rituals were rituals concerned with the use of the sruti texts. Srauta Sutras contain detailed and meticulous guidance to the priests for performing solemn sacrificial rites

categories of priests, such as Hotṛ (Ṛgvedic rituals), Adhvaryu (Yajus ritual), Udgāṭṛ (Sāma rituals) and Brahman (Atharva Vedic rituals). The Srauta reform led to rivalry between the Hotṛ priests and the Adhvaryu priests as regards their relative importance in the conduct of the rituals. The importance that the Hotṛ priest enjoyed during the Ṛgvedic period saw a decline due to such division of priestly functions and standardization of Śrauta ritual under the Kuru tribe. The Adhvaryu priests, however, gained in prominence in the new Śrauta ritual. The enhanced features of new Srauta rituals, apart from strengthening the bond between the king and the priestly class also ensured the latter's pre-eminence in the social structure as they alone possessed the ability to conduct such complex rituals. One of the important fall-outs of this development was further deepening of social divisions as the Vaiṣyas and the Sūdras were precluded from any substantive role in such rituals.

As we proceed further, we find the Vedic canon evolving further and its impact is discernible on the polity during the hegemony of the Pañcālas, the Kosalas and the Videhas. After the Kurus, the realm of the Pañcālas, situated eastwards into what is currently Uttar Pradesh, emerged as the ritual and political centre of the post-Ṛgvedic period. The Pañcāla period witnessed further innovations in ritualistic practices which is reflected in the Brāhmaṇa texts. Following the Kuru-Pañcāla period, the Kosala-Videha realm which flourished in eastern Uttar Pradesh (Oudh) and in Bihar north of the Ganges respectively, come into prominence. These kingdoms sported a mix of tribes and are credited with introducing further developments in political, social and religious spheres. While the society during this period retained the Kuru-Pañcāla pattern, it also reflected greater influence of religious practices of the western region. This is evident from the marked preference shown by the Kosalas and the Videhas for priests from the western region, including their religious texts and rituals for proper conduct of Srauta rituals. This preference for western religious practices was reflected in the decision of the King of Videha to obtain the services of the Brahmins (Aitareyins) from the west who were also asked to be his Śrauta priests. Likewise, in the Kosala area, the Kāṇvas (priestly clan) assumed a dominant position. This led to the shifting of various prominent schools of the Brahmins in the West to the East. This proximity to the western religious order in the texts and religious practices is seen in Baudhāyana Śrautasūtra and the Kāṇva version of the Śatapatha Brāhmaṇa whose composition occurred between the geographical region of the Kuru-Pañcālas and the Videha. The composition of the early part of Aitareya Brāhmaṇa bears the imprint of the Punjab region while its later part, which deals with royal consecration/ royal rituals such as the Aśvamedha and Rājasūya and the role of the royal priest, bears the stamp of eastern and the south-eastern regions. The above discussion shows that the religious practices obtaining in the western region significantly influenced the canon formation in the eastern region during the late Brāhmaṇa period. Indeed as Witzel[52] points out that the eastern territories witnessed during this period a complete reorganization of the brahmana style texts and a fresh thinking on earlier theological positions. The canon formation was not without glitches and was frequently affected by the competitive style of different schools. This period produced a clash of ideas and the emergence of new thinking and concepts that finally led to creation of a body of Upaniṣadic literature. The early Upaniṣads, according to Brian Black[53] reflected "a shift in geographical orientation, changing attitudes about the sacrifice, and the changing definitions about the status of Brahmins". There was rivalry among the kingdoms on the east on two issues: 1) How to enhance their position and authority vis-à-vis the other; and 2) how to use the process of textual reform to further their end. In this context, the ritual of sacrifice also acquired a degree of standardization and entailed performance of sacrifice by any Brahmin who was well-equipped to do so. The Upaniṣads signaled the end of the Vedic literature and therefore, are given the appellation of Vedānta. Concurrently, the composition of Sūtras followed suit. The period suggested for the composition of the Sūtras are supposed to be between 500 BCE and 200 BCE.

There was also a noticeable difference in the language of the earlier and the later texts. The views of E.J. Rapson[54] in this regard, are given in the footnote.

---

[52] Inside the Texts Beyond the Texts, Ed. Michael Witzel,Harvard Oriental Series,Opera Minora Vol.2,P.328

[53] The Character of the Self in Ancient India,Brian Black,State University of New York Press, 2007, P.13

[54] The Cambridge History of India, Vol. I, Edited by E.J. Rapson, P.57, The Macmillan Company, New York, 1922. Prof. Rapson notices considerable difference and states – "the language of the Rgveda, the oldest form of Vedic Sanskrit, belongs to the country of the Seven Rivers..." and the language of the post Rig-Vedic text precedes that of Panini circa 4th century B.C.

It appears from the above discussion that the development of Vedic canon in successive phases and evolvement of Vedic polity are closely inter-related and reflects the social, religious and political aspects of the polity that obtained at the time of the redaction of respective Vedic texts.

Chapter IV

Vedic Concepts of Nationalism and Sovereignty

Historically speaking, the meaning and context of concepts like polity, nation, and nationalism, have been continuously evolving in successive stages as we go from the ancient to the medieval and further to the modern periods. It is evident both in European and Indian context.

In Europe, the concept of nationalism grew in phases. During the middle ages, the tenets of the Holy Roman Empire acted as a centripetal force and the Church played a pivotal role in enforcing common religion, language, and culture. As the middle age progressed, several factors eventually led to the decay of the church primacy; the vacuum was filled by the emergence of royalty in some European states as a focal point of effective authority. Nationalism as a political doctrine, however, developed in Europe in the late 18th century[55] which, according to Bruno Leone[56], was a liberal reaction to the autocracy exemplified by the dynastic states of Europe. In the place of personal allegiance to the monarch, which was the flavor prior to the 19th century – "the idea of allegiance to a geographical nation, composed of people joined by language, custom and a common historical tradition, evolved." According to a Report on Nationalism by a Study Group of the Members of the Royal Institute of International Affairs (OUP, 1939, London), the factors responsible for its growth included invention of printing that helped quick dissemination of secular ideas and democratization of political structure in the aftermath of the French Revolution and Act of Settlement (1701) in England. In the modern context, there is a broad degree of consensus over the salient features of these concepts. A nation, for example, is generally characterized by a defined territory, inheritance of common heritage and bond by the people, as well as the existence of a

---

[55] H. Kohn, The Idea of Nationalism: A Study of its Origins and Background. (Macmillan, New York,1951)P3-6, C.J. H. Hayes, The Historic Evolution of Modern Nationalism (Macmillan, New York 1931) P. 6

[56] . Bruno Leone, The Isms: Modern Doctrines and Movements, Nationalism Opposing View points, Revised second edition, 1986, Greenhaven Press, 577 Shore view road, St. Paul, Minnesota, 55126.

common superintending authority which goes by the name of government. Nationalism is the spirit, expressed in terms of a distinctive culture, values, language, or religion, that binds people together in their quest for furthering common objectives and mutual well-being.

In India, we have to examine the various phases of its history to understand the approach to nationalism in different time-line. Here, we shall deal with the Vedic concept of nationalism and attempt to discover the nucleus of this concept in the various aspects of Vedic polity. The period between1500 and 500 BCE, which corresponds to the Vedic age, witnessed significant political and social transformations in north and eastern India. This period covers the Ṛgvedic phase of tribal society and extends up to the emerging state society of the later Vedic period. The lineage factor was pervasive in the Ṛgvedic polity (Romila Thapar[57]), and served as an important ingredient for legitimizing the authority of the tribal chief or the ruling elite. This factor also set them apart from the people who were outside the elite group. The later phase which corresponds to the movement of Vedic Aryans and the spread of Vedic culture by osmosis from the Northwest region to the Gangetic plain and further to the east, witnessed a change in the nature and structure of the tribal polity. The merger of tribes led to the emergence of super tribes who exercised control over a larger territory. The mix of tribes, both Vedic Aryans and pre-Aryans in such a political dispensation, lent the polity a more inclusive character with the lineage factor losing its pre-eminence. The structural change also involved stratification of society on occupational lines with clear division of functions between the upper rung represented by the Brahmins and the kṣatriyas and the lower order represented by the vaiśyas and the śūdras (which also included the non-Aryan tribes). Taking the Ṛgvedic and Mantra (Post Ṛgvedic) periods together, one can surmise that the concept of nationalism was identified with the persona of the tribal chief or the ruler of the emerging state [in the post-Ṛgvedic period]. The privileges arising from birth or notions of status invariably subjugated the rights of common man. The mahājanapadas of 5th century BCE reflected the same tendencies with perhaps the exception of some tribal "republics" such as those of the Mallas and Vṛijis in which the polity was more broad-based and enjoyed a measure of internal autonomy. The rise of regional centres of power in the middle ages, such as the Palas of the east, Pallavas of Kanchipuram in the south and Chalukyas of Badami in the central India also reflected similar

[57] From Lineage to State, Romila Thapar, OUP, New Delhi, 1990, P.18

centralized monarchical trends during the early medieval period. In all these cases, the concept of nationalism was subsumed in the expression of allegiance towards the ruler and protection of territorial sovereignty.

The question whether the concept of sovereignty existed in the Vedic polity has been a subject-matter of debate. Professor V.P. Varma, an eminent scholar, discounts the presence of the concept of sovereignty in ancient Hindu thought[58] but at the same time he has not questioned the existence of sovereign states in ancient India. Further, according to him, "nothing but the creation of kingship is meant" in the ancient texts. Such a view is contestable on the ground that the concept of sovereignty (which, according to standard definition implies self-governing state) and sovereign states are not mutually exclusive. It is true that during the Vedic period the concept of sovereignty revolved round the persona of the tribal chief or the king as the case may be and cannot be equated to the meaning attached to this term in the modern context. However, we can discover a semblance of sovereignty in its rudimentary aspect in Vedic polity if we interpret this concept to mean the exercise of supreme power or final authority in the process of decision-making. This, it seems, is embedded in the structure of society prevailing during the Ṛgvedic period and the exercise of authority by its different segments. These segments consisted of the extended family at the bottom, viś (clan) at the middle level and the tribe where all segments were coalesced into one under a common leadership. As would happen in a patriarchal system, the final authority in all matters in the family was vested in the master of the house (grhápati). A group of families, bound by common ancestry constituted a clan and all the clans together constituted a tribe. It finally devolved on the leaders of various clans to elect or select a leader of tribe who exercised the sovereign power on behalf of the tribe as a whole. This exercise of power was not absolute or unfettered and had to be within the confines of Ṛta (cosmic and social law). Ṛta is viewed as something more than truth. It has a positive orientation and not only forbids action exceeding its purview but also ensures action to fall within its ambit.[59] Thus every social and political act had to be cosmic law compliant. The roles assigned to other political institutions, such as, the Sabhā, Samiti, Vidhata (which we shall discuss later) also acted as a check against the exercise of authority in an unfettered manner. Hence, the exercise of sovereign power by the leader

---

[58] Hindu Political Thought, V.P. Varma, P.182

[59] RV. X. 10.4

of the tribe had to fit into his role as a protector of the tribe and as an upholder of Ṛta.

The cult of fire rituals, which pervades the Ṛgvedic hymns, the texts of Yajur and Sāma Saṃhitās was a potent instrument for all the three levels of societal structure to propitiate gods and seek blessings for their well-being. In the practice of rituals, Agni, a terrestrial god, emerges as a central figure. He is perceived as a messenger between gods and men and as one who brings prosperity and happiness to dedicated devotees. Theodore Proferes[60], has provided a new perspective on the Vedic concept of sovereignty and relates it to the three-fold hierarchy of fires which reflect the structure of the early Vedic society. Elucidating this perspective, he observes that "the sovereignty was constructed through the interactions of three primary social units", namely, the household, the clan and the tribe and that each of the three levels was required to perform fire ritual specific to that category. Thus fire occupies a central place within a household and accords the master of the household primacy in the conduct of fire rituals which makes him virtually a sovereign limited to household matters. As we go progressively up the ladder, we find the leader of the clans associated with fire ritual corresponding to that level. Since association of the leader of the clan with fire ritual is a visible manifestation of his authority vis-à-vis the clans, he becomes a symbol of clan sovereignty. Similarly, association of the leader of the tribe with fire ritual at tribe level symbolizes his sovereign authority over the affairs of the entire tribe. Thus, fire ritual provided a visible symbol of identity at the family, clan and tribe levels with all the three levels having an organic relationship through kinship ties. The inter-relationship between the three levels also became an instrument for expression of collective sovereignty.

The concept of sovereignty was also reflected in sacrifices and ceremonials connected with the king's accession and his acceptance by the people. To be a lawful ruler, he had to go through various ceremonies to establish his credentials and also obtain gods' sanction to the exercise of royal authority. The various ceremonies undertaken by the king in this behalf included Rājasūya, Daśapeya as part of Rājasūya (the ceremony of drinking Soma in the Rājasūya), the Kṣatradhṛti (wielding of royal power), Vājapeya sacrifice etc. The winning of chariot race, which is intimately connected with the performance of Vājapeya sacrifice, was supposed to

---

[60] Vedic Ideals of Sovereignty and the Poetics of Power, Theodore N. Proferes, American Oriental Series, Vol.90,New Haven, Connecticut, 2007. P.23

endow the king with supreme power and strengthen his position as a sovereign (ŚB V.1.1.3). The priests also played a great part in deification of royal authority and the Purohita came to be regarded as the *alter ego* of the king. The status of the king during the early Vedic was that of a war lord and collector of tributes. This position subsequently changed to that of a sovereign having control over his people in the territory. The concept of territorial sovereignty was taking root in the later part of the Ṛgvedic period and acquired a definite shape during the post-Ṛgvedic period. The kingdoms came to have more or less a defined territorial limits where the tribes led a settled life, a far cry from the nomadic life of the early Vedic period. The consolidation of tribes under the leadership of the Kurūs leading to its emergence as a super tribe, having control over a larger territorial domain provides a good example in this respect. The other realms like the Pancālas, the Kosalas, the Videhas and the Kasi are examples of the emerging state forms during the post Ṛgvedic phase. In these cases, the concept of sovereignty denoted independence of action enjoyed by these rulers in the affairs of the territory under their control.

Chapter V

Vedic Rāṣṭra

We have seen how the societal structure and the cult of fire rituals practiced during the Vedic period convey a sense of sovereignty in its very rudimentary form but does not take us anywhere near the modern concept of sovereignty. The same is true of the concept of Rāṣṭra as discerned from the Vedic texts which is not the same as understood in modern sense. The modern concept of state broadly postulates a well-defined territory; a common heritage and organized governance. During the early Vedic period, we do find evidence of a tribal chief having a flexible territorial jurisdiction. Initially, *grāma* (later came to be identified with a village) did not represent a fixed settlement. This stands to reason since the Indo-Aryan tribes were going through the phase of pastoral nomadism. According to Wilhelm Rau[61] the term *grāma* in early Vedic literature, represented "a train of herdsmen roaming about with cattle, oxcarts and chariots in quest of fresh pastures and booty" and as "a temporary camp of such a train, sometimes used for a few days only and sometimes for a few months at the most". Rau's views find support from MacDonnell and Keith[62] who discount the description of *grāma* as a legal or a political unit. In their view the assumptions to treat a *grāma* as a fixed dwelling place under the king's control on the basis of its association with the various occupational classes of people, seem to be unattested. The scenario changes as the Ṛgvedic period progressed and the Aryan tribes continued to expand their political control and cultural influence vis-à-vis the indigenous tribes. During the later part of the Ṛgvedic period, they appeared to have moved forward from the semi-nomadic stage, as the occurrence of the term *Grāma* at several places in the RV as the stay place of the tribes seems to suggest. According to H.N. Sinha, another scholar, the occurrence of the term *grām*a in the Ṛgveda, seems to suggest a possible dwelling place of the people and has not ruled out the possibility of the people inhabiting a *grāma* or *grāmas* of taking part in military

61 Wilhelm Rau's The earliest literary evidence for Permanent Vedic Settlement, in Inside the Texts and Beyond the Texts, Vol.2 Cambridge, 1997, P.203

62 Vedic Index of Names and Subjects: Macdonell and Keith, Vol.I, P.246

operations[63] in the context of the likely role of the *Grāmaṇī* (Village headman) in civil and military matters. Further, the association of *grāma* with the various occupational classes of people, such as the cultivators, the chariot-makers (Rathakāras), the carpenters etc., as also payment of tributes to the king for the land held by the *Brāhmins* (Priestly class) and Kṣatriyas (Warrior class), also suggests that the *grāma* increasingly represented a territory over which the king exercised his authority. The concept of *grāma,* did not remain static and further evolved during the Mantra (Post Ṛgvedic) period. During the early Vedic phase, as indicated earlier, it signified a wagon train of the Vedic Aryans moving towards the east. Subsequently, however, it came to represent small indigenous settlements along the Gangetic plain where the Vedic Aryans eventually settled down. This was a time when the merger of tribes took place; small kingdoms emerged and there was an expansion of economic activities with agriculture gaining in prominence. The changed scenario required changes at structural, political and administrative levels. The change at the structural level was reflected in transition of Vedic polity from being a lineage-based clan organization to a more inclusive polity, as the confederation of Kuru-Pañcālas, consisting of a mix of tribes, would seem to suggest. Romila Thapar[64] describes the change as a gradual transition from identity derived from "the lineage of the ruling family ... to identification with territory and new forms of political authority...". At the political level, the Kuru tribe in the Kurukṣetra region assimilated within its fold a large number of smaller Ṛgvedic and other tribes. This event enhanced its stature as a super tribe while at the same time it also challenged their acumen and obligated them to meet the aspirations of merging tribes and their chieftains for proper accommodation within the system. Further, keeping in view the changes in the structure of the economy following practice of new vocations, changes in the mode of production and ritualistic practices, corresponding administrative support was required to be created at the administrative level. Close on the heels of this transition between the 6th and the 4th centuries BCE, a new urban culture, also called 'Second Urbanization' which we shall discuss later, started sweeping the Gangetic plain and the political sky was dotted with small/big kingdoms which is reckoned as the early stage of

---

[63] Development of Indian Polity, H.N.Sinha, Asia Publishing House, New York, 1972, P.25

[64] The Penguin History of Early India, From the Origins to AD 1300, 2003. Romila Thapar,P.137

state formation. The term 'State', however, received a wider treatment (seven elements of state) only when we come to Kautilya's Arthaśāstra and Pali texts of roughly 250 BCE.

The Vedic literature does not give us much details about the political institutions that existed during the early Vedic period nor do we get much idea about their political persuasion during that period. Some of the hymns of the Ṛgveda and the Atharva-Veda as well as the Brāhmaṇas, however, do throw light on the institution of kingship and the executive machinery associated with it. We do hear about the Rājan (King or a noble), Rathakāras (the chariot maker), the *Grāma* [65] signifying, during the Ṛgvedic period (according to Wilhelm Rau), a wagon train on the move, the *Grāmaṇī*, the leader of a grāma, Ratnins,[66] and other officials , such as, Akṣāvāpa(the dice player), the senānī (the commander of the army) the Saṃgrahītṛ (the tax collector or treasurer), the Purohita (The Priest) etc., as also the institutions of the Sabhā(meeting place) and the Samiti (folk assembly). The existence of all these institutions also suggests that the king had a sway over an undefined geographical area, since boundaries were never clarified except by certain rivers during that period. Further, the existence of these institutions also shows that the king had the military capability to defend the territory besides an executive/representative machinery to assist him in the task of governance. These institutions also testify to the fact that they must have been a part of an organic whole, that is, "*Rāṣṭra*" in its embryonic form. This impression further gets reinforced when we find different expressions for the term 'Rāṣṭra' in the Vedic literature, such as 'Rāṣṭrabhrt' (upholder of the kingdom) in Śatapatha Brāhmaṇa (VII.1.1.4), 'Rāṣṭra' in the Śatapatha Brāhmaṇa (5.3.4.5,6,10,11), and in RV 10.173.5 and in Atharva-Vedic Saṃhitā (8.9.13, 1.29.4,5.19.10; 12.1.8, and 20.127.9). These expressions have been used in various contexts, such as awakening of rāṣṭra, dedication to rāṣṭra, enhancing the

---

65 Wilhelm Rau is credited with elucidating the concept of *grāma* as "a train of herdsmen roaming about with cattle, oxcarts and chariots in quest of fresh pastures and booty" and as "a temporary camp of such a train, sometimes used for a few days only and sometimes for a few months at the most". This interpretation of the *grāma* is the only one, according to him, attested in early Vedic literature but still known to Patanjali (150 BCE). Refer Wilhelm Rau's The earliest literary evidence for Permanent Vedic Settlement, in Inside the Texts and Beyond the Texts, Vol.2 Cambridge, 1997, P.203

66 Ratnins- a person who owns a jewel; regarded as an important person in the King's court.

prosperity of rāṣṭra, responsibility of citizens and the king etc. It is important here to deal with the usage of the term Ksatra (dominion) in the context of the early and the later Vedic phases. While the term Kṣatra was earlier understood in the sense of dominion or sphere of influence, it came to acquire a different connotation during the later Vedic phase. One of the objectives of the iniation ceremony performed by the king during the rājasūya was to encourage him to acquire kṣatra which implied extending his area of influence, both with reference to people inhabiting his domain and in territorial terms. The equation between kṣatra and rāṣṭra became more pronounced during the later Vedic period. Some post Ṛgvedic texts also identify Rāṣṭra in terms of Kṣatra[67] used in the general sense of dominion. However, we also notice a trend where "the rāṣṭra, apart from indicating the sphere of influence of the raja [king] was tending to be identified with specific social and economic configurations". (Kumkum Roy, P134). This is evident from a qualitative change in the natural relationship expressed in terms of kinship bond that existed between the king and the *viś* during the early Vedic phase. This change served a dual purpose: First, absorption of more people in the *viś*, not necessarily bound by kinship, was expected to strengthen the king's base and secondly, it would have also helped him to expand his "access to a range productive resources". Induction of a mix of tribe in the polity also had a negative fall-out as it emphasized social differences which affected the homogeneous character of the polity.

Yasuhiro Tsuchiyama, a Japanese scholar, has examined the meaning of the term 'Rāṣṭra'(Nation) with reference to PS(Paippalada Samhita) of the Atharva-Veda. In his paper, he refers to some verses in PS 10.4.1, 10.4.3, 10.4.6, 10.4.5d, 10.4.7a, 10.4.8, 10.4.12c, and 10.4.13 that describe the various facets of Rāṣṭra(Nation) as well as early forms of rituals connected with royal consecration.). The verses in the PS seem to equate Rāṣṭra with the king himself and also indicate the king's responsibility relating to enrichment of his kingdom (PS10.4.1). Exhortations are made therein for making the rāṣṭra 'powerful, victorious and strong' so that the other chieftains pay tributes (PS 10.4.3). Such exhortations also require king to protect the chieftains in return for tributes. In one of these verses, not only the king but also the tribal alliance constituting the kingdom, symbolizes a Rāṣṭra (PS 10.4.6). In the early Vedic period, the king and the tribal alliance submissive to him seem to be the basic ingredients of a Rāṣṭra. This seems

---

[67] Vedic Index of Names and Subjects: Macdonell and Keith, Vol.I, P.202

to resonate with the view of V.P. Varma, earlier referred to, that the ancient texts only mention about the creation of kingship [which perhaps epitomized the concept of rāṣṭra]. However, in the later Vedic period, with the consolidation of tribes and the emergence of kingdoms, and alliance between the Kṣatriyas and Brahmins in their mutual self-interest, also called the brahma-kṣatra alliance and increase in the complexity of rituals, there was a change in the power structure and nature of governance. The brahma-kṣatra alliance was posited against the Vaiśya (who formed the third tier in the society), the Śūdra (the lowest class in the society performing a motley of inferior services) and the dāsa (aboriginal population). The 'Brahma-kṣatra alliance' brought about a change in the role of the king and placed the institution of kingship on a more stable footing. The concept of Rāṣṭra came to be associated with the authority of kingship or in other words, according to Tsuchiyama, the term Rāṣṭra came to symbolize a person endowed with sovereignty. This raises an important question of interpretation. If the king is treated as representing sovereignty, it has to relate to some entity. This entity could be a tribal polity or a state. Perhaps, Theodore Proferes was expressing a similar view when he analysed how the construct of sovereignty was intimately linked with fire ritual. He[68] held that the " fire can represent the lord of the house the clan lord, as well as the tribal leader who exerts control over these lesser entities..." Thus the fire ritual at the tribe level symbolized tribal kingship in whom the ultimate tribal sovereignty was vested.

We also find the word "Rāṣṭra" occurring in various books of the Ṛgveda in different contexts; for example, the Book IV hymn 42.1 and BK VII hymn 84.2 dealing with invocation to Indra and Varuṇa and Book VII hymn 34.11 dealing with invocation to Viśvedevas. The term 'Rāṣṭra' also occurs in AV 13.1.34; 13.1.35, in Taittirīya Saṁhitā 1.8.11, in Maitrāyaṇī Saṁhitā 2.6.7, in Kāṇva Saṃhitā 15.6 and in Āpastamba Gṛhyasūtra 18.13.20 etc., etc.

It, therefore, seems plausible that certain elements of a 'Rāṣṭra' were present in the Vedic polity. Such a view finds support from K.P. Jayaswal, a noted Indologist, who in his work Hindu Polity, equates the occurrence of the term Rāṣṭra in the Vedic texts with the word state. . V.P. Varma[69]

---

68 Vedic Ideals of Sovereignty and the Poetics of Power, Theodore N. Proferes, American Oriental Series 90, New Haven, Connecticut, 2007. P.25

69 Studies in Hindu Political Thought and its Metaphysical Foundations, Dr V.P. Varma, Motilal Banarsidass, Delhi, 1974, pp.8-9

earlier referred to, however, does not support Jayaswal's assumptions and observes that "the Vedic Rashtra was not an exactly defined political term and to translate it by the modern word state would imply an amount of legal precision which did not obtain in those days." Thus, in view of the above, it seems reasonable to assume that while the Vedic concept of Rastra cannot be equated to its modern equivalent, it did contain some basic governance structure which could be related to the features of a state in its embryonic form. This assumption gains ground if we identify the early Vedic Rāṣṭra with the ruler/king who ruled over a group of people moving around in an undefined territory or headed a tribal alliance. This meaning also seems to fit in with nomadic pastoralism which characterized the Indo-Aryans' way of life during the Rig-Vedic Period. However, during the post Rig-Vedic period, we come to the stage of early state formation when the concept of Rāṣṭra underwent a qualitative change. The concept of Rāṣṭra emphasized both the institution of king vested with independence of action with reference to his realm and a defined territory under the king's control. Further, management of a larger domain and diversified economic, political and social activities enhanced the king's role and necessitated a more elaborate governance structure. This stood in contrast to the role of the king during the early Vedic period who managed the polity with a fairly simple governance structure which was in tune with the limited range of his responsibilities.

Chapter VI

Important Ṛgvedic Tribes

A study of Vedic polity would not be complete unless we discuss the principal actors in the polity who were the Vedic tribes. These tribes were instrumental in bringing about a qualitative change in the nature of Vedic polity as they endeavored to move over from a purely pastoral vocation to a mix of occupations which included pastoralism, agriculture and crafts during the post Rig-Vedic phase. This qualitative change between Rig-Vedic and the Post Rig-Vedic periods is clearly reflected in the nature of polity as it existed during the two periods.

The Rig-Vedic period is a saga of efforts put in by the Rig-Vedic tribes to put in place initially a basic system of governance as they struggled to find food and shelter and overcome the vagaries of nature and antagonism from their adversaries. Their constant preoccupation with such mundane activities was an important pursuit basic to their survival, but their thought process went much beyond that as they sought to indulge in religious and philosophical speculation as reflected in Vedic texts. The Vedic tribes were unique in this respect and have absolutely no parallel elsewhere. So were also the Rig-Vedic seers and their clans who through the composition of Vedic texts mirrored the religious and philosophical speculation of the Indian mind and also captured in their compositions the political, social, and economic aspects of life pursued by Vedic Aryans.

The Ṛgvedic polity was essentially tribal in nature and interspersed with the presence of a few big and many smaller tribes. As stated earlier, five or six generations of kings belonging to two major tribes, namely, the Pūrus and later the Bharatas, dominated the entire Ṛgvedic period. Keith and MacDonnell in Vedic Index [70] have identified 66 tribes for the entire Vedic period. According to them, the following were the prominent Vedic tribes: 1) the Kambojas, Gandharis, Ālinās, Pakthās, Bhalānas and Viṣāṇins in the extreme west and beyond the Indus; 2) the Arjikiyas, Śivas, Kekayas, Vṛcīvants, Yadus, immediately to the east of the Indus; 3) the Mahāvṛṣas to the east of the Vitastā and the extreme hill region, Uttara-Kurus and Uttara Madra beyond the region of Shivalik hills.; 4) the Balhikas, the Druhyus, Turvaśas and the Anus between Asiknī and Paruṣṇī; 5) the

[70] Vedic Index of Names and Subjects: A.A. Macdonell and A.B Keith

Bharata,Tṛtsus, the Pūrus and the Pārāvatas to the east of the Śutudrī; 6) the Uśīnaras, Vaśas, the Śalvas, the Krivis to the east of Yamuna, and 7) south of the Dṛsadvati were the Matsyas. The other prominent tribes included the Yadus-Turvaśas; Anus-Druhyus and the Purus. Michael Witzel, in his Paper, titled "Rigvedic history: poets, chieftains and politics" has identified about 30 Rig-Vedic tribes and clans and focused particularly on the above-mentioned "Five tribes."

It is a stupendous task to present a detailed profile of each of the Vedic tribes, since scanty details are available about them as regards their geographical locations, the names of their chieftains or kings and the priestly clans with which they were associated. We do get some information about these tribes from the Rig-Vedic hymns and other Vedic texts including the Brāhmaṇas and some secondary sources. In order to substantiate the likely locations where these tribes settled, we have necessarily to turn to Vedic rivers, mountains / hill ranges and plain lands associated with them. The Vedic tribes find a mention in the texts in a somewhat vague manner and finding their approximate location with reference to the rivers with which they seem to be linked, provides the best option. This is also because towns do not find any mention in the Ṛgvedic hymns except for the word '*Pur*'[71] and since the people were on the move, we do not get the names of permanent villages. The plain lands as such do not have names at that time and received the names of the tribes who roamed in that area. It is so typical down to the period of the Upaniṣads or even later that certain areas, for example, the Videha areas were called the Videhas and not the other way.

The riverine areas included the banks of the Indus, its sister streams – Vitastā (Jhelum), Asiknī (Chenab), Paruṣṇī (Ravi), Vipāś (Beas), and Śutudrī (Sutlej) – alongside the banks of the Sarasvatī, the Yamuna, and the Ganges. For example, referring to Sarasvatī, the hymn 96.2 in Book VIII of the Ṛgveda mentions about the Pūrus, an Aryan tribe settled on both banks of the Sarasvatī or Indus. RV book IV hymn 30.14 also alludes to another tribe which dwelt in a hilly region. It refers to Kulitara's son Sambara as the dasa from the lofty hill.

The geographical locations, where the tribes settled down, acquired the names of those tribes. Some other features like physical characteristics,

---

71 Rau, W. (1976)"The Meaning of *pur* in Vedic Literature," *Abhandlungen der Marburger Gelehrten Gesellschaft* III/1, München: W. Finck.

analogous cultural pattern or common ancestry also were the other identifying factors in this respect.

Keeping the above background in view, an attempt has been made to provide on the basis of information as available, the details of each tribe, the approximate locations of their habitat, the names of their chieftains, the books of the Ṛgveda to which they relate as also their linkages with poets and chieftains identified from the hymns.

An attempt has also been made to construct a Vedic grid and graphically present the above information. The geographical features would take into account the rivers and mountainous areas to which the tribes gravitated for settlement.

First, we take up the "Five tribes" – Anus, Druhyus, Purus, Turvaśas and Yadus – that figure prominently in the various hymns of the Ṛgveda

For example, these 'Five tribes' figure in the Book I, hymn 108.8 of the Ṛgveda which relates to the "Battle of Ten Kings". These tribes again appear in the Book VII, hymn 18 of the Ṛgveda. The relevant stanzas 5 to 10 of this hymn as translated into English by Schmidts [72] also mention these tribes. Similarly, Book VII hymns 18.6 and 18.7 specifically mention Turvaśa, Druhyus, the Pakthās, the Bhalānas, the Ālinā-s besides the Śivās and the Visāṇins.

There are also allusion to five tribes in the Book III hymns 37.9, 59.8, Book V hymn 86.2, Book VI hymn 61.12, Book VII hymn 15.2, Book VIII hymn 32.22, Book IX, hymns 65.23,92.3, 101.9 and Book X hymns 45.6, 53.4 and 53.5 of the Ṛgveda. [73] The above-mentioned hymns of the books of the Ṛgvedic Saṃhitā where these tribes figure also give an indication of their possible dwelling places on the plains of the Punjab. For example, the possible locale of Yadu-Turvaśa and Anu-Druhyu is stated to be in the Punjab region when the Pūrus and the Bharatas arrived there. The locale

72 H.P. Schmidt's article, "Notes on Ṛgveda 7.18.5-10. Indica (Organ of the Heras Institute of Indian History and Culture, Bombay) 17, 41-47. (1980)

73 The 'five tribes' who figure prominently in Book VII of the Ṛgveda, participated in the famous 'Battle of Ten Kings'. The scene of the battle was on the banks of the Paruṣṇī (Ravi). In this battle, the Pūru tribes under the guidance of sage Viśvāmitra together with other Indo-Aryan tribes such as theTurvaśas, the Yadus, the Matsyas, the Druyus, the Pakthās, the Bhalānas, the Ālinās, the Śhivas and the Visāṇiṇs were arraigned against the Tṛtsu clan led by Sudas. The latter under the guidance of the sage Vasistha inflicted defeat on the confederation of 'Ten Kings'.

of Anus could possibly be alongside the river Paruṣṇī with the Druhyus to the north-west and the Yadus near Yamuna. Their original habitat is stated to be in the mountainous country of Afghanistan along Helmand river. The Pūrus came later into the subcontinent and according to the Jaiminīya Brāhmaṇa, the Pūru king Trasadasyu and the Bharata king Divodāsa inhabited on the western side of the river Indus at the time of the composition of Book IV. The Pūru king, Trasadasyu is believed to have 'moulded the defeated Anu-Druhyu and Turvaśa-Yadu [in the battle of Ten kings] into the 'Five Peoples' [representing 'Five tribes]. The Bharatas were a subtribe of the Pūru who, later, came into prominence. These migrations into the sub-continent witnessed frequent strife and shifting alliances, prominently highlighted in the 'Battle of Ten Kings', which also saw replacement of the Bharata purohita(Priest) Viśvāmitra by Vasiṣtha and the break-up of the Bharata-Pūru alliance.

We discuss below each of these five tribes first and thereafter follow it up with the other tribes of the Ṛgvedic period.[74] The details about each of the tribes are also given in a table form under five heads. In some cases the table is partially populated for want of information under a particular head.

a) Anus

As per the Vedic Index of Names, Anus denote a special people and find mention along with the Druhyus in RV Book VII, hymn 18.14 and with the Turvaśas, Yadus, and Druhyus in RV Book VIII, hymn 10.5. All these five tribes are supposed to have had their dwelling place on the banks of the river Paruṣṇī (Ravi). Anus were connected with the priestly families of Madhuchchandas, Viśvāmitra, Vasiṣtha, Kaṇvas, Āṅgiras, and Atri and the name of their chieftain was Anu.

In tracing the genealogy of Anu, one has to turn to book I, hymn 31.4 of the Ṛgveda, where Pururavaśa finds a mention. One of his descendants, was Yayati who figure in RV I, hymn 31.17 [75] .

---

[74] A.A. Macdonell & A.B. Keith: Vedic Index of Names and Subjects, Vols. I&II Motilal Banarsidass, Delhi Reprint 1982.

[75] According to epic-puranic tradition, Yayati had five sons, namely, Yadu, Turvaśa, Druhyu, Anu, and Puru. After a long rule, Yayati is said to have divided his territories among his sons and Anu got territories to the north of the Sarasvatī region (on the banks of Paruṣṇī).

Anu along with some others find mention in RV Book VIII, hymns 10.5 and 10.6.

Anu figures in the "Battle of Ten Kings" where the five tribes and a few other tribes joined hands on the banks of Paruṣṇī to defeat king Sudās but the confederacy arraigned against Sudās lost the battle. In this battle the Anus and the other members of the confederacy received support from the sage Viśvāmitra while the king Sūdas was supported by the sage Vasiṣtha.

Table I: Anus

Name of the tribe	Geographical location	Period	Chieftain/ King	Priestly family
Anus	on the banks of Paruṣṇī	RV Books I, V,VII and VIII	Anu	Priestly families of Madhuchchandas, Viśvāmitra, Vasiṣtha, Kaṇvas, Āṅgiras, Atri

b) Druhyus

As per the Vedic Index of Names and Subjects, the name of this tribe occurs several times in the Ṛgveda along with the four other tribes which go by the nomenclature of "Five Tribes." [76] They may be situated in the North-west region between Vitastā &Asiknī and later, according to the epics, moved to Gandhara. Druhyus were connected with the priestly families of Vāmadeva-Āṅgi-rasa, Atri, Vasiṣtha, and Kaṇvas and the name

[76] Druhyu was one of the sons of Yayati, the famous king belonging to Sudyumna dynasty, who ruled on the banks of Sarasvati. RV Book VII, hymn 96.2 lends credence to this location which speaks of Purus, another son of Yayati who lived on the banks of the Sarasvati (North-western region). The English translation of this hymn is as follows: *"When in the fulness of their strength the Purus dwell, Beauteous One, on thy two grassy banks, Favour us thou who hast the Maruts for thy friends: stir up the bounty of our chiefs."* (Trans. R.T.H. Griffiths: Hymns of the Rgveda. According to the Puranic tradition (Vayu Puran and Brahmand Puran), the sons of Yayati established their kingdoms in the adjoining areas with Druhyu moving to further west in the north-western region, the territory situated between the Vitasta and the Askini. This is corroborated by the fact that the Druhyus later migrated to Gandhara where a kingdom was established. Drhuyu figures in the "Battle of Ten Kings" fought on the Parsuni where he along with the others lost the battle to king Sudas.

of their chieftain was Druhyu. They figure in RV books I, IV, VI, VII, IX and X.

Table II: Druyhus

Name of the tribe	Geographical location	Period	Chieftain /King	Priestly family
Druhyus	North-Western region between Vitastā&Asikni	RVBooks I, IV, VI, VII, VIII,IX &X	Druhyu	Vāmadeva-Āṅgi-rasa, Atri, Vasiṣtha, Kaṇvas & Rishis of various other families.

c) Pūrus:

The Pūrus represent a group of tribes who along with the Bharatas are prominent in the Ṛgveda and appeared on the scene succeeding earlier groups of migrants such as the Turvaśas and the Yadus. As per the Vedic Index of Names and Subjects, the Pūrus were located in the area along the Sarasvatī [77] and their great kings were Purukutsa and Trasadasyu.[78] The Jaiminīya Brāhmaṇa places Pūru king Trasadasyu on the western side of the river Indus at the time of composition of Book 4 of the RV. Trasadasyu occupies the place of principal chieftain in Book 4 of the Ṛgveda where he is also referred to as Paurukutsya, the son of Purukutsa(4.42). Pūru is presented in a favourable light in book V of the Ṛgveda and also figures frequently in Book 6 of RV together with the Druhyu, Yadu and Turvaśa (6.46.7-8). After the Bharatas inflicted defeat on Pūru tribe in the 'Battle of Ten Kings', their importance diminished considerably. They were connected to the priestly family of Vasiṣtha and figure prominently in Book VII of the Ṛgveda.

---

[77] Rgveda Book VII, hymn 96.2

[78] RV Book VII. hymn 8.4 , As per Puranic tradition, Pu¯ru was one of the five sons of Yayati whom he installed as his successor of the kingdom he ruled on the banks of Sarasvati. Five of Yayati's sons including Pu¯ru were members of the confederacy along with a few other tribes and fought on the banks of the river Paruṣṇi¯ against King Su¯das, who was in the genealogical line of the Ṭrtsu king Divoda¯sa, but were defeated. This is known as the "Battle of Ten Kings" and finds mention in the RV Book VII, hymns 18,33, and 83(belonging to the priestly family of Vasiṣtha) where Indra, impressed with the libation and exhortations of Vasiṣtha helped Suda¯s defeat the confederacy of ten tribes.

TableIII: Pūrus

Name of the tribe	Geographical location	Period	Chieftain/ King	Priestly family
The Pūrus represent a group of tribes who along with the Bharatas are prominent in the Ṛgveda and appeared on the scene succeeding earlier groups of migrants such as the Turvaśa and the Yadu. As per the Vedic Index, Pūru inhabited in the region of the Sarasvatī and their great kings were Purukutsa and Trasadasyu.	Region of river Sarasvatī(as per Vedic Index); During the late Vedic period, the location is eastern U.P. or Bihar border.; JB places Pūru king Trasadasyu on the western side of the Sindhu at the time of composition of BK.4	RVBook VII	Trasadasyu	Vasiṣtha

d) Turvaśas

This name occurs several times in the Ṛgveda representing people of a tribe or a person.[79] Turvaśa is also clubbed with Yadu in the Rig-Vedic hymns. Turvaśa was among the ten kings who formed a confederacy and fought against king Sūdas on the banks of river Paruṣṇī where he lost the battle. They are supposed to be situated towards South east of Sarasvatī. The precise location is, however, not known, except that they were in the Punjab region at the time of arrival of the Pūrus and Bharatas. They figure in RVBooks I, VIII, IX and X and their chieftain was Turvaśa. They were connected with various priestly families including Kaṇva-Āṅgiras As per Vedic Index, there is a reference to Turvaśa in the Śatapatha Brāhmaṇa (Xiii. 5.4.16) as having been allies of the Pañcālas. Nothing further is known about this tribe in the Ṛgveda.

---

[79] Vedic Index of Names and Subjects, A. A. Macdonell & A.B. Keith, vol.I 1st ed. London, 1912. According to Puranic evidence, Turvaśa is believed to be one of the sons of Yayati, the famous king belonging to Sudyumna dynasty, who ruled on the banks of theSarasvatī. Yayati divided his kingdom after a long rule among his sons and Turavaśa perhaps got territory to the south-east of Sarasvatī, on the banks of Dṛstadvati.

Table IV: Turvaśas

Name of the tribe	Geographical location	Period	Chieftain/ King	Priestly family
Turvaśas	South east of Sarasvatī. The precise location is not known, but is supposed to be in the Punjab region at the time of arrival of the Pūrus & Bharatas.	RVBooks I,VIII, IX and X	Turvaśa	I,IX&X- Various priestly families;VIII- Kaṇva-Āṅgiras

e) Yadus

Yadus represents an ancient Vedic tribe with Yadu as the name of its king. Yadu and Turvaśa appear together in several Ṛgvedic hymns, such as Book I, hymns 36.18; 54.6 and 174.9; Book IV, hymn 30.17;Book V, hymn 31.8 ; Book VI, hymn 45.1. They are mentioned together in several other hymns in books VIII, IX and X of the Ṛgveda.[80] They were situated on Yamuna towards south-west of Sarasvatī and connected with various priestly families including Vāmadeva; Atri; Bhāradvāja, and Kāṇva-Āṅgiras.

Table V: Yadus

Name of the tribe	Geographical location	Period	Chieftain/ King	Priestly family
Yadus	Yamuna,South-West of Sarasvatī	RV Books I,IV,V,VI, VIII,IX and X	Yadu	I,IX&X- Various families;IV-Vāmadeva;V-Atri;VI-Bhāradvāja, VIII-Kāṇva-Āṅgiras

Of the five tribes mentioned above, various Rig-Vedic hymns put Anu-Druhyu and Yadu-Turvaśa together; for example, Book VII hymn 18. 13 in the former case and Book VI hymn 20.12 in the case of Yadu and Turavaśa. This may be on account of common ancestry, contiguous territories, and

[80] According to Puranic evidence, Yadu is one of the five sons of Yayati, the famous king belonging to Sudyumna dynasty who ruled on the banks of the river Sarasvatī. When Yayati divided his territories among his sons, Yadu got south-west part of Yayati's outlying territories. Yadu along with his brothers was also a member of a confederacy of ten tribes which fought against King Sudās on the banks of the river Paruṣṇī, but lost the battle.

common cultural pattern. These five tribes find mention in the hymns of Books I, IV, VI, VII, VIII, IX, and X of the Ṛgveda.

Different priestly families are connected with the composition of hymns of various books of the Ṛgveda. Book I containing 191 hymns is ascribed to the rishis belonging to various families; Book II containing 43 hymns is attributed to a single priestly family, that of Gṛtsamāda; Book III is ascribed to the family of Viśvāmitra ; Book IV to Vāmadeva ; Book V mainly to the family of Atri; book VI to Bhāradvāja; Book VII to Vasiṣtha ; Book VIII jointly to Kāṇva and Āṅgirasa; and Books IX and X are believed to have been composed by rishis of various families.

f) Other Ṛgvedic Tribes

The particulars of the other Ṛgvedic tribes are given below:

Table VI: Other Ṛgvedic Tribes

Name of the tribe	Geographical location	Period	Chieftain/ King	Priestly family
Ajas (a dasa tribe) figures in RVVII 18.19(XX)	Northern India, Bank of Yamuna	Book VII	Aja	Vasiṣtha

It appears that Aja brought tribute to Indra after he was defeated by Tṛtsus [81] on the banks of the Yamuna. Tṛutsus are perceived as helpers of Sudas in this battle.

Name of the tribe	Geographical location	Period	Chieftain/ King	Priestly family
Ālinā-s Took part in the Battle of Ten Kings against King Sudās (RV VII, 18.7)	Sindhu & sister streams	Book VII	Alina	Vasiṣtha
Ayus figures in RV I, 53.10, 31.11 and RVII, 14.7;also	Western side of the Sindhu	Books I &VII	AYU	BKI- Various families ,

[81] Vedic Index of Names and Subjects,Vol.I A.A. Macdonell, A.B. Keith,Motilal Banarsidass, Delhi,P.320

described as the ancestors of the Ayava tribes[82]; Succeeded Purūravas as "King"				BK VII-Vasiṣtha
Bhalānas One of the tribes ranged with the enemies of king Sudās in the Battle of Ten Kings (RV VII, 18.7)	Bolan Pass(Quetta)	Book VII	Not known	BK VII-Vasiṣtha
Bharatas prominent in RV III&VII in conjunction with Sudās and Tṛitsus; associated with Divodāsa of Tṛtsu Dynasty(RV VI,16.45)	Original settlement somewhere in the north-west; around the Indus and then between Sarasvatī and Dṛsadvati; later moved to Ganga-Yamuna belt	Books III, 23.4 & VII	ŚB &AB mention Bharata Daushani as king	Dirghatmas, Viśvāmitra, Bhāradvāj a, Vasiṣtha
Cedis Name of tribal people mentioned in Danastuti RV VIII 5,37-39, also in late Vedic texts Cedis occur with the Matsyas .	Inhabitants of greater Punjab; moved south of Yamuna in later Vedic period.	RV VIII	Kasu	Kāṇva
Gandhāris the name of the people in the north-western region of India during the RV period; also mentioned with Mūjavants, An˙gas and Magadhas in AV(22.14),also figure in	the north-west region [83,84] According to Zimmer,[85] Gandharis were settled in Vedic times on the south bank of the Kubhā up to its mouth in	Book I	Druhyu (as per Aitareya Brāhmaṇa (VII,34), SB 8.1.4.10	Various authors

[82] The Indo-Aryans of Ancient South Asia: Ed. by George Erdosy, Walter de Gruyter, Berlin. New York 1995,P.328-29

[83] Tribes in Ancient India: B.C. Law, Bhandarkar Oriental Research Institute, Poona,1943, p.9

[84] Ibid, According to D.R. Bhandarkar, it included the western Punjab and E.Afghanistan.

[85] Vedic Index of Names and Subjects, Vol.I, P. 219

Baudhāyana Śrauta Sūtra(xxxi.13)	the Indus			
Ikṣvāku finds mention in RV Book X 60.4. and in AV XIV 30.9.	Western bank of Sindhu; later in east Kosala	Book X	Ikṣvāku, laterPurukutsa	X-Various authors
Krivi As per SB XIII 5, 4,7, Krivi is the older name of a section of the Pañcālas; It finds mention in RV Book VIII, 20.24, according to which they appear to be based on the banks of Sindhu /Asiknī.	Original settlement in the region between the Sindhu and the Asiknī (Chenab)[86], later migrated to the land of the Pañcālas; had their habitat in districts of Barielly, Budaun, Farukkhabad.	RV Book VIII	Kraivya Pañcāla(mentioned in SB Xiii.5,4,7) as the king of Krivis	Kāṇva Section of Book VIII
Kikaṭas [87]	Southern outskirts of Kurukṣetra; a northern Rajasthani tribe.[88]	RV Book III	[89]	Viśvāmitra
Kurus In the Rgveda, Kurus do not appear as a name in RV BK X &VIII but only the nameKuruśravana appears. The Kurus are usually mentioned as Kuru-Pañcāla which is	The territory according to Aitareya Brāhmaṇa viii.14 is Madhyadesa which corresponds to western U.P. Kurus are frequently mentioned for being	RV books VIII&X (only the name Kuruśravana finds mention)	Kuruśravana (RVX,33.4); Kuruśravana connection with the Kurus is also recognized in the RV as	BK VIII-Kāṇva section BK X-ascribed to various families. (Kavaṣa

86 Vedic Index Vol. I. p.198

87 According to Nirukta (VI, 32), it was the name of non-Aryan country and later this name was given as synonym of Magadha. They also appear in RV III, 53.14

88 According to Weber (Indische Studien I, 186) Kikata were based in Magadha and were also Aryans but at variance with other Aryan tribes.

89 Pramaganda figures in RV Book III Hymn 53.14 as follows: *"Among the Kikatas what do thy cattle? They pour no milky draught, they heat no caldron. Bring thou to us the wealth of Pramaganda; give up to us, O Maghavan, the low-born"*

post Rig-Vedic. They are repeatedly mentioned together in Jaiminīya Brāhmaṇa vol.I 163(iii 7.6; 8.7; iv, 7.2).	in occupation of Kurukṣetra.		Trasadasyava, a descendant of Trasadasyu, king of the Pūrus.Then we have Parikshit in AV XX and RV Khila section V	and Alusha)
Matsya As per Vedic Index[90], Matsya as a name of people figures in RV VII, 18.6. and in the Kauṣitāki Upaniṣad (IV.1) together with the Vaśas, name of a tribe which finds mention in AB (VIII,14.3) as being based in Madhyadesa.[91]	Western U.P. In RV VII, 18.6, "fish" alluding to the Matsyas seems to suggest their habitat by the side of the river Paruṣnī	Book VII	Dhvasan Dvaitavana (SB xiii. 5,4, 9)	Vasiṣtha
Mūjavant The name of this tribe finds mention in AV, V 22.5.7.8.14 along with the Gandhāris, the Mahāvṛṣas and the Balhikas.	In the RV X 34.1, Soma is described as Maujavata (as indicated in Vedic Index Vol.II (p.170) They are believed to be the inhabitant of Mūjavat in the northern most Kashmir	RV Book X	Not known	Ascribed to various authors
Nahuṣa[92]	Around the region of	Book IX,	Nahus	Bhāradvāj

---

90 Ibid Vol.II pp 121-122

91 This tribe derives its name from "fish" (SB XIII. 5.4.9) and is often seen in ancient texts as paired with Sursenas and Pancalas on grounds of territorial contiguity

92 Nahusa finds mention as an author of RV IX, 101. He was one of the celebrated early Saudyumna kings. Also finds mention in' India in the Vedic Age': P.L. Bhargava, The Upper India Publishing House Ltd, Lucknow,1956, p. 81

	the Sarasvatī[93]	also in RV I, VI, and VIII		a, Kāṇva-Āṅgirasa
Paktha[94]	Extreme west beyond the Indus	RV Books I,VII & Kāṇva section of BK VIII	Paktha[95]	Vasiṣtha, and Kāṇvas
Pañcajanah As per Vedic Index vol. I P.466-468, Panca-janah represents 'Five Peoples' variously described in the Vedic literature.[96]				
Pārāvata It finds mention in RV VIII, 34.18 and Pañcaviṃśa Brāhmaṇa, IX, 4.11 as the proper name of a people on the river Yamuna.	Habitat in the region of river Yamuna	Books VI & VIII	Not known	Book VI-Bhāradvāj a; Book VIII-Kāṇva

93 Ibid, P. 134 this was the territory of Sudyumna dynasty.

94The name this tribe occurs in RV VII, 18.7 as one which supported the confederacy of ten tribes against King Sudas in the f'Battle of the ten kings'. RV VIII, 22.10; 49.10 and RV X. 61.1, identify Paktha¯ as a protégé of Aśvin, as also connected toTrasadasyu and asTurvayana (opposed to Cyavana,a rishi) respectively .-Vedic Index Vol.I, P.463-464

95 Vedic Index Vol. I , P.464

96 Vedic Index Vol. I, P. 465-466. According to AB, iii.31 and iv, 27, they represent gods, men, Gandharva, snakes and the Fathers. They also refer to five tribes on the Sarasvati¯ (RV VI 61.2). Indra is also represented as *Pancajanya* in RV V, 32.11. Zimmer (Altindisches Leben, p.119-123) and others are of the view that *Pancajanya* in RV V, 32.11. refers to five tribes of the Anus, Druhyus, Yadus, Turvaśas and Pu¯rus who figure together in RV I, 108.8.

Parśu[97]	Original settlement in the Panjab along the western sister streams of the Indus.[98]	RV Book VIII	Not known	Kāṇva section of Bk VIII
Ruśama[99] Ruśama is mentioned in RV VIII, 3.13; 4.2 and 51.9 as a protégé of Indra. Also finds mention in RV Khila (section V). The Ruśmas are also mentioned in RV V, 30, 12.15 with King Rnamcaya and in AV XX. 127.1 with king Kaurama	Areas surrounding Kurukṣetra.	Books V&VIII Valakhilya Hymn III.9	Rnamcaya; Kaurama	Atri; Kāṇva section of Bk VIII
Sārasvatas They occur in RV III, 4.8 together with river Sarasvatī. This tribe is also identified with Ābhīras who were a Central Asiatic people and settled near the Vinaśana region, Gujarat and the lower Indus valley.[100]	[101]	RV III	Not known	Viśvāmitr a

[97] Vedic Index Vol.I, P. 504-505, According to Zimmer, Parśus were known to Panini as a warrior tribe. The name appears in one passage in the Rgveda (VIII, 6.46) as the name of a man. Ludwig (Trans. Of the Rgveda) finds in RV X, 33.2 a reference to the defeat of Kuruśravaṇa, a Kuru king, by the Parśus

[98] Tribes of Ancient India: Mamata Choudhury, Indian Museum, Calcutta, 1977, P.41, are believed to have moved over to the south-western region during the Puranic period.

[99] Vedic Index Vol. II, P.225

[100] Racial Affinities of Early North Indian Tribes, Sudhakar Chattopadhyaya, Munshiram Manoharlal, New Delhi,1973,P.99

Satvants They figure in AB VIII. 14.3 and S.B XIII 5,4,21. According to S.B. they were defeated by Bharata.	South of Yamuna. According to AB VIII 14, 3.[102] , they are supposed to belong to the south.	AB & SB	Not known	Not Known
Śigru[103] This tribe occurs in RV VIII. 5.25 and again in RV X 40.7 together with the Ajas and the Yakṣus in connection with the battle they lost to King Sūdas.	As per RV VII, 18.9, the Śigrus lived on the banks of the Yamuna . This was also the habitat of the Ajas and the Yakṣus	RV Books VII, VIII & X	Not known	BK.VII- Vasiṣtha, BK VIII- Ka¯ṇva section BK.X- ascribed to various authors.
Śimyu As per R.T. H. Griffiths translation of RV Hymns (P.64), this tribe represents men of indigenous hostile race and figures in RV Book I, 30.18 together with Dasyus. They are supposed to be enemies of Sanskrit- speaking people. This tribe[104] is also mentioned in the RV VII. 18.5 in connection with its defeat in the battle of the 'Ten Kings' at the hands of Sudās.	The Śimyus probably inhabited in the region along the tributaries of the Indus as seems to be alluded to in (RV I. 100.18).	RV Books I & VII	Not known	BKI- ascribed to various authors; BK.VII- Vasiṣtha

101 According to Vayu Purana, Sārasvatas are the people dwelling along the Sarasvati¯, which goes into the sea past modern Somnath. Finds mention in Tribes in Ancient India: B.C. Law, Bhandarkar Oriental Series, Poona, 1943, P.397

102 Vedic Index Vol. II, P.421

103 Ibid, P.378

104 Vedic Index Vol. II, P.381

Śiva Śivas find mention in RV VII, 18.7 where they are "grouped together with four other minor tribes, viz., the Ālinās, Pakhtās, Bhalānas and Visāṇiṇs"[105] as having been defeated by King Sudās.	[106] Also between the Indus and Asikni rivers	RV Book VII	Saibya[107] (a designation of king Amitratapan a Susmina and finds mention in the Aitareya Brāhmaṇa (viii.23,10))	Vasiṣtha
Sṛñjaya[108] Finds mention in RV, VI. 27.7 and IV. 15.4. Sṛñjaya Daivavata's Victory over the Turvaśas and the Vṛcīvants is celebrated in RV VI. 27.7. The Sṛn¯jayas and Tṛtsus were close to each other as would be evident from the common celebration of Divodāsa and Sṛñjaya prince in the above hymn. In JB paragraph 196, they are mentioned as a part of the Kurus.	Ibid[109] The location of this tribe is uncertain. Having regard to their proximity to Divodāsa, their location may be in the region west of the Indus. Their location could even be farther east than the Indus since their allies Tṛtsus were located in Madhyadesa.	BooksIV & VI	Daivavata; Somaka Sahadevya and his father Sahadeva Sṛñjaya[110] (Ibid)	BK IV- Vāmadev a BK. VI- Bhāradvāj a

105 Ibid. P.381 They are also associated with Uśīnaras and this is evident from the Anukramini of the Rgveda, ascribing hymn X , 119 to Sivi Ausinara

106 The Śivas are believed to be inhabitants of the region lying between the Iravati and Chandrabhaga, in the northern region. Later, they seem to have migrated southwards to Rajputana.

107 Vedic Index Vol. II, P.394

108 Vedic Index Vol.II, P.469-470

109 Ibid

110 Ibid

Ṭṛtsus As per the Vedic Index Vol. I, P.320-323) Ṭṛtsus are a name of a tribe of great importance in RV where it finds mention in several hymns of the seventh book. They are shown as helpers of Sudās in the battle against the ten kings. [111], [112],[113].	East of Saptasindhu	Book VII	Ṭṛtsu	Vasiṣtha
Uśīnaras In the Kauṣitaki Upaniṣad (iv.I) the Uśīnaras are associated with the Kuru-Pañcālas and Vaśas. AB (ii. 7, 5; x. 91, 14) also indicate that the Vaśa tribe was based in Madhyadesa along with the Kurus, the Pañcālas and the Uśīnaras.	[114],[115]	RV Book X	Queen Uśīnarani (finds mention in RV X, 59.10	BK. X-ascribed to various authors.

[111] Translation of the Rgveda 3.175: Ludwig identifies Ṭṛtsus with the Bharatas

[112] Buddha: Oldenberg p.406, Oldenberg holds Ṭṛtsus as the priests of the Bharata people on the basis of RV vii. 33.1.

[113] Vedische Studien, 2, 136: Geldner holds that in singular, Ṭṛtsu stands for king, that is, Suda¯s. (on the basis of the RV vii, 18.3)

[114] Ancient Indian Historical Tradition, p.109 According to Pragiter, Uśi¯naras initially were settled in the Punjab region. But according to AB (VIII 14) they were located in Madhyadesa together with the Vaśas.

[115] According to Cambridge History of India, Vol. I (p.84), the Uśi¯naras lived to the north of the Kuru country.

Vaśas[116] It is a name of a tribe, mentioned in AB V111,14.3, located in Madhyadesa along with the Kurus, the Pañcālas and the Uśīnaras. Kauṣitāki Upaniṣad (IV.1) also links them with the Matsyas. Vaśas and Uśi¯naras are linked together in the AV. VII, 113.	Madhyadesha	AV & AB	Not Known	Not Known
Vṛcīvants[117] This tribe finds mention in the RV VI, 27.5, where it is stated that the Sṛñjaya king Daivavata conquered Vṛcīvants and Turvaśas. Hariyūpīyā river finds mention in the RV VI, 27.5 where Vṛcīvants were defeated by Abhyavartin Cayamana.	Probably west of the Indus. The position is not quite clear	RV VI	Not known	Bhāradvāj a
Visāṇiṇ[118] The name of this tribe occurs once in RV VII, 18.7 as an enemy of Tṛtsus. This tribe figures as a member of the confederacy that fought and lost the battle of the ten kings against Sudās	They appear to be situated in the north western region.	RV VII	Not known	Vasiṣtha

[116] Vedic Index Vol. II, P.273.

[117] Vedic Index Vol. II, P. 319, 499.

[118] Ibid. P.313

Chapter VII
Vedic Grid

A graphic representation of the Ṛgvedic tribes, their locations, names of their kings/chieftains, linkages with the books of the Ṛgveda and priestly families are given in the three maps below:

Map 1: Rig-Vedic Tribes - Geographical Location

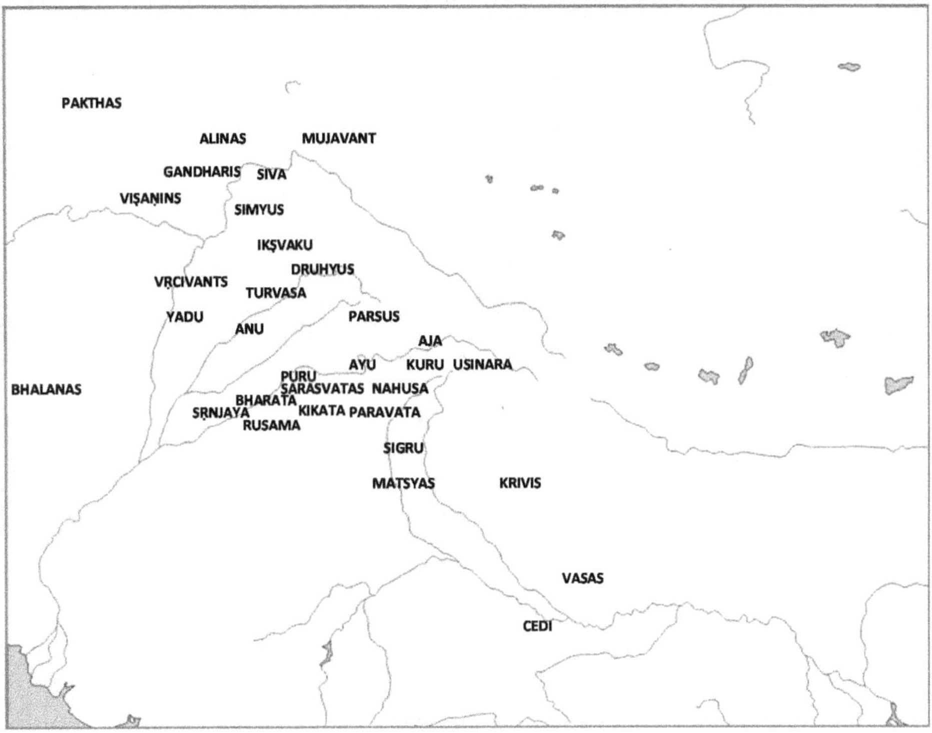

Map 2: Rig-Vedic Tribes/ Kings or Chieftains/Priestly Families

Names of Rig-Vedic Tribes (Kings or Chieftains) / Priestly Families

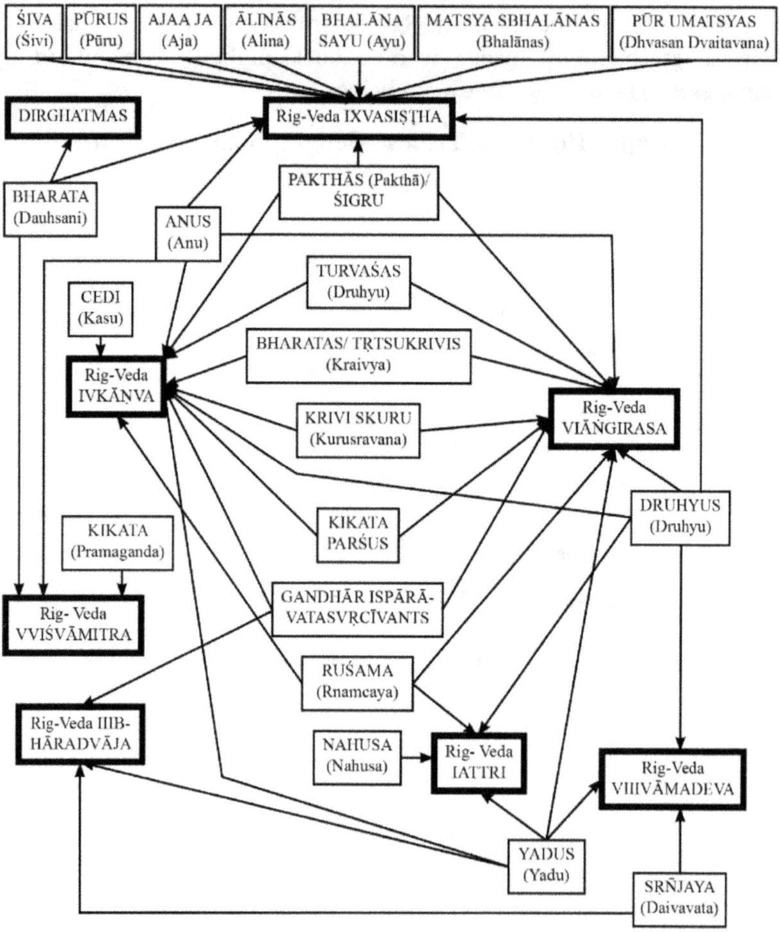

Map 3: Name of Rig-Vedic Tribes/Books of Rig-Veda

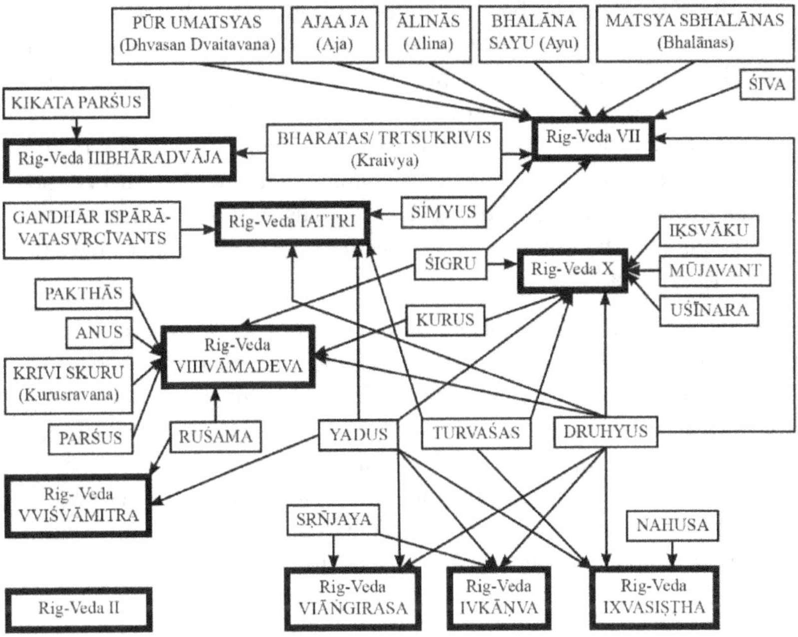

It would appear from the above three graphic representations that the Ṛgvedic tribes mainly inhabited in different locations towards the north-west in the region of the Sapta-Sindhu. The Yadus-Turvaśas inhabited in the North-West, Pūrus in the West, and Anus-Druhyus in the South-west. They were closely connected with the priestly families which composed Books II-VII of the Ṛgveda. These priestly families were: Gṛtsamāda (Book II); Viśvāmitra (Book III); Vāmadeva (Book IV); Atri (Book V); Bhāradvāja (Book VI); and Vasiṣtha (Book VII). Book I represents a group of 9 poets; Book VIII is ascribed to two priestly families, namely, the Kāṇvas and Āṅgirasas; and Book X is attributed to various authors, such as, Atri, Bhāradvāja, Vasiṣtha. Book IX is a collection of Soma rituals culled out from various books of the Ṛgveda

The graphic representation also shows the alignment of various books to different locations in the subcontinent and beyond. Most of the imagery and content of these books are associated with the Punjab and the north-western region and with the rivers such as the Indus, the Sarasvatī, the Paruṣṇī, the Sarayu and the Ganges. The authorship of these Vedic texts is attributed to various priestly families inhabiting different geographical locations in the aforesaid region. The home of these families may, however, represent sometimes a much wider area in geographical terms.

Chapter VIII

The Post-Ṛgvedic Tribes

During the post-Ṛgvedic period, the Aryan tribes had moved away from the valley of the Sapta-Sindhu and the hilly tracts of the northwest to the vast and expansive plain land in the eastern region. The number of such tribes increased following induction of many non-Aryan tribes which find mention in the later Saṃhitās and the Brāhmaṇas. Further, during this period regrouping of tribes also occurred and on account of such mergers, we find super tribes emerging on the scene. The Kūrus, the Pañcālas, theKosalas, the Kāśis and the Videhas acquired prominence as the leading tribes. The prominent post Ṛgvedic tribes along with their places of habitat, names of their kings/chieftains (wherever known) and their time frame are indicated below:

Table VII: Summary of Post Ṛgvedic Tribes

Name of the Tribe	Geographical location	Period	Chieftain/King
The Kambojas	Extreme North-West.	500 B. C.	Sudaksina/ Kamboja
The Pañcālas	Madhyadesha	800 B.C.	Kaiśina, Kraivya, Satrasaha, Durmukha
The Kosalas	Eastern Region of UttarPradesh	Brāhmanạ Period	Para Antara Hairanyanabha, Pasendi (during Buddha's time).
The Videha	Tirhut or North Bihar	Brāhmanạ Period may be 800 B.C	King Nami Sapya, Janak
The Kāśi	east of the Central region.(Madhyadesa)	Brāhmanạ Period	Ajātaśatru
The Śālvas	On theYamuna	Brāhmanạ period	Yaugandhari
The Kiratas	Initially in the Himalayan region, then Magadha (Bihar) or Odisha coast	Later Vedic period	Not known
The	Somewhere in Bihar	Period of Aitareya Brāhmaṇa, Not	

Pulindas		known	
The Puṇḍras	Eastern region	Aitareya Brāhmaṇa	Not known
The Śavaras	Eastern region; , in Odisha , as per the later texts.	Aitareya Brāhmaṇa	Not known
The Bāhīkas	The Punjab region	Brāhmaṇa period	Balhika Pratipiya
The Mahāvṛṣa	Eastern Punjab/Haryana region	Brāhmaṇa period	Hṛtsvasaya
The Aṅgas	on the Sone and the Ganges	Late Vedic Period	Not known

During the early 6th century BCE, 16 important states, also called Mahajanapada flourished in ancient India. Some of these were monarchies and the others were oligarchical in character. The list of such states included Kamboja, Pañcāla, Kāśī, Kosala. The Kambojas find mention in several ancient texts, particularly, in the works of the grammarian Panini and in the other brahmanic and Buddhist literature. H.A. Rose[119] subscribes to the view that they were of Iranian origin and that their territory lay in the extreme north-west. This tribe also finds mention in the epics (Shanti Parva of Mahabharata) and the Puranic literature. They were known for their fine breed of horses and excelled as cavalry men[120]. According to traditions, their king Sudakshina was a great warrior who had participated in the Mahabharata war. The Pañcālas inhabited the Madhyadesha region and find mention along with the Kurus. After the Kurus, the kingdom of this tribe had emerged as an important political and cultural centre during the late Vedic period. There is further discussion on this tribe later in the book. The Kosalas find mention in the later Vedic texts, particularly, the Satapatha Brahmana. The Kosalas also figure in the Puranic, the epic and the Buddisht literature. They were located in the eastern region of modern Uttar Pradesh (one of the major states of India) and Shravasti was a flourishing city of this kingdom. Prasenjit (also called Pasendi) was an important king

[119] A Glossary of the Tribes and Castes of the Punjab and North-West Frontier Province, H.A. Rose, p.p. 25-26, 1997,Nirmal Publishers and Distributors, New Delhi-110027.

[120] Hindu Polity, K.P. Jayaswal, ,2nd ed., Bangalore,1943

of the Kosala kingdom and also a contemporary of the Buddha. The Videhas were located in the northern region of Bihar(a state in India), also called Tirhut region and find mention in the later Vedic texts, particularly, the Satapatha Brahmana. It emerged as a prominent political and cultural centre under their king Janaka, who was a great patron of the Vedic culture and philosophy. King Janaka patronised learned Brahmins, seers and all wise men and the celebrated Brahmin priest Yājñāvalkya graced his court. The Kāśī refers to the people who were based on the banks of Varuna and Asi rivers from which its capital city Varanasi derives its name. The name of Ajātaśatru finds mention as the king of Kāśī in the Bṛhadāraṇyaka Upaniṣad. The Kāśīs and the Videhas shared close relations. The kingdom of Kāśī , a powerful kingdom of north India, was later subdued by the Kosalas and became a part of the latter's territory. The Śālvas find mention in the Śatapatha Brāhmaṇa and appear to be closely connected with the Kuru-Pañcālas. We do not have much information on this tribe. The Kiratas figure in both early and later Vedic texts. They inhabited initially in the Himalayan region and later moved to the eastern region (Bihar and Odisha). According to one view[121] they had a good military organization and to some extent were advanced in civilization and thus could not be put in the category of "barbarians". They are also mentioned along with the other tribes such as, Śavaras, Puṇḍras, Yavanas as Mleccha tribes. Not much is known about the Pulindas except that they were an outcast tribe who find mention in Aitareya Brāhmaṇa[122]. Some scholars associate this tribe with the Vindhya region and also maintain that they had multiple branches. The Puṇḍras find mention in Aitareya Brāhmaṇa as well as Baudhayana Dharma Sūtra. In the Aitareya Brāhmaṇa they are portrayed as outcasts. They are supposed to be non-Aryan people and were located in eastern region, most probably, Purnia region of Bihar. According to traditions, the Puṇḍras figured in the list of five eastern kingdoms[123] and shared with them a common ancestry. Śavaras, according to Edgar Thurston, were an important tribe who lived in Ganjam district of Odisha. As per Aitareya Brāhmaṇa, they are supposed be the descendants of the sons of the sage

---

121 Mlecchas in Early India, Aloka Parasher,P.188, Munshiram Manoharlal Publishers, New Delhi, 1991.

122 Vedic Index of Names and Subjects, Vol. II, A.A. Macdonell & A.B. Keith, p.8

123 These five eastern kingdom besides the Pundras were Kalinga, Suhma, Anga and Vanga

Viśvāmitra. The language spoken by them belonged to the Munda family. Vedic Index[124] places Bāhīkas in the Punjab region and they come to notice during the Brāhmaṇa period. However, according to Sir Edward Blunt[125], the Bāhīkas occupied part of the Punjab in the 4th century A.D. and figure as a Hindu caste in the Puranic lists H.A. Rose[126] identifies Bāhīkas with Bahilkas who came from the Balkh (N.W. Province). Mahāvṛṣa finds mention as a tribe in the Atharva-Veda along with another tribe Mujavants. Vedic Index of Names and Subjects refers to Jaiminiya Upaniṣad Brāhmaṇa (iii, 40.2) where Hṛtsvāśaya is identified as the king of this tribe. The Aṅgas find mention in the Atharva-Veda (V.22,14) and the Gopatha Brāhmaṇa(ii.9). Vedic Index refers to the views of Zimmer and Bloomfield to identify the settlement of this tribe in the vicinity of the rivers Sone and the Ganges.

---

124 Vedic Index of Names and Subjects, Vol. II, P.67

125 The Caste System of Northern India, CSir Edward Blunt, pp.24-25, Reprinted in 2010 by Isha Books, Delhi-110009.

126 A Glossary of the Tribes and Castes of the Punjab and North West Frontier Province, H.A. Rose, Nirmal Publishers ad Distributors, New Delhi- 110027, 1997, P.54

The Post-Rig-Vedic tribes, their geographical locations and time-frame are graphically represented below:

Map 4: Post Rig-Vedic Tribes

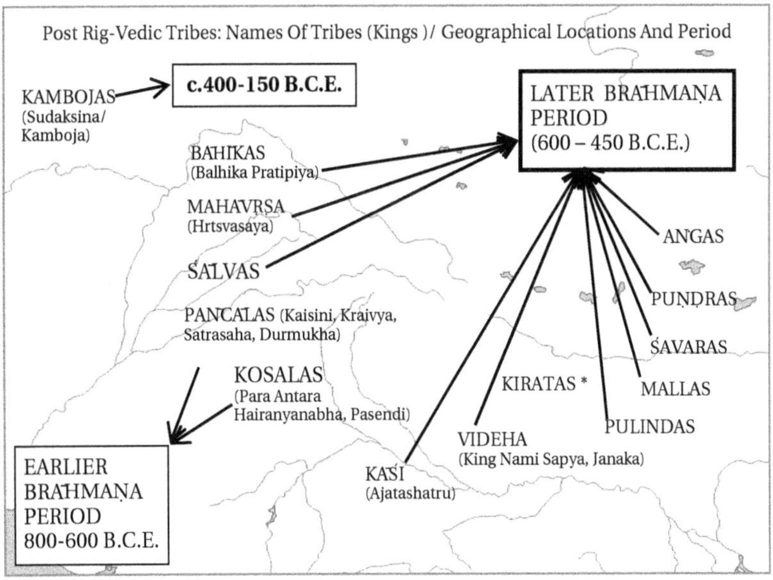

*** Later Vedic Period**

Having discussed the nature and linkages of the tribes during the Ṛgvedic and post Ṛgvedic periods, it is time now to reflect upon the political, social and religious aspects of the polity that prevailed during these two periods. We will discuss the features of the developments in the above spheres in the two time-frames together in order to ensure better appreciation of changes that occurred as the polity evolved from the Ṛgvedic to the post Ṛgvedic phase.

Chapter IX

Political System and Institutions during the Rig-Vedic and Post Rig-Vedic Periods

We have already seen that the Aryans came from different directions from the north and north-west of India and made their initial habitat in the region of the Sapta-Sindhu and lower regions of the Himalayan range. These people were Vedic tribes who came in groups and cattle-rearing was their main occupation. Thus the society during the early Vedic period assumed a tribal and pastoral character. The early Vedic phase witnessed proliferation of a few major but many smaller tribal units headed by tribal chiefs. These tribes had to contend with each other and also with the indigenous tribes on a continual basis. There was hardly any harmony among them which accounted for their frequent movement from one place to another either as a process of aggrandizement or in search of safer grazing locations or collection of grains from the local population (Dasyus). The tribes clashed amongst each other and also with the indigenous tribes in their search for cows. The later texts also testify to the march of Aryan tribes eastward to rob people of their grains. The society during the Ṛgvedic phase retained a tribal character where the people had the freedom to choose their occupations. The practice of occupations based on hereditary lines had not yet taken roots notwithstanding higher status enjoyed by the Brahmins and kṣatriyas in the society. The kingship in the tribal structure did not imply territorial monarchy and there are conflicting instances of heredity playing a role in anointment as a king or the viś having a say in the selection of a king. We come across various terms in Vedic texts such as, *rajan or viśpati* used to describe chiefship of a tribe. The meaning of the term *Rajan,* according to R.S. Sharma[127] during the Ṛgvedic period denoted "a tribal leader who combined the functions of both priest and warlord". He finds support for this view in the expression 'Gopati' applied to rajan for his role as a protector of the tribe. Similarly, according to him, the term viśpati also meant "head of a clan

[127] As pects of Political Ideas and Institutions in Ancient India, R.S. Sharma,Motilal Banarsidass,Delhi, Reprint 2009,Pp.186-187

comprising kinsmen". The use of both the terms for the chief in the context of the Ṛgvedic period implied head of a clan and "not the lord of a settlement" as was the case in the later Vedic period. The kingship evolved towards the later part of the Vedic period when territorial features came to be attached to kingship. Limited material resources were available to the king during the Ṛgvedic period as the practice of agriculture had not developed to a stage where it could become a source of income. Pastoralism could yield only meagre income which was insufficient to support any moderately large administrative machinery. That explains the existence of a few officials like the Purohita (Priest), Taksan (the carpenter), Mahisi (the queen) etc. who assisted the king in the performance of various tasks. The number of such officials grew in strength in the later Vedic period as would be apparent from the list of Ratnins (King's jewels) which we shall discuss later in the book under subsidiary administrative apparatus. In order to overcome the resource crunch, the chief had to take recourse to collecting tributes called "Bali" presumably in the form of cattle or agricultural produce, from the defeated tribes or from his own tribe's men. Initially, "Bali" was deemed as a voluntary contribution to the king made on ritualistic occasions but later acquired a coercive character. The quantum of resources, thus generated depended upon the prowess of the chief or the ability of those involved in the process on behalf of the chief. However, collection of tributes in the form "Bali" was not something akin to the practice of collection of taxes on a regular basis that we notice in the later Vedic period. Perhaps, during the later Vedic period the king had bigger claim on resources due an increase in agricultural production or diversification of economic activities as also a larger size of tribal population due to merger of tribes which included non-Aryan tribes also. The resource crunch during the Ṛgvedic period again, perhaps, was a factor in not having a regular defence support in place. The mention of the term 'Senani' in the Ṛgveda does support the existence of a basic type of defence mechanism comprising the tribes who were put in action whenever situation so demanded. Thus, during the Ṛgvedic period, the king operated within a tribal framework, handicapped by meagre resources, bereft of a standing army and control over any defined territory. He was mostly occupied with dealing with the prevailing situation of inter and intra tribal strife which invested the polity with the features of a military establishment. This also explains why the polity required a strong leadership which could provide a protective cover to the tribe and also help in securing its objectives. This was something akin to the mythical situation when even gods realized the need for strong leadership, a king among gods, when faced with successive defeats inflicted by Asuras (demons). This is how, according to tradition, Indra, a Vedic god, was anointed as king by the Devas (gods). Some scholars maintain that this mythical description of Indra's anointment is open to question. They do, however, recognize that Indra is one of the of Rājans in the Vedas and each of the godly Rājans has its own realm, like Rājan Varuṇa, a super lord of Ṛta, Rājan Yama, a lord of departed ancestors, and Rājan Soma, a presiding deity of plants. In a similar vein, the chiefs of tribal units felt the necessity of buttressing their authority through performance of rituals and donning the mantle of chief sacrificer, in which the priests, in mutual self-interest also actively collaborated. According to Kumkum Roy[128], the concept of kingship during Vedic period envisaged two things; first he has to be unique vis-a-vis those over whom he exercised control and authority and secondly, his role as the leader and protector should be viewed as "vital for the proper functioning of the society". This has been, according to her, the underlying feature of kingship "throughout the brahminical tradition", notwithstanding the form of kingship which was not uniform and carried various nomenclatures. This view finds support from the practice of coronation rituals as well as from the role the Vedic king as a protector of the tribe. We find from the Vedic texts that the king chose the ritual route and performed highly visible sacrifices in order to assert his high status and differentiate his exalted position with the rest. The king also had to contend with his peers and overcome any challenge to his authority in the realm besides successfully playing the role of a strong leader of the tribe. This explains numerous designations the king came to acquire in successfully acquitting his responsibilities and overcoming challenges from within and outside. In fact, the various nomenclature attached to kingship qualified his standing in the polity. For instance, the term '*Rājan*' in the Vedic context ,does not refer to the ruler of a well-established kingdom, rather it stands for the tribal chieftain, one who possesses the requisite attributes to lead a tribe. However, in several hymns of the Ṛgveda (RV I, 40.8; 108.7; RV X, 42.10 and 97.6), the term '*Rājan*' denotes a noble belonging to the royal family or just a 'noble'. Hartmut Scharfe[129] maintains that the word "*Rājan*" denoted members of higher nobility who alone were eligible to become rulers. The word "*Rājanya*" according to

---

[128] The Emergence of Monarchy in North India. OUP, 1994, P.24

[129] The State in Indian Tradition, Hartmut Scharfe, E.J. Brill, Leiden, The Netherlands, 1989, P.59

him, suggests members of lower nobility who were ineligible to hold the position of a ruler. Wilhelm Rau[130] defines *rājan* in terms of three usage categories: 1) the nobility in general i.e., kinsman of the royalty/aristocracy, 2) a man of the royal lineage i.e. a representative of high-nobility, and 3) the monarchs/kings. Therefore, the *rājans* belonged to high nobility through their birth and were eligible for kingship. Wilhelm Rau has also cited[131] certain denotations occurring in the Vedic texts, for the Regents such as adhipati, adhiraja, uttama, ekaraj etc.; for the denotation of their ranks, such as adhipatya, adhirajya, kṣatra, janarajya, jyesthya etc.and for the men from the royalty/aristocracy, such as rājan, rājaputra, samana (bandhu), Sva etc.

Hartmut Scharfe[132] has also referred to AB VIII 23 and 23.10 to suggest that there also existed rulers who had no claim to nobility and there were also Brahmin kings. Here he highlights the role of Ratnin-s as a king maker. Ratnin-s included Brahmins, noblemen, the Queen and other officials.

The post Ṛgvedic period witnessed a distinct transformation in the nature of kingship. With the merger of tribes and the emergence of super tribes, the king came to exercise his authority over a much larger territory, and hence, the kingdom acquired a territorial base, a far cry from the Ṛgvedic phase when the king was a master of undefined territory. Social differentiation on Varṇa (class) lines also got accentuated during this period. The Brahmins and the kṣatriyas by virtue of their occupations cornered the top slots in the society with the Vaiṣyas and the Sūdras getting relegated to the lower order. With the breakdown of kinship structure, the polity came to acquire a more inclusive character. This was reflected in the coronation rituals which were designed to get the support of all sections of the society and not only of the clan of the king. The status of women witnessed a decline with the strengthening of patriarchal system in the society. The polity also acquired a sound base due to expansion in agricultural activities and the resultant accrual of more income from agricultural produce as well as diversification of economic activities. This enabled the king to institute a taxation system to augment

---

[130] Staat Und GesellSchaft In Alten Indien: Wilhelm Rau, Otto Harrassowitz. Wiesbaden, 1957, P.70.

[131] Ibid, P.72

[132] The State in Indian Tradition, Hartmut Scharfe, P.59

his income on a regular basis and have a better organized defence mechanism. Pastoralism and collection of spoils of battle no longer remained the king's sole source of income. It was now possible for the king to have a much larger administrative machinery to support his varied functions and responsibilities.

This provides a background for understanding the nature of polity that existed during the Ṛgvedic period and its further evolvement in the post Ṛgvedic phase. Now we shall turn to specific institutions in the polity in particular, the kingship and discuss them in some details drawing from the Ṛgvedic and post Ṛgvedic texts. We will deal with subject for both the periods together in an integrated and holistic manner along with the interpretations given by some noted scholars on the subject. Similar approach has been adopted for dealing with the subjects relating to social practices during the Ṛgvedic and post Ṛgvedic periods.

a) Institution of Kingship

The evolvement of the institution of kingship during the span of the Ṛgvedic period and thereafter in the post Ṛgvedic period can be better appreciated if we examine the issue further through the prism of changes in the kinship structure and the changing relationship between the king and the priestly class. The early Vedic phase was characterized by strong ties of kinship that held the king and his tribe together and the major responsibility of the tribal chief was to provide a protective cover to his tribesmen. This relationship between the king and the *viś* served well so long the king exercised control over a small polity and the requirement of generating additional resources had not yet become an important consideration. This, however, changed in the post Ṛgvedic period for two reasons, first, attempts by the tribal chief to expand his area of influence which could not have happened without bringing more tribes, not necessarily bound by kinship, under his fold; and secondly, induction of more tribes in the fold presented an opportunity to the king to expand his resource base by laying claims on their productive resources. This changed the nature of kinship structure of the society which was no longer homogenous but the presence of multi tribal polity presented its own problems of command and control and highlighted the need to define new relationship between the king and the *viś*.

Side by side with the above development, the mutual dependency between the Brahmin class and the king seen at a basic level during the early Vedic phase, assumed a critical level in the post Ṛgvedic period and witnessed a strong ties developing between the two driven by considerations of serving larger mutual interest. The king turned to the priestly class for legitimizing his status through ritualistic practices, and for providing a linkage with the god as well as for garnering additional productive resources through occasions provided by complex sacrificial rituals, such as, rājasūya and aśvamedha. The priestly class also depended upon the king for gifts though this was not overtly acknowledged. The performance of the complex rituals also put the brahmins in a different class as they alone possessed the ability to conduct such rituals. The doctrine of mutual self-interest practiced by the king and the Brahmins (from which class the priests were drawn) brought them much closer to each other to the exclusion of others and this development came to acquire the nomenclature of 'brama-kṣatra alliance.

Kumkum Roy [133] has sought to provide a new angle to the rituals connected with the institution of kingship. She has observed that the rituals connected with the rājasūya and áśvamedha provided an occasion for the king to display his opulence and also to control "a range of distributive mechanisms". A part of the resources collected on such occasions were distributed by the king amongst those who were present and participated in the rituals. However, such redistribution was not on a uniform basis and the priests benefitted the most as they were crucial to the execution of such rituals which were intended to strengthen the position of the king. This differential approach led to strengthening of the bond between the king and the priests and weakening of kinship structure which had provided an important support base for the king during the early Vedic period. This also had another important fall-out. While the occasions for performance of sacrifice was overtly intended to enhance the support base of the king, these actually had the opposite effect. The differential approach adopted by the king in the matter of redistribution of resources, accentuated "social differences" which had considerable impact on institutionalization of class system seen during the later Vedic period and thereafter.

[133] Emergence of Monarchy in North India, Kumkum Roy, OUP, 1994

b) Origin of Kingship

As regards the origin of kingship during the Vedic period, various theories have been advanced by the scholars, such as the doctrine of divine origin or the theory of social contract or just the view that the evolvement or conferment of kingship/chieftainship on a person in a tribal society depended upon his leadership qualities and martial prowess. Both the Bṛhad Āraṇayaka Upaniṣad (B, U I, 4.II) and the Aitareya Brāhmaṇa (AB VII, 17, VIII, 13,14,19), which are later Vedic texts, allude to divine appointment of the king.[134] There are other two important references in Aitareya Brāhmaṇa which throw light on this subject. AB I.14 attributes the creation of the institution of king to the defeat of the gods in the battle against Asuras (demons) and ascribing the success of the demons in the battle to the fact they had a king while the gods had none. Another reference in Aitareya Brāhmaṇa (AB viii 12) refers to the consecration of Indra which was a result of a conscious decision among gods. These references underlie the importance of having a king to obtain success against the adversaries. While these two references do not clearly establish the theory of the divine origin of kingship, they do in a way, implicitly, indicate what is expected of a king and what he is expected to do as a master of the realm. The consecration ceremonies and invocations made during such ceremonies invested the king with certain elements of divinity and thus it is plausible to explain this development as divinity by extension.

Keith[135] has a mixed view on this issue. He refers to ŚB. V.1.5.14 where Rājanya has been shown as a representative of Prajapati, entitling him "... to rule over many". This, he asserts, should not be regarded "as precisely a doctrine of the divine origin of the kingship in any specific sense." He buttresses this point by stating that even the Brāhmaṇas do not expound a doctrine of hereditary divinity and "the ceremony of Rajasūya hints at . . . an elective kingship by the consent of the people." Hence, it cannot be

134 Even hymn 9 of Book IV of the Rgveda mentions how Trasadasyu, son of Purukutsa of Pu¯ru dynasty, attained the status of a demi-god through oblations given by the spouse of Purukutas to Indra and Varuna. This hymn reads as follows: *"The spouse of Purukutsa gave oblations to you, O Indra-Varuna, With homage. Then unto her ye gave King Trasadasyu, a demi-god, the slayer of the foeman"* (Griffiths Trans.).

135 The Religion and Philosophy of Veda and Upanishads, Vol.II P.481, A.B. Keith, Motilal Banarsidass, Delhi, Reprint 2007

conclusively stated that the institution of king owed its origin to divine dispensation. There is a greater probability that as a result of a strong coalition between the Brāhmana and Kṣatriya during the Brāhmaṇa period, the king came to be eulogized in various ways and the priests ensured that the king virtually acquires an aura of divinity in the eyes of his people.

We could locate the genesis of this trend even during the Ṛgvedic period. Hymn 50.9 of the Book IV of the Ṛgveda clearly states "*...the Gods uphold that King with their protection who helps the Brahman when he seeks his favor*" (Griffiths Trans.). Scharfe[136] maintains that during the Vedic period the chiefs/kings 'assumed identity with various gods during certain state rituals' but never any divine parentage has been alluded to. The Vedic king however, "attained and maintained his quasi-divine stature through ritualized worship with the help of his Brahmin priests". According to ŚB V 4,4, 9-12, on the occasion of the royal consecration, the king was represented as personification of gods, such as, Indra, Varuṇa, Rudra etc. In view of the above, the doctrine of divine origin of king seems to fail. Even though the term 'Rājan' was associated with kingship, it was at best understood during the Ṛgvedic period, in the sense of control over a particular tribe or a chief of chieftains without any claim to a defined territory. This assertion fits in well with the mobile structure of tribal polity.

Some scholars also refer to theories of Social Contract as a possible explanation for the origin of kingship. A closer look at the application of this theory during the Vedic period, however, reveals that the basic ingredients of a social contractual theory as we know them, such as, ability to contract, performance of action on the basis of contract, are not satisfied. Nevertheless, there are passages in T.B. and AB which may allude to a contract in its most rudimentary form. For example, AB V111,15 mentions about the king taking an oath after coronation (which may obligate him to govern righteously); T.B.1, 713 mentions about the role of Ratnin-s in offering *rāṣṭra* to the king during the Rājasūya ceremony (This again casts an obligation on the king to justify his selection by the Ratnin-s). Thus, the application of the social contract theory as regards the origin of chieftainship or kingship can be stretched to an extent.

---

[136] State in Indian Tradition, Hartmut Scharfe, E.J. Brill, Leiden, The Netherlands, 1989, P.92

Leaving aside the contentious views on the divine origin of the kingship as well as application of the social contract theory, it can be reasonably asserted that the turbulence within and among the tribes as also constant strife against the aborigines created a similar situation earlier faced by gods that required a strong leadership. We discern in this situation the genesis of the institution of chieftainship/kingship in the early Vedic period. Spellman [137] has vividly explained the concept of the institution of kingship by expounding "Matsyaya doctrine" where he has given the analogy of "the big fish eating up the little fish." He has traced this concept to Śatapatha Brāhmaṇa passage XI, I.6.24 which states: "Whenever there is drought, then the stronger seizes the weaker, for waters are the law." This doctrine, according to him, operates in the absence of a king or when there is no fear of punishment. The institution of kingship during the early Vedic period was, therefore, a response to the prevailing turbulent situation that required a strong leadership to secure the polity from external aggression and internal disturbance. This also shows that the early Vedic society was plagued by strife and dissensions and military prowess evidently became a key factor in governing a tribal polity.

The concept of kingship, even though it related to tribal polity, was fairly well-established during the early Vedic period. Elucidating the position of 'Vedic King', Hartmut Scharfe[138] holds that the position did not imply his being the 'lord of earth (Bhū-pati)' but the 'lord of men or the lord of cattle (Go-pati)'. He refers to RV IV 38, 2 and RV VI 28.3 respectively in support of his observations which, inter-alia, are in line with the semi-nomadic character of early vedic pastoral society. He further adds that it was important for the king to be endowed with 'charisma' which could be a factor in sustaining his kingship. In the Ṛgvedic hymns there are invocations to Indra, Agni and Maruts for bestowing 'charisma' on the king. Further, the lineage also seems to be a factor in the evolvement of kingship. The rulers of tribes, such as, the Yadu, Pūru, Anu, Druhyu or Turvaśa carried the names of their respective tribes. Thus, the Yadu king is simply described as Yadu, the king of the Turvaśas simply as Turvaśa. Epithets like Caidya applied to king Kāsu; Sṛñjaya applied to Daivavata. Kingship seems to have been confined to a particular family but had not assumed a hereditary character. The laws of primogeniture were not yet

[137] Political Theory of Ancient India,John W. Spellman, Clarendon Press, Oxford, 1964 P4-5

[138] The State in Indian Tradition, Harmut Scharfe, E.J Brill, Leiden, the Netherlands, P.34, P.36

universally applied. The kingship was not equated with chieftainship of a particular tribe since he was held as a leader of chieftains.

The kingship, however, did not acquire an autocratic character due to the pre-eminence of the ruling clan and the vested rights of princes claiming common ancestry. The people, who enjoyed a dominant position through effective institutions like the Sabhā and the Samiti, also acted as a bulwark against any irresponsible exercise of authority by the king. In the body politic, the personal element also had a sway and personal relation between the king and the subject acted as political bond. Hence, popular discontent was viewed as fatal to the king. The king, therefore, was bound to rely on the goodwill of both these elements and this is confirmed by the evidence provided by the hymns of the Atharva Veda, such as, I.9, 3&49 (the priest here invokes the help of Indra, Varuṇa, Agni and other gods to "prostrate beneath our feet the king's enemies and rivals and to exalt him high above his kinsmen"). Thus, it would not be an exaggeration to suggest that a system of checks and balances operated even during such a distant past. The role of *ṛta,* as 'an assertion of an absolute and true reality and order', was also crucial in regulating social and political actions and acted as a check on all the stakeholders in the polity. The 'universal power' of the king was circumscribed by the imperative to adhere to *ṛta* which devolved an obligation on him to adhere to truth while dispensing justice and performing regal duties. This was considered essential for strengthening 'the cosmic truths and orders around him.'[139] Conduct of an arbitrary nature, whether it related to collection of tributes or impairing the role of representative institutions like the Sabhā/Samiti, was frowned upon.

The institution of kingship further evolved during the post Ṛgvedic phase and this was reflected in the changing relationship on the one hand between the king and the viś and stronger ties between the king and the priestly class. The breakdown of kinship structure during the post Ṛgvedic phase presented its own problems of accommodating and meeting the aspirations of new tribes who were brought within the fold. The king, in addition, had to meet new challenges arising from his expanded jurisdiction and finding resources for ensuring proper governance. We, therefore, find hymns both in the Ṛgveda and the Atharva-Veda in which exhortations are made for strengthening the institution of monarchy. PS 10.4. 3 exhorts that the kingdom be possessed of power, rich in heroes,

[139] Ibid, P.48-49

victorious and strong... and the chieftains pay tribute to the kingdom . . . A king also promises the chieftains to protect them in return for receiving tributes. AV VII.34 refers to use of charms and magical formulae for destruction of rivals, living or yet to be born); AV,I. XXIX mentions about the king invoking the amulet to "increase the strength of the regal sway, to put down all who menaced the king and to make him the sole ruler of the tribe." It needs to be stated here that the relationship among the rājanyas was not always a peaceful one and bitter quarrels occurred amongst them. But they would resort to compromise when threatened by an external enemy.

c) Selection or Election of a King

Both the Ṛgvedic and post Ṛgvedic texts throw considerable light regarding the nature of kingship. To be chosen or elected as a king, certain criteria were required to be met. For instance, a priest or a noble belonging to lower category or a vaiṣya were excluded from the zone of consideration. So were those who suffered from any physical or psychic handicaps. Great importance was laid on the ancestry aspect as the king's name was pronounced as in the family tree on the occasion of his coronation. Apart from ancestry, military prowess was deemed as an important qualification for the position of king.

The Vedic hymns have been variously interpreted to determine whether the kingship during the early Vedic period was an elective position or otherwise. The Vedic Index cites the view of Zimmer and Geldner in this context. According to Zimmer[140] this position was sometimes hereditary where the descent could be traced but he also adds that this position could even be elective. In the latter case, according to him, the process and ambit of selection was not clear; whether the king was selected by the people from amongst the members of the royal family only or the field of selection also included members of the "noble clans." Geldner[141] is of the view that elevation to the position of king should be seen not as 'choice by the cantons (*Viś*), but as acceptance by the subjects. It is apt here to refer to various hymns in order to appreciate the position pertaining to this issue. In AV III.4 (on the occasion of royal inauguration) the king is told that the "tribesmen shall elect thee for kingship... and kinsmen inviting

140 Vedic Index of Names and Subjects, Vol. II P.211

141 Vedische Studien

thee shall go to meet thee; with thee will also go to Agni as an active herald;" AV III.5, 6, 7 mention about participation of some prominent people in the nomination of the king-elect; Ṛgveda X.124.8 refers to subjects choosing a king. Translated in English (Griffiths) this hymn reads as follows: *"These wait upon his loftiest power and vigour: he dwells in these who triumph in their Godhead; and they, like people who elect their ruler, have in abhorrence turned away from Vrtra."* The celebrated Coronation Hymn of the R.V. X.173.1 [142] and AV VI, 87.1 & 87.2[143] also speak of the acceptance of the king by the *Viśaḥ*. This acceptance of the king by the people has been interpreted by some scholars to mean that the institution of kingship was elective in nature and this election was done by the people assembled in the Samiti. The hymn in AV VI 73 shows the king telling the clansmen how invaluable to him was the allegiance of the subjects.

All these amply demonstrate the people's role in the selection of their king. Thus, the royalty seems to be dependent on popular choice for accession to office as well as retaining people's allegiance for continuance in authority. In such a situation, the king could not claim divinity nor could he exercise his prerogatives in an unfettered manner. This also implied that there was an obligation cast on the king to ensure safety of the people at all times since this was the rationale behind his continuance in office. Thus, for being anointed as a king, possession of military qualities was deemed as essential.

d) Deposition of a King

There are references in the Saṃhitās and Brāhmaṇas to exiled kings and how they tried to regain power. Vedic Index Vol.II (P.211) also mentions about expulsion of king. The people's role was important in this context. One also comes across instances of the king's effort to retain support of the people as this was crucial for regaining authority in the event of his expulsion. According to Pañcaviṃśa Brāhmaṇa, (2,3,7), since internecine tribal strife was common, there was always a lurking apprehension that

[142] R.V. X.173.1 "*Be with us; I have chosen thee: stand stedfast and immovable. Let all the people wish for thee let not thy kingship fall away*"(Grifffiths Trans.)

[143] AV87.1 Here art thou: I have chosen thee. Stand steadfast and immovable. Let all the clans desire thee: let not thy kingdom fall away.AV87.2- Be even here: fall not away: be like a mountain unremoved. Stand steadfast here like Indra's self, and hold the kingship in thy grasp'. (Griffiths Trans.).

the king could be dethroned or exiled by the ruler of another tribe . In the event of expulsion, certain magical rituals had to be performed by the exiled king to regain his position. The king's *purohita* was usually entrusted with the task of executing such rituals. The Vedic texts assign an important role for Ratnin-s on the occasion of the royal consecration but are silent as regards their role if any, in the expulsion of a king. However, this much is clear that the king was required to perform certain rituals for regaining his position.

e) The King's Consecration

The royal consecration was a fairly simple affair during the Ṛgvedic period in which the king's associates and the people, apart from the priest participated. The rājasūya, according to J.C. Heesterman,[144] "did not represent a special type of sacrifice, nor was it surrounded with the pomp and prestige of the horse sacrifice, the Aśvamedha, the 'king of sacrifices' ". It consisted of one-day Soma sacrifices, offering of cakes, occasional animal sacrifice and some special rites 'such as the unction, the chariot drive, the dicing ceremony and the use of some special formulas'. In this ritual, the main focus is on the sacrifice and not the king who is treated on par with a common sacrificer, without in any way detracting from the royal dignity. In the post-Ṛgvedic period, however, the rituals, as we learn from the hymns of the Atharva-Veda and the Brāhmaṇas, assumed a complex character, lasting several days, where the Purohita played an important part. The coronation rituals signified two important aspects; first, it tested the prowess of the person who was to be anointed as the king or a chieftain; secondly, it ensured that the person so anointed does not carry any baggage with him while assuming the position of chieftainship. This is evident from the formulae for Rājasūya as given in MS mantras 2.6.3 and MS Brāhmaṇa 4.3-4[145] The ceremonies, such as a game of dice or chariot race, connected with Rājasūya, according to R.S. Sharma[146], are reflective of "the tribal and primitive character of the

---

[144] The Ancient Indian Royal Consecration, J.C. Heesterman,Mouton & Co. 's-Gravenhage, P.3

[145] The Maitra¯yaṇi¯ Saṃhita¯: its rituals, Dharmadhikari, T.N., Adarsha Sanskrit Shodha Samstha, Pune. P.21

[146] Aspects of Political Ideas and Institutions in Ancient India, R.S. Sharma, Motilal Banarsidass Publishers, Reprint, Delhi, 2009. P.163.

rituals" intended "as ordeals for establishing the qualifications... for kingship or chieftainship." There is further discussion on the subject in the later part of this book.

f) The King's Duties

The king had an important role to play during war and in times of peace in return for taxes received. His chief duties involved protection of the people against foreign invaders which also was his best qualification for the royal office. The king had an important role in a war-like situation where he had to show leadership in battles and raids. Attacks on the aborigines find frequent mention in the Ṛgveda, e.g., RV II, 12.11; RV IV, 26.33; RV VI, 26.5. The king's another duty was to defend his territory, take defensive action against raids and ensure protection of his tribe and also to expand his territorial limit by resorting to attacks on the neighbouring tribes. The Vedic Index cites references to war situation in the Ṛgveda, e.g., RV. VII, 18.33; RV III, 33. 53. During the time of peace, the king received contributions from the people for services rendered during the war and he also had a claim on the booty of the war. The king's duties also involved participation in rituals to ensure the well-being of the clan as well as for strengthening his own position. Ensuring compliance with ṛta also figured as a part of his important duties. There is, however, no evidence to support that the king performed any legislative function during the early Vedic period.

During the post Ṛgvedic phase, there was considerable enlargement in the scope of his functions and responsibilities of the king. He had to reckon with the problem of managing a much larger territorial domain, inhabited by tribes no longer bound by the ties of kinship, keep an eye on augmenting his resources to meet varied tasks and ensure proper compliance with the edicts of dharma in his capacity as an upholder of Varṇa order. The dimension of his responsibilities grew manifold as he was required to grapple with security, economic and social issues, all together unlike the situation that obtained in the primitive Ṛgvedic polity.

Wilhelm Rau[147] has succinctly put across the various duties of the king by grouping them under three heads : i) Performing magical sacrifices to ensure righteous conduct on the part of subjects; ii) upholding law and

[147] Staat Und Gesell Schaft In Alten Indien: Wilhelm Rau, Otto Harrassowitz. Wiesbaden, 1957, P.90

meting out justice; and iii) maintaining social order among the tribe. The description of king as 'Dharmapati' finds mention in ŚB (5,3,3,9) and this related to his role in formulating rules for maintaining purity in conduct, food habits and marriage. There are indications in ŚB (5,4,7) which suggest that the king was viewed as above the law but in exceptional cases he was answerable to a collegium of his regents (subordinate kings). The other duties of the king involved exercising his jurisdiction in civil and criminal matters, such as civil processes relating to land, cattle and breach of contract; and criminal processes related to theft, dacoity, murder, causing bodily injuries, and feud between a brahmin and non-brahmin etc. Different levels of punishments were prescribed for commission of such offences as would be apparent from various references in ŚB and TS on this account. As regards death penalty, there is every possibility that the king could also award this penalty. ŚB (v. 4,4,7) also mentions about immunity to king from punishment but this did not prevent him from punishing others.

The king's role in the management of land is not clear and there is not enough evidence to attest conclusively his status as a landowner. Scholars have viewed this subject in different perspectives Hopkins declares the king to be the owner of all lands While Baden-Powell views the king's status as a land owner a later development (Vedic Index (Vol.II, P.14). Irrespective of these views, we do know that the ownership of land also devolved upon an individual or joint family.

g) Subsidiary Political Institutions and Administrative Apparatus

Not much information is available on the nature of administration that existed in the Ṛgvedic polity, but we do know that the early Vedic chief did possess a modest number of administrative staff whose strength grew manifold during the post-Ṛgvedic period due to an increase in the size of the tribal kingdoms and diversification of economic and social activities. During the Ṛgvedic period, we come across the names of certain entities which performed various types of functions connected with the affairs of the polity. Besides the king, we hear of the Sabhā and the Samiti, the Rathakāras, the Ratnins, the dice player, the Grāmaṇīs, the Senānī and the Purohita etc. These entities had an assigned role in the system. The king enjoyed the pre-eminent position in the Vedic polity, but as we shall see the members of the royal family, learned Brahmins besides those mentioned above also had their place in the system. A number of the political institutions mentioned above and discussed below like the Sabhā and the Samiti, Ratnins, Purohita, Rathakara (Chariot maker), Gramani, Senani etc. also spilled over to the post Rig-Vedic phase.

The king had the following ministerials[148], apart from Purohita and noblemen, who performed various functions namely, i) Senānī (commander); ii) Grāmaṇī (Head of the village); iii) Sūta (One who heralds the king); iv)); iv) Ksattṛ[149] (doorkeeper); v) Bhāgadugha(Distributor of shares); vi) Sovikarta (Cook); vii) Akṣāvāpa (Dice-thrower); viii) Takṣan (Carpenter); ix) Ratha-kāra (Chariot-maker); x)Saṃgrahītṛ (Tax collector) and xi) Pālāgala (messenger). Among these Senānī had only military duties; Grāmiṇī, Sūta and Charioteer had both civil and military duties but the rest only performed peace-related tasks. For instance, the Bhagadugha distributed spoils or tributes which the chieftain received. According to Wilhelm Rau, the above were not the only court nobles. The King had other personnel also to assist him in his duties as land lord, or in the conduct of trade or performance of religious acts. The character and functions of the various political institutions are elucidated as hereunder:

The Sabhā. Not enough details are available regarding the character, composition and functions of this institution which finds mention in the hymns of the Ṛgveda and Atharva-Veda. But there is no ambiguity about the existence of such an institution. Zimmer describes the word *Sabhā* as the assembly of the village community which also denotes village community hall where gatherings take place. He also calls it 'the general social amphitheatre for the men'. Wilhelm Rau[150] has cited Grassman's view that the word Sabheya occurring in RV hymn 1,91.20 is an adjective to Sabhā which means "to qualify for an assembly, to be distinguished in it." He[151] further adds that according to many instances in the Brāhmaṇas the word Sabhā has multifaceted meaning. "It denotes a barn building, an un-timbered hall with a fire-place and dice game for the banquets or game in the house of rich men, the society, the community, a place where

---

148 Ibid. P.107

149 As perVedic Index(Vol.I P.201)both in the Rgveda and AV, this term is used of a god as a distributor of good things.This term is also interpreted to mean a doorkeeper or a 'Chamberlain'.

150 Ibid. P.77

151 Ibid, P.81

aristocratic people grant official audience, the hall in the palace of the regents, where they together with aristocratic men and assessor-brahmans dispense justice."

There are divergent views among the scholars about this institution, some treat the Sabhā and Samiti as one and the same institution; some prefer to describe it as a place where the members of the tribe meet to discuss matters of their concern. It figures in the RV VI 28.6 and RV VIII, 4.9 where the Sabhā is supposed to comprise elders and influential men. V.P. Varma, an eminent scholar, has cited the opinion of Ludwig, a German scholar according to whom the Sabhā consisted of Brahmins and rich people. But, according to the Vedic Index, its real role is not explicit. R.S. Sharma suggests that it could have been in earlier phase, merely a "clan assembly." when there was not much distinction between the rich and the poor. This institution, he further adds, may have acquired a different connotation as an advisory body when economic inequalities developed, and the king emerged as a "principal factor in the political system." This becomes clear when we refer to RV VIII, 4.9, SB III.3.5.14 or AV VII.12. The Sabhā grew in importance due to the king's presence and participation. A reference to this effect is found in RV IX, 92.6. This is also evident from a reference in Chāndogya Upaniṣad (V.3.6) about the king having his own Sabhā. RV X 71.10 also credits the Sabhā with a judicial role. This role acquired prominence in the later Vedic period.

The Samiti. The word Samiti seems to suggest a meeting place for common people. This is reflected in RV X, 191.2 and 191.3[152] Ludwig in his translation of the Ṛgveda has also observed that the Samiti comprised primarily the *viśaḥ* (the common people) but could also include the Brahmins and the rich. Authors of the Vedic Index have indicated greater probability of the Sabhā and the Samiti being the same body (Vol.II P.430). However, N.C Bandyopadhaya has discounted this assertion by referring to AV VII.12 where the "the Samiti along with the Sabha has been described as one of the two daughters of Prajapati." In his[153] view, there

---

152 RVX,191.2 and 191.3"this is the meeting where the Gods are worshipped. Assemble, speak together: let your minds be all of one accord, As ancient Gods unanimous sit down to their appointed share. The place is common, common the assembly, common the mind, so be their thought united. A common purpose do I lay before you, and worship with your general oblation."

153 Development of Hindu Polity and Political Theories: N.C. Bandyopadhaya P. R.Cambray & Co. , Book-Sellers and Publishers, 15, College Square, Calcutta, 1927

are allusions to this word in several places in the Ṛgveda and the Atharva-Veda. For example, RVIX, 92.6 refers to the word Samiti:

Griffiths Trans.

92.6 As the priest seeks the station rich in cattle, like a true King who goes to great assemblies, Soma hath sought the beakers while they cleansed him, and like a wild bull, in the wood hath settled.|

The context here is about a king entering the Samiti while the priest was entering the house which had the sacrificial animal. There is a more explicit narration of the Samiti's role in RV X 166.4:

Griffiths Trans.

166.4 Hither I came as conqueror with mighty all-effecting power,

And I have mastered all your thought, your synod, and your holy work.

Here the king talks about the enemy's destruction and conquering the Samiti.

In AV VI 88 (Griffiths trans.) the term 'assembly' occurs which may stand for the Samiti. The Priest invokes the following:

1. *Firm is the sky, firm is the earth, and firm is all this living world; Firm are these mountains on their base, and stedfast is this King of men.*
2. *Stedfast may Varuna the King, stedfast the God Brihaspati, Stedfast may Indra stedfast, too, may Agni keep thy stedfast reign.*
3. *Firm, never to be shaken, crush thy foemen, under thy feet lay those who strive against thee c. One-minded, true to thee be all the regions: faithful to thee, the firm, be this assembly! (Here the assembly stands for Samiti in the Sanskrit version)*

The Samiti seems to be the larger version of the Sabhā and served as the meeting place for the entire community. The occasion for its meeting used to be on issues of common concern or interest, such as coronation of a king or to meet the situation arising from external threat or a calamity. K.P.Jayaswal[154] has pointed out that electing a *Rājan* was an important business of the Samiti and in this context, has referred to AV III, 345 to substantiate this point. It is relevant here to refer to another meaning attached to the Samiti, i.e., Sam-grāma, understood in the context of a war assembly of tribesmen. The Samiti does not figure in the later saṃhitās, the reasons for which are not clear. It could be a fall out of the strengthened position of the king in the later Vedic period that may have enabled him to function independently of the Samiti, in consultation with

---

[154] Hindu Polity: K.P. Jayaswal, P.12, 2nd ed., The Bangalore Printing and Publishing Co. Ltd., Bangalore, 1943

his advisors and the Sabhā. The Samiti, however, resurfaces as the Janapada assembly during the period between 600 B.C and 600 A.C.[155]

Vidhata. Vedic Index Vol. II (pp.296-297) refers to various interpretations of this word given by the scholars. Roth describes Vidhata as a body which gives orders as also an assembly for secular or religious ends. According to Bloomfield, Vidhata refers to the patriarchal house and then to sacrifice connected with the house. It is difficult to surmise whether it was a regular body or an occasional one. However, this institution finds mention in the Ṛgveda several times more than the Sabhā and the Samiti which reflects its importance. Some of the hymns in the Ṛgveda provide a clue to its military and religious character. (RV, VI.8.1).

The other entities which wielded influence in the political system were:

- **The Purohita** in the Ṛgvedic period was taken as a learned Brahmin specially close to the king and as someone employed by the king to perform priestly duties. JB III 94 also mentions another role for the priest, that is to act as the king's charioteer. This role, seen in a positive light, brings him very close to the king, as someone who is trustworthy and enjoys the confidence of the king. The role of the Purohita during the Ṛgvedic period was extremely important as he was viewed as a specialist in the performance of sacrificial rituals including rituals for the king's consecration. The Ṛgvedic hymns, as stated earlier, are woven around sacrificial rituals and fire-cult, where the fire god Agni occupies an important place like the God Indra. The Purohita provided a link between the sacrificer and the god. RV IV, 50, 8 seems to allude to the importance of the institution of Purohita .It has been stated therein that the king rules safely where a Brahman leads the way. The grip of this institution and the Brahmins in general over the polity continued to grow matching the pace in the growth of complexity in the body of rituals. This happened during the Bra¯hmaṇa period, as we shall see later in the discussions on the post-Ṛgvedic polity. During this period, the institution of Purohita evolved further and there was considerable enhancement in his status as a symbol of spiritual power and as one who knew how to handle 'the forces of living and non-living nature

[155] Ibid, P.239, 2nd ed., The Bangalore Printing and Publishing Co. Ltd., Bangalore, 1943

through magical sacrifices'[156].ABVIII 24 mentions about the gods returning a king's offerings who has no purohita. Scharfe[157] refers to ŚB IV 1.4 to describe the standing of the purohita vis-à-vis the king as the same as between the gods Varuṇa and Mitra. The Purohita is also stated to have acquired the epithet of "Rastra Gopa", the protector of the realm during the Brāhmaṇa period (AB VIII. 25), which reflects the growing importance of this institution.

The Grāmaṇī is cited as the leader of the village (which could be geographically described as a tract without denoting a fixed settlement) both for civil and military purposes and was regarded as a jewel of the royal establishment. It finds mention in RV X, 62.11 and 107.55 and is also mentioned in the later Saṃhitās and the Brāhmaṇas.

The Grāmya-vādin. A village judge who finds mention in Yajur-Veda I, 12.1.3;

- **The Saṃgrahītṛ** or the treasurer of the king;
- **The Saṃgrāma**, primarily a collection of tribal military units[158];
- **The Rathakāra**, or Chariot maker did not belong to one of the higher classes but had a difficult job of making light-weight chariots. The institution of Rathakāra finds mention in Atharva-Veda III, 5.6 and also in Yajur Saṃhitās. The eligibility of Rathakāras to perform Vedic sacrifices has been variously treated in later Vedic literature. It is stated therein that "while the Brahmin may set the sacred fires in the spring, the Rājanya in the hot season, and the Vaishya in the autumn, the Rathakāra may do so in the rainy season"[159] The status of this functionary has much to do with the importance of chariot to the king in a war-like situation.

---

156 Staat Und GesellSchaft In Alten Indien: Wilhelm Rau, Otto Harrassowitz. Wiesbaden, 1957 , P.117

157 State in Indian Tradition, Hartmut Scharfe, E.J. Brill, Leiden-New York, 1989,P113-114

158 Aspects of Political Ideas and Institutions in Ancient India, R.S. Sharma, Motilal Banarsidass Publishers, Reprint, Delhi, 2009. P.p. 112-113

159 Indo-Iranian Journal, Vol.32, No.3. July 1989. Article on 'The Rathakara's Eligibility to Sacrifice' by Christopher Minkowski. P.178.

- **The Senānī,** He led the army and is regarded as a jewel in the royal establishment. This term finds mention in the Rgveda VII, 20.5, IX, 96.1 and X, 84.2. It also figures in the Yajur-Vedic Saṃhitās and Brāhmaṇas.
- **Ratnins:** also called jewel-holders; they represented a conglomerate of individuals/functionaries in the king's court who were assigned different duties. These functionaries performed two types of functions, namely, first, the assigned roles and secondly, in their ritual context pertaining to Rājasūya ceremony. There exists no unanimity regarding the list of Ratnins. The Vedic Index of names and subjects refers to the list of names as contained in TS, TB, ŚB, MS and KS. There is a difference in the total number of functionaries/personages who constituted the list of Ratnins in the aforesaid texts. For example, both TS and TB include twelve names in the list, namely, the Purohita, the Rājanya, the Mahisi (the first wife of king), the Vāvātā (chief wife of king), the Parivṛkti (the secondary queen), the Senānī,the Commander of the army; the Su¯ta,(one who heralds the king); the Grāmaṇi, the village headman; the Kṣattr,(assigned the meaning of chamberlain); the Samgrahitṛ, the treasurer; the Bhāgadugha, distributor of shares or divider of food; and the Akṣāvāpa, the thrower of dice. The ŚB retains all the above in the list excepting the Vāvātā and the Parivṛkti but adds Govikartana, (butcher) slayer of cow; and the Pālāgala, the messenger. Hence, the total number of Ratnins remains the same, that is, twelve. The MS mentions thirteen names which are in common with TS and TB but omitting, the Vāvātā, the Grāmaṇi and replacing the latter by adding Vaishyagramani; Taksa-Rathakarau, carpenter and chariot-maker; and Govikartana(chief huntsman)[160]. The KS substitutes Go-vyacha for Govikartana and omits Taksa-Rathakarau.

A word here is called for on the role of the king's mother who was referred to as Indra's mother. This was deemed as the highest possible honour for a woman in Vedic times. The king's principal wife was called' Mahisi'. We find no mention of King's father or his brother. The children of the first wife were eligible for throne but there is no supporting evidence to confirm this position.

The above lists seem to represent the king's household and different functionaries deployed in the administration of the kingdom. They all take

---

160 Aspects of Political Ideas and Institutions in Ancient India, R.S. Sharma, Motilal Banarsidass Publishers, Reprint Delhi, 2009. P.149

part in rituals connected with Ra¯jasu¯ya or royal consecration. Such participation is reflective of the bond the king attempted to establish with his subject and other levels.

In the post-Ṛgvedic period, far reaching developments take place in the political and social spheres. Later Vedic literature gives us more information on consolidation of the position of the king, addition of new entities in the governance structure and further enhancement in the status of the Purohita. The polity, during this period, witnessed significant changes in political, social and religious spheres. Pastoral nomadism had characterized the early Vedic period even though a transition to settled agriculture was seen in the Punjab region where the Vedic Aryans grew barley and millets. During the post-Ṛgvedic period, the tribal settlements were more focused on agriculture and a variety of other occupations relating to trade, metal work and crafts. In other words, the post Ṛgvedic polity, though tribal in character, had enhanced features. Kulke [161]maintains that the transition from the nomadic life of early Vedic period to settled agriculture during the late Vedic period also signified a change in the meaning of the term *grāma*. While in the early Vedic period, as analysed by Wilhelm Rau, *Grāma* stood for a train of vehicles used by nomadic tribes constantly on the move for better pastures, in the later Vedic period this term came to mean a village where the tribes eventually settled down.

At the political level, the merger of Ṛgvedic clans and tribes in areas in Eastern Punjab/Haryana and Western Uttar Pradesh into the Kuru confederacy resulted in the emergence of the Kurus as a super tribe with larger territorial base and expanded jurisdiction. The Kurus, further strengthened their area of influence eastwards into the Ganges region by entering into a tribal union with the Pañcālas, their eastern ally. The Kurus, thus empowered, were able to introduce far-reaching changes in social, linguistics and religious spheres. The centre of the Kuru realm, the Kurukṣetra area became the hub of activities.

During this phase, several factors contributed towards strengthening the King's position. Apart from presiding over a larger kingdom, sacerdotal support was deemed crucial for strengthening his position. The Brahmin class, which performed priestly duties, viewed the royal rituals as the terrestrial counterpart of the divine rituals. Rituals during the post Ṛgvedic

[161] A History of India, Hermann Kulke and Dietmar Rothermund, Routledge, 2004, 4th Ed.pp.40-41

period indicate rājanya and brahmin working in tandem to ensure a mutually beneficial arrangement to the disadvantage of the ordinary kinsmen and the Śūdras. Elucidating the Sacrificial Theory of the State, Spellman[162] has emphasized the key role of sacrifice "in the scheme of things" in ancient India and referring to the king, he has added that "he was the foundation upon which all religious activities rested." The centrality of rituals in Vedic texts, particularly the enhanced role of rituals as evidenced in the Brāhmaṇa, served twin purposes. It strengthened the position of the king and also placed the priestly class on a high pedestal. Kulke [163]rightly observes that "in the late Vedic period the king usually emerged from a struggle for power among the nobility and then derived his legitimacy from the ritual investiture by their Brahmin priests." There was, therefore, a natural expectation on the part of the Brahmins, that in return the king would ensure them a pre-eminent position in the class hierarchy. The emergence of Brahmins as a key supporter of the king is evident from the many hymns that recognize the sanctity of this class in the body-politic. Hymn 19 of the Book V[164] of the Atharva-Veda is entirely devoted to implications of oppressing a Brahmin. A further accretion to and consolidation of the king's prerogatives and privileges are seen in the Atharva-Vedic hymns such as AV IV. 22, where he is variously described as the "sole lord of the people," the "head and chief of princes" and the beloved of cattle, plants and animals. Thus the king was not only the head of body-politic but also symbolized the aspirations and the dignity of the tribe. In the post-Ṛgvedic period, according to R.S. Sharma, [165] "power structure had assumed a character which was that of a proto-state. The society stood at the threshold of the formation of the state which originated in settlements inhabited by agriculturists." The strengthened position of the king of such a super tribe, however, did not preclude

---

[162] Ibid P.9-10

[163] A History of India,4th ed., Hermann Kulke and Dietmar Rothermund, Routledge, N.Y., 2004, P.44

[164] Griffiths Trans. 19.6 – *"If any King who deems himself mighty would eat a Brahman up, Rent and disrupted is that realm wherein a Brahman is oppressed."* 19.7 – *"She (the cow) grows eight-footed, and four-eyed, four-eared, four-jawed, two-faced, two-tongued, And shatters down the kingdom of the man who doth the Brahman wrong."* 19.8 – *"As water swamps a leaky ship so ruin overflows that realm, Misfortune smites the realm wherein a Brahman suffers scath and harm."*

[165] Ibid. pp.29-30

conflict within the tribal structure. According to R.S. Sharma[166] the later Vedic rituals also depict such conflicts between the raja and the clan chiefs. Conflict also occurred on regular basis between the kin aristocracy and ordinary kinsmen (peasants) over collection and distribution of tributes. In order to meet such situations, the ruling chief took recourse to seeking outside help including from those belonging to "non-Vedic" groups.

166 Origin of the State in India: R.S. Sharma, Department of History, University of Bombay Publication, 1989, P.15

Chapter X

Ṛgvedic and Post Ṛgvedic Social Practices

a) Social Characteristics

A clear differentiation needs to be made between the nature of society as it existed during the Ṛgvedic period and as it evolved in the post-Ṛgvedic period. The society underwent a qualitative change from being a tribal organization based on kinship to a more stratified society based on social differences reflected in the emergence and later institutionalization of four varṇas. Similarly, the political sky was dotted with little kingdoms and later bigger monarchical states from what used to be the chief dominated tribal polity during the Ṛgvedic period. This progression is clearly evident from the later Vedas and the Brāhmaṇas.

The semi-nomadic character of the Ṛgvedic people, constantly on the move, did not favour consolidation and hence they became groups of scattered tribes where kinship provided a major cementing force. Common language (Ṛgvedic Sanskrit), common rituals and common beliefs were the other contributing factors in strengthening their mutual bond. In the RV hymn 1. 33 .18, the names of the tribe Yadu and Turvaśa occur in the context of seeking help to subdue the enemy: *"We call on Ugradeva, Yadu, Turvasa, by means of Agni, from afar; Agni, bring Navavastva and Brhadratba, Turviti, to subdue the foe."* (Griffiths. Trans.). This shows the bond that existed among the Aryan tribes in the face of the common enemy (Dasyus). It was a clan organization based on patrilineal system that derived its strength from shared social and political identity.

The Ṛgvedic society[167] was patriarchal in nature where the father was regarded as the head of the family. He was entitled to take decisions in all important matters concerning the family. Men were fond of music and were also familiar with use of liquor. Despite high standard of morality, crimes like robbery were not unknown. Commitment of such crimes invited punishment; even gods were invoked through prayers to grant

[167] A History of Sanskrit Literature: A.A. Macdonell, Munshi Ram Manoharlal, 3rd Indian edition, Delhi, 1972, pp. 163-166.

protection from thieves and robbers. The staple diet of the people was milk and butter along with fruits and vegetables. Meat was taken on special occasions.

Romila Thapar, a noted historian, prefers to describe the Ṛgvedic tribal society as "lineage society"[168]. In political terms, lineage guaranteed a share in the power structure in the normal course. The social dimensions of lineage are seen in the stratification of social structure during the post-Ṛgvedic period, into four Varṇas. The economic dimension involved diversification in the modes of production/occupation, with the addition of agriculture and later commerce to pastoralism and alignment of the vaiṣyas and the śūdras with such economic activities. The society, during the Ṛgvedic period consisted of two categories of inhabitants, namely, the Aryans and Dasyus (aborigines). The Aryan tribes were able to subdue the local population due to their military prowess and ability to marshal better resources as reflected in the use of horse and light spoked wheel chariots. However, this was not enough to stabilize their dominance. Hence, they initiated a process to assimilate the indigenous people in the Aryan milieu which gathered momentum during the post-Ṛgvedic period. Such blending of indigenous people, however, did not extend to ritualistic sphere during the Ṛgvedic period as we know that the non-Aryans were not permitted to perform sacrifices or rites during that period. MacDonnell and Keith,[169] maintain that Dasyus did not perform sacrifices or rites and were non-believer in gods while the Aryans were just the opposite. We, however, do not have any significant details regarding the impact, if any, of non-Aryans' religious beliefs and practices on the Aryan tribes during the Ṛgvedic period.

Further, social stratification into four classes in the society was beginning to germinate during the Ṛgvedic period in which the non-Aryans found themselves in the lowest rung of the order performing a motley of inferior services. Even though the social occupations had not assumed a hereditary character and there was freedom to choose occupations of one's choice but this freedom did not imply movement to professions across the Varṇas. For example, a Vaiṣya could not choose to be a noble man and engage in battle or raids. Likewise, a Kṣatriya could be a nobleman and engage in war-like pursuits.

---

[168] From Lineage to State, Romila Thapar, Oxford University Press, New Delhi, 1984, Paperback 1990, pp.18

[169] Vedic Index of Names and Subjects, vol. I, P.347

The Ṛgvedic society, though essentially pastoral, also engaged in production of barley. Their entry into agricultural production was, however, at slower pace. Clearing forest areas for agriculture with copper and bronze implements presented serious problem. Discovery of iron had not yet taken place. The invocation to Puṣan in Book 1 hymns 42.7, 42.8 does suggest the pastoral nature of the society: 42.7 – *"Past all pursuers lead us, make pleasant our path and fair to tread: O Pusan, find thou power for this."* 42.8 – *"Lead us to meadows rich in grass: send on our way no early heat."* (Griffiths Trans). R.S. Sharma[170] describes the Ṛgvedic people as "semi-nomadic" at pastoral stage. They depended on cattle rearing and not agriculture as the main source of their livelihood. Sharma further adds that possession of cattle was a frequent issue in inter-tribal strife. According to him, the importance of cattle in the social life of the Ṛgvedic people can also be discerned from the fact that the people living together with the cattle acquired the same *gotra,* but it did not mean "descent from the same ancestor." The *gotra* was, perhaps, understood in the sense of a cowpen and acquired the meaning of a clan at a later date.

H.H. Wilson,[171] as explained in the footnote, also holds that the Aryan tribes engaged in agricultural pursuits besides cattle-rearing. According to Wilhelm Rau,[172] "there cannot be the slightest doubt that the Vedic Aryans practiced agriculture from the very beginning. We find words for the plough, the furrow, the club to break clods of earth after ploughing, the sickle."

Harry Falk [173] argues that there is a good deal of similarity between the pastoral economy of the Ṛgvedic period and that of proto Ṛgvedic Aryans,

---

170 Aspects of Political Ideas and Institutions in Ancient India: R.S. Sharma, Fifth Revised Edition, 2005, Motilal Banarsidass Publishers Private Ltd, Delhi. Pp. 350-351

171 Rgveda Samhita (First Book), Translated from the original Sanskrit, Allen &Co., London, 1850, P. Xii. Wilson hasobserved that the Aryan tribes at the time of the composition of the hymns, may have been a pastoral people to some extent but "they were also , and, perhaps, in a still greater degree, an agricultural people, as is evidenced by their supplications for abundant rain and for the fertility of the earth..."

172 Permanent Vedic Settlements in Inside the Text Beyond Texts, Wilhelm Rau, Cambridge, 1997, P.205

173 The Purpose of RGVedic Ritual: H.Falk in Inside the Texts Beyond the Texts, Ed. Michael Witzel, Harvard Oriental Series, Opera Minora Vol. II, Cambridge, P.87.

in this case, the Gaudar tribes who lived in Seistan region on Helmand river. These Gaudar tribes also tended cattle and lived in reed houses.

However, during the post Ṛgvedic period, the society reflected increasing social stratification and differentiation among the four varṇas on vocational lines which eventually led to the emergence of divisions in the society on hierarchy- based caste lines. The social order came to be dominated by the Brahmins, who being well-versed in scriptures and in the performance of complicated rituals, could alone claim prerogative for performing priestly functions. The Kṣatriyas grew next in importance by virtue of their role as a protector in the society. The respective roles of the Vaiśyas and the Śūdras were also delineated with the king emerging as the seat of effective authority. The Varṇa system, thus, evolved into caste system at this time and the Brahmins and kṣatriya welded together to form 'Brahma-kṣatra' against the lower echelons of the society. The system of governance also underwent a change with the streamlining of functions related to collection of land revenue and tributes. Running of administration and military operations no longer remained the prerogative of the king's kinsmen but paid personnel also shared this responsibility.

Other activities relating to trade and crafts as well as agriculture also gained in prominence during the post Ṛgvedic period. The people engaged in such activities constituted the third tier of the society and belonged to the category of Vaiṣyas. The Śu¯dra class which also included the non-Aryans, formed the fourth tier which was at the lowest echelon of the society. They were entrusted with inferior jobs.

b) Status of Women

In the early Vedic society, the women enjoyed a better status and led a life of dignity and honour. But this did not imply that women could occupy higher positions of authority. The Women took part in the Vedic rituals, but this participation was in their minor aspects. Stephanie Jamison highlights the importance of the women's role in Vedic rituals as also in the area of sexuality and fertility. According to her,[174] women were 'necessary ritual participants not only in the domestic but also in the solemn rites...' and that a householder's wife performed a 'structural role'

[174] Sacrificed Wife and Sacrificer's Wife, Women, Ritual and Hospitality in Ancient India, Stephanie W. Jamison, OUP,Newyork, 1996, P.30

in ritual with clear delineation of functions which she could only perform and none else. She refers to TB II.2.2.6 which enjoins as necessary the participation of wife in rituals [including Śrauta rituals] without which the basic purpose of performing a ritual is lost. This explains the enhanced position of women in the early Vedic society. The women also played a key role through begetting children, in fulfilling an important objective of Vedic rituals which is to enhance fertility. The women also enjoyed certain rights and privileges in domestic sphere. The women were allowed to participate in tribal assemblies and could join certain economic activities, such as, agriculture, making of baskets, embroidery etc. Widow remarriage constituted another important feature of the early Vedic society. The Purdah system was non-existent and perhaps, there was no bar to inter-caste marriages. The practice of young maiden performing certain rituals to find a husband was not unknown during Vedic period. AV VI. 60.2 alludes to this practice where benediction of Aryaman (Marriage god) is sought in this regard. However, we also get mixed signals from the Ṛgveda regarding the status of women in early Vedic society. The predominance of male deities in the Ṛgveda and assignment of minor role to female deities seem to get replicated in the structure of the Vedic society. Indra (Warrior god) and Agni (Fire god) figure in 254 and 204 hymns of the Ṛgveda respectively while Uṣas (the goddess of dawn), a female deity figures in 18 hymns only. There is a stanza in the Ṛgveda which describes the plight of a brotherless woman (RV 1.124.)

We also notice the beginning of certain deterioration in the status of women during the post Ṛgvedic phase which got further accentuated when we come across the Manu Smṛti. This is evident from the practice of celebrating the birth of a son in the family as a more welcome event than the birth of a daughter. Hanns-Peter Schmidt[175] refers to Manu's passage (9. 137-138) which succinctly describes the fate of a person with a son and that of a person without a son. The passage, translated into English, reads as follows: "Through a son one wins the worlds, through a grandson one gains eternity, and through grandson's son one reaches the realm of the Sun. Because a son saves the father from the hell named *put*, he was called

[175] Some Women's Rites and Rights in the Veda, Hanns-Peter Schmidt, Bhandarkar Oriental Research Institute,Poona, India, 1987, P.45

putra by Svayambhu himself." There are passages[176] in the Atharva-Veda (AV III, 23; VI, 11, VII, 48) which advocate practice of rituals for birth of a son. Such a preference for a son may be seen in the context of his greater usefulness not only for reasons of military operations but also for perpetuating lineages and performance of rites As regards participation in Vedic rituals, it was restricted to only to a married woman. There is an indication to this effect in hymn 3 of Book XII of the Atharva-Veda. Griffiths English translation of this hymn runs as follows: *"An accompaniment to the preparation and presentation of sacrificial offerings by a householder and his wife, with prayer for prosperity and happiness on earth and in heaven."* It is true that a woman could participate in Śrauta rituals but this she could not do independently of her husband. Further, elucidating on the position of women, Dr Altekar[177] , a well-kown Indologist, refers to Bṛhad Āraṇyaka Upaniṣad (IV.4.18) where a certain ritual has been recommended for begetting a scholarly daughter. This highlights the importance of a girl's education and provides a clue to the fact that the women could take up teaching profession. [178] It is also a common belief that some women studied Vedic texts. But this is hardly attested and evidence for this is rather flimsy. We, however, do find evidence of conversation of two women, namely, Gargi Vacaknavi and Maitreyi discussing with Yājñavalkya deep philosophical issues. These conversations appear in Bṛhad Āraṇyaka Upaniṣad in chapter 3 (3.5,1 ; 3.7.22;3.8.11) and in chapter 4 (4.5.6; 4.5.15) respectively. Some people did wish to have a learned daughter like Maitreyi but it required a special ritual to accomplish this feat. It did not happen automatically. The magical rituals required to be performed in this respect have been described in chapter 6 of the Bṛhad Āaraṇyaka Upaniṣad.

---

[176] Griffiths English Translation of AV III, hymn 23.3 reads as follows: *"Bring forth a male, bring forth a son. Another male shall follow him. The mother thou shalt be of sons born and hereafter to be born."* Hymn 23.6 reads as follows: *"May those celestial herbs whose sire was Heaven, the Earth their mother, and their root the ocean. May those celestial healing Plants assist thee to obtain a son."*

[177] The Position of Women in Hindu Civilization, A.S. Altekar, Motilal Banarsidass, Delhi. 2nd edition, Reprint, 1987

[178] We also find references in the Rgveda about enlightened women who attained great spiritual heights. Some of these women rshis include Aditi (4.18), Yami (10.154), Lopamudra (1.171), Vishvavara Atreyi (5.28) etc. The women were also allowed to participate in tribal assemblies and could join certain economic activities, such as, agriculture, making of baskets, embroidery etc.

On the question of inheritance, Schmidt refers to Manu's observations according to which "the right to inheritance belongs to both children (son and daughter) without distinction." However, the *putrika*[179] inherits not in her own right but only as a trustee for her son. Book II.17.7 of the Ṛgveda mentions about the share of a daughter in her father's property. The later Vedic literature, however, discount a woman's right in this respect. There is a clear statement in the Śatapatha Brāhmaṇa in this regard. The deteriorating status of women is also reflected in Manu's injunctions (Manusmṛti IX.3) regarding protection to be afforded to a woman throughout her life, first by the father during her maidenhood, then by her husband in her youth (after she gets married) and lastly by her son in her old age or when she becomes a widow. During the post-Vedic period the egalitarian character of the early Vedic period slowly melted away. This is also evident from Manu's advocacy of child marriage, polygamy and rigorous discipline for widows. Even on the question of disposal of Stridhana and inheritance of property, views are divided among the authorities.

c) Varṇa System

During the early Ṛgvedic period, we notice intermingling between the Aryan tribes and the local population. The results of such intermingling were seen in social interaction between these two groups. There are instances of inter-marriage and acceptance of local poets and chieftains in the fold of Aryan tribes. For example, the name of chieftain Bṛbu, clearly a non-Aryan name, occurs in book VI, hymn 45 and stanzas 31 and 33 of the Rgveda. Another example is Varo-Susa man, another non-Aryan, whose name occurs in RV book 8, hymn 23 and stanza 28. The term Varṇa finds frequent mention in the Ṛgveda but there was no rigidity in observing class distinction. Absolute restriction in allowing mobility across Varṇa also did not exist. It is only towards the later part of the Ṛgvedic period when Book X was added that one finds some contemplation regarding

179 Some Women's rites and Rights in the Veda, Hanns-Peter Schmidt, p38-39, The term *putrika* suggests that the brotherless daughter herself is considered a son. This provision was probably made 'in order to secure her right to inheritance in case she had not yet borne a son when the father died'. In Schmidt's words, the explicit appointment of the *putrika* could not be revoked and this is testified in Manu 9.140 (" The son of a Putrika should first offer the funeral cake to his mother, the second (cake) to her father, the third to the father of her father")

four classes in the Puruṣa-Sukta (RV 10. 90.12)[180]. Mention of four classes, however, did not mean formalization of caste system. It is generally held that the Puruṣa hymns were a late addition and "its evidence is not cogent with the rest of the Rgveda." Max Muller[181]also held the view that "... that the 90th hymn of the tenth Book is modern both in its character and in its diction..." Similar views have been expressed by Muir[182]. Beni Prasad [183] has also observed that "the weight of cumulative evidence lies on the side of those who hold that the institution (of caste) is taking shape in the early hymns." He has cited RV Book IV hymns 12.3; 42.1, book V hymn 69.1 and book VII hymn 64.2 to buttress this point. From many Ṛgvedic hymns, however, it can be inferred that Varṇa implied class distinction based on role assigned to a particular class in the society. For example, a Brahmin is described by his priestly profession, (RV Book I, 108.7, IV, 50.8; VIII, 81.30, 7.20; IX 112.1 and RV X 85.29 refer).The Brahmins, thus, formed a distinct class. Similarly, the Kṣatriyas, by virtue of their warrior status and as a protector of the tribe, occupied the next place in social classification. These examples clearly show that both Brahmins and kṣatriyas were already positioning themselves in the upper rung of the Varṇa system. The influence of indigenous peoples on the Varṇa system is also visible. Initially, the influence was mostly restricted to economic activities and performance of inferior services but in the post-Ṛgvedic period, more and more indigenous people were accepted in the Vedic fold. Kulke[184] holds that the dark-skinned people subjugated by the Aryans were skilled artisans and the Aryans lacked the artisan skills they possessed. This in his

[180] Vedic Index of Names and Subjects Vol.II, pp 247-48. Hymn 90.12 together with hymn 90.11 reads as follows: 90.11 – *"When they divided Purusa how many portions did they make? What do they call his mouth, his arms? What do they call his thighs and feet? 90.12 The Brahman was his mouth, of both his arms was the Rajanya made.His thighs became the Vaisya, from his feet the Sudra was produced"* (Griffiths Trans.).

[181] Ancient Sanskrit Literature: F. Maxmuller, P.570

[182] Original Sanskrit Texts on the Origin and History of the People of India, their Religion and Institutions, vol.I, 2nd ed., Amsterdam Oriental Press, 1967. Muir is also of the view that the Purusha-Sukta hymn does not belong to the most ancient portion of the Rgveda

[183] The State in Ancient India: Beni Prasad, P.19-20, Arthur Probsthain, Oriental Book Seller and Publisher, 41 Gt.Russel Street, London, W.C.I., 1928.

[184] A History of India, 4th ed., Hermann Kulke and Dietmar Rothermund, Routledge, N.Y., 2004. P.43

view was, perhaps, 'one of the important reasons for the emergence of the caste system, which was designed to maintain the social and political superiority of the Aryans.'

The Varṇa system, observed in a very rudimentary form during the Ṛgvedic period, however, evolved further and took a concrete shape in the later Vedic period. The attempt on the part of the king to widen his sphere of influence by incorporating diverse tribes in the polity and generate additional resource was an important factor in the establishment of a hierarchical order among the four varṇas (classes). Kumkum Roy[185] has succinctly illustrated this aspect from the rituals associated with the rājasūya where according to her, "the four distinct chants symbolic of brahma, ksatra, viś and sūdra conceived of as endowed with... luster, valour, procreative power and stability, respectively, represented the incorporation of the four varṇas with what were defined as their proper attributes". The increasing stratification of society in the post-Ṛgvedic period is seen as a result of evolvement of roles of different classes in the society. The performance of complex Śrauta rituals required specialized handling which led to the emergence of a class of priests who were well-versed in this respect. Here in also lay the genesis of the emergence of this class on hereditary lines and the complexity of rituals to a great extent, accounted for the division of priestly functions among four categories of priests. This also explains the growing importance of the Brahmin class who had the sole responsibility to perform rituals. Some scholars, however, discount the enhanced status of priestly class in religious and temporal spheres. They, on the strength of Brāhmaṇa texts, hold that they just performed priestly duties like an employee and the purohita also acted as a chariot driver for the king. Brian Smith ("The Veda and the Authority of Class"), however, has attributed to the Vedas as "the sanctifying source of a hierarchical social order" in which the Brahmins occupied the highest status, [presumably because of their key role in the performance of rituals]. Similarly, the responsibility for protecting the community devolved on the Kṣatriya class who were noblemen, and occasionally fought wars besides taking part in raids. The functions attached to their station in life ensured them a pre-eminent place in the society. The other two categories, namely, the Vaishyas and the Sudras occupied lower positions in the social hierarchy. The Vaiṣyas engaged in economic activities while the Sudras performed a motley of inferior

[185] The Emergence of Monarchy in North India, Kumkum Roy, OUP, 1994, Pp. 152-153

services. It was, however, in the post-Ṛgvedic period that the Varṇa assumed an institutionalized form where it got aligned with the nature of function performed and heredity became a determining factor. Beni Prasad[186] observes that "the theory of function, as crystallized in caste acquired a conspicuous position in Hindu speculation and determined the trend of social literature." Diverse economic activities [187]seen during the post-Ṛgvedic phase which, inter-alia, encouraged trading activities, also introduced some measure of elasticity in the otherwise evolving rigidity in the Varṇa system. Such trading activities were not viewed as inferior activities. This allowed people situated in the upper rung of the society to participate in such activities. Kulke holds that this impacted the future development of social order and explains how this factor accounts for the importance of trading class in the society at a later date.

[186] The State in Ancient India: Beni Prasad, Arthur Probsthain, Oriental Book Seller and Publisher, 41 Gt.Russel Street, London, W.C.I., 1928., P-9

[187] A History of India, 4th ed., Hermann Kulke and Dietmar Rothermund, Routledge, 2004, P.43

Chapter XI

Vedic Values and Religious Practices

In the midst of seemingly mundane activities, like organizing cattle raids to enrich cattle stock, engagement with various types of economic activities, such as crafts, metal work or cultivation of land, the Vedic Aryans never lost sight of higher principles which guided them to stay on the course. This is writ large in the hymns of the Vedas, philosophical speculation enshrined in the Upaniṣads and the various rituals practiced by the Vedic Aryans to seek the benediction of deities.

a) Concept of Ṛta

Adherence to *Ṛta* (Cosmic law and Social law) and the performance of Yajna assumed a central place in their thought process and had an all-pervasive influence in moulding the tenor of their social and religious life. H.N. Sinha[188] credits the Ṛgvedic Aryans with having brought with them these two concepts. Bloomfield[189] maintains that in relation to "man's activity the *.rta* manifests itself as a moral law" and likens it to the Confucian idea of order, harmony, and absence of disturbance. RV II,24,8 likens the magical power of *.rta to Brhaspati's string of bows* which never misses the mark and is effective in destroying the enemies.[190] The concept of *.rta* is not riveted to any particular deity as such but flows from what such deities symbolize. For example, *Ṛta* is embedded in the statutes of Varuṇa and Mitra relating to cosmic order or in the regulations of Adityas determining the course of the nature or in the power of Indra who acted as a saviour for the Vedic Aryans and helped them to overcome obstacles. *Ṛta* stands out as a symbol of orderliness in the realm of nature or as influencing actions in the mundane world and exempts none from its

188 The Development of Indian Polity: H.N. Sinha, Asia Publishing House, New York, 1962,pp.16-18

189 Ibid, pp.126-128

190 The Religion of the Veda, Hermann Oldenberg, English Trans.by S.B. Shrotri, Motilal Banarsidass,Delhi, 1998,P.35

purview. According to Beni Prasad,[191] an eminent historian, "ethical motive" characterized the Indian social thought which was reflected in social order and orientation of the polity. Gṛhyasūtra and Dharmasūtra stand testimony to ethical bent of mind of the Vedic Aryans.

The concept of *ṛta* which was the bedrock of political and social orientation of Vedic Aryans during the early phase was morphed into *dharma* at a later stage and became an essential feature of brahmanical tradition. It no longer expounded higher ethical principles but essentially ensured that each social category performs duties as envisaged for that category in the context of Varṇa system. Observance of brahminical tradition in the place of adherence to Ṛta dented the higher ethical values earlier professed by the Vedic Aryans. This development also impacted the role of the king who no longer remained an upholder of Ṛta and became a conformist to brahminical ideology and practices as exemplified in the brahminical tradition. This development enhanced the social responsibilities of the king as a guardian of a new Varṇa order which emphasized social difference and is still reflected in the social orientation of the Indian polity.

b) Cult of Sacrifice

The ritual of sacrifice practiced by the Vedic Aryans was central to their social and religious life, nay, even entered the political arena in a significant manner. Rituals at domestic level were performed and offerings were made to gods to seek their benediction. The Vedic Aryans propitiated the heavenly bodies in the belief that they may come to their succour in their fight against the Dasyus (demons), and, at the same time, also contribute towards maintaining cosmic order. To this end the sacrificial rituals were performed for a long series of gods. Among these, Varuṇa and Indra were the prominent ones, followed by Agni, the fire god. Soma sacrifices also occupied a pride of place since the great gods were in their foreground. The Vedic Aryans could not have performed these rituals by themselves and needed a medium to connect with the gods. Hence, the Brahmins who formed the priestly class and were well-versed in the practice of rituals, served the purpose of a medium through which such a link with the gods could be established. The Hotṛ establishment (a

---

[191] Theory of Government in Ancient India: Dr Beni Prasad, The india Press Ltd., Allahabad

priestly class during the Ṛgvedic period) played a prominent role in the performance of such rituals during the Ṛgvedic period. However, during the post Ṛgvedic period, other categories of the priests also gained in importance. This happened on account of the transformation of the Ṛgvedic ritual into Śrauta ritual which led to a division of priestly functions among the four categories of priests, such as Hotṛ (Ṛgvedic rituals), Adhvaryu (Yajus ritual), Udgātṛ (Sāma rituals) and Brahman (Atharva Vedic rituals). The division of priestly functions underlies the growing importance of rituals as also emphasizes the degree of complexity in the performance of such rituals which could not have been left to only Ṛgvedic hotṛ and the other categories of priests had to step in. The fire ritual is accorded great importance because the Vedic Aryans believed that the offerings put into fire are partaken by gods as the fire consumes them. Thus the objects of sacrifice acquired divine connotation and a potent element in obtaining god's benediction. Whitaker[192] while highlighting the importance of the Ṛgvedic rituals, maintains that these rituals also symbolized a man's identity in terms of power, masculinity and dominance and were reflected at family, clan, tribe and mythological levels. According to him, the focus on masculinity is evident in the practice of Vedic rituals and the prominence accorded to masculine gods in the Ṛgveda. He further explains that on the occasion of fire ritual, masculinity is represented by the head of the household at family level, the clan leader at clan level and the tribal chief at tribe level. At the mythological level, god Indra is projected as a symbol of masculinity and similarly, other gods, such as Agni and Soma are also accorded high status in the Ṛgveda. Such a view accords well with the fact that Indra and Agni figure in 254 and 204 hymns of the Ṛgveda respectively; in the Sāma-Veda, too, Agni is invoked in 114 verses and 189 verses are devoted to Indra alone and in approximately 153 verses , Indra is joined by other gods. The goddess of dawn, namely, Uṣas, however, figures in only 18 hymns of the Ṛgveda. Further, the patriarchal nature of the early Vedic society, did not allow women, despite enjoying a better status, to occupy higher positions of authority. They did take part in the Vedic rituals, but this participation was in their minor aspects For the Ṛgvedic Aryans, the performance of *yajna* was a relatively a simple affair with an altar of one fire and the Soma ritual, which was moderately elaborate, was, perhaps, the only exception . There also appears to be no uniformity of views regarding association of magical actions in the early Vedic period with sacrifice rituals. Oldenberg

---

[192] Strong Arms and Drinking Strength, Jarrod L. Whitaker, OUP, 2011. P.5

discounts the presence of such magical actions in the Ṛgveda or even animal sacrifice other than Aśvamedha, i.e., Horse-sacrifice.[193] Keith[194], however, adduces to RV iv 50.8 to show that the prosperity of the realm of the king depended on the Purohita as he performed "all the domestic ritual of the king's household, with its many formulae and magic rites to secure the success of the king's undertakings in war and peace, the correctness of his judgments, and the prosperity of his subjects." Further, it appears from RV vii, 18 that the Purohita was supposed to use his magic power to secure the king's success in the battle. The later Vedic literature mention about cattle, goats and sheep being commonly used as sacrificial animals.

The cult of sacrifice was practiced to seek god's blessings and ward off evils. Great gods, in particular, were perceived as repository of benevolent powers. Offerings during the course of sacrificial rituals was the usual way of showing veneration towards them and reaping rewards in return. Recital of hymns in the praise of gods on such occasions was believed to obtain for the sacrificer the god's blessings for achieving the desired objectives and also god's mercy for sinful acts committed. Both the rituals pertaining to gift offering and seeking mercy for committing violation of divine were seen as a method for expiating gods and also to ensure the well-being of the clan. There were certain conditionalities attached to being a patron of a sacrifice. One of such conditionalities envisaged that only a person with a wife could be eligible to be patron of a sacrifice. This reflects the importance of the institution of marriage in Vedic rituals.

During the post-Ṛgvedic period, under the Kurus, the sacrifice rituals acquired the character of a cult as they evolved from simple rituals to Srauta rituals. The rituals became more elaborate and complex. The mantras (verses) recited on the occasion were invested with magical quality and the priestly class became the sole competent authority to infuse such magic into the mantras. The transition from the Ṛgvedic sacrifice rituals to new Śrauta rituals created ripples in the priestly establishment which were reflected in the rivalry between the Hotṛ establishment and YV Adhvaryu. The result of this rivalry and the increasing complexities in the performance of rituals saw the division of

193 The Religion of the Veda, Hermann Oldenberg, English Trans.by S.B. Shrotri, Motilal Banarsidass,Delhi,1998,P.5-6

194 The Religion and Philosophy of the Veda and Upaniṣads, Part I, A.B. Keith, P.292, Motilal Banarsidass, Delhi, Reprint 2007.

priestly work into four groups with the Hoṭṛ establishment losing its pre-eminent position.

The fire rituals came to symbolize both social status as well as political power. There also occurred a structural change in the performance of sacrificial fire. Śrauta rituals required three fires instead of one Domestic fire which was staged within the home premises on occasions like a woman giving birth to a child[195], marriage rites and various other similar ceremonies to grant protection. Srauta rituals were performed with three fires outside the home premises. Brian Smith[196] describes domestic ritualism as "basic to the ritualism of ancient Vedic Indians" and that some of such rituals were "pre-requisites for the Śrauta sacrifices". The three fires of Śrauta rituals consisted of householder's fire (Gārhapatya), Āhavanīya and Dakṣiṇa. As Brian Smith puts it[197], the śrauta fires were first established "by expanding the Domestic fire into the householder's (Gārhapatya) fire. This perhaps meant rekindling the household fire from the last [domestic] fire tended by the householder.[198]The Gārhapatya thus, represented the fire of the householder which was located in the west. The next stage was carrying the embers of householder's fire to the other two śrauta fires, namely, Āhavanīya and Dakṣiṇa. Āhavanīya ritual involved carrying offerings to gods while Dakṣiṇa (southern fire) ritual, involved offerings to the ancestors or was intended to ward off evil spirits. Patrick Olivelle[199] maintains that "the brahminical theology invested the Dakṣiṇa [ritual] with enormous power and importance" which persuaded "the patrons to give generously." This practice ostensibly benefitted the priestly class enormously. The performance of Śrauta rituals was not exclusively in the domain of men. The wife of a householder was an essential part of this ritual but she could do so only in the company of her husband.

---

[195] There is a special fire, Sūtikāgni, for woman in child birth for driving off evil spirit. (Keith in Religion and Philosophy of Rgveda, Pt. I,P.285)

[196] Reflections on Resemblance, Ritual, and Religion, Brian K. Smith,Motilal Banarsidass, Delhi,1998. P.145

[197] Reflections on Resemblance, Ritual, and Religion, Brian K. Smith,Motilal Banarsidass, Delhi,1998. P.152

[198] The Religion and Philosophy of the Veda and Upanishads, Pt. I, A.B. Keith,P.289

[199] The Early Upaniṣads, Patrick Olivelle, OUP, N.Y., P.18

Sacrifice rituals also acquired a political overtone as an occasion to display the king's authority. These occasions strengthened the position of the priestly class as it was seen as the only group possessed of magical power with ability to perform complex rituals for conferring boon on the king and the clan. The king also benefitted by granting patronage to holding of rituals on a large scale. For him the priest became a medium to connect with the divine for obtaining the latter's benediction. The patronage of rituals also enhanced his stature as the chief sacrificer and provided him with the rationale for collecting gifts from the clan. Describing the complex relationship between the priestly and royal classes, Patrick Olivelle[200] has observed that "the entire Brahminical ideology of society and the science and practice of ritual were designed, on the one hand, to enhance kṣatriya power and on the other, to ensure the recognition by the kṣatriyas that the source of their power was the Brahmin". Such a trend, clearly discernible in the early Vedic period became a dominant feature of the society during the post-Ṛgvedic period.

Srauta reforms during the post Ṛgvedic period also had implications on the social plane. The respective roles of the Brahmins and Kṣatriyas, Vaiśyas and the Śūdras in the system were clearly delineated with the king emerging as a seat of effective authority. The Varṇa evolved into caste system at this time and the Brahmins and kṣatriya welded together to form 'Brahma-kṣatra' against the lower echelons of the society. The system of governance also underwent a change with the streamlining of functions relating to collection of land revenue and tributes. Running of administration and military operations no longer remained the prerogative of the king's kinsmen but paid personnel also shared this responsibility.

[200] The Early Upaniṣads, Patrick Olivelle, OUP, New York, 1998. P.11.

Chapter XII

Tribal Kingdoms

During the later Vedic period, a number of tribal kingdoms came to be established, the prominent amongst them were: a) The Kurus around Kurukṣetra region; b)the Pañcālas in the Rohilkhand region; c) the Matsyas who occupied the lands now known as Alwar, Jaipur and Bharatpur;[201] d) the Uśinaras near the Kuru country; e) the Kosalas in the region of Oudh and Faizabad; f) the Kāśi around the modern city of Varanasi; g)the Videha in the north-eastern Bihar; h) the Aṅgas near the modern Bhagalpur; i) the Magadhas in South Bihar; j) the Cedis in modern Bundelkhand to the north of the Vindhya; k) the Vidarbha near the Narmada region; and l) the Uttara-Kuru, and m) the Uttara-Madras in the Himalayan region. We shall now focus on Kurus-Pañcālas and Kosala-Videha, which throw considerable light on the polity of the period.

a) The Kuru-Pañcālas Ascendancy

A major development of political significance during the Brāhmaṇa period was Kuru's assumption of leadership of the Kuru-Pañcāla group after they moved from the greater Punjab region to further east alongside the belt of the two rivers, the Ganges and the Yamuna. The Kuru ascendancy was facilitated by the innate strength of the Kuru tribe and the opportunity offered by the process of merger and consolidation which the Ṛgvedic tribes were going through on their arrival in the eastern region. The integration of the Ṛgvedic tribes and clans of the eastern Punjab, Haryana and Western Uttar Pradesh with the Kuru tribe was an event of great political and social significance. The assumption of leadership position of these motley group of tribes by the Kurus had two broad implications: First, the Kurus emerged as a Super tribe with its leadership exercising control over an expanded jurisdiction which became a nucleus for Kuru-Pāñcāla alliance in the Madhyadesha, and second, the enhanced status enabled the Kurus to introduce major changes on social and religious fronts. This is evident from the references we find in Book X of the Ṛgveda as also in the later Vedic literature, particularly, Aitareya Brāhmaṇa, Śatapatha Brāhmaṇa and the earlier Upaniṣads. This event

[201] The Cambridge History of India,Vol.I, p.84

also exerted strong influence on Kosala and Videha, situated in areas corresponding to modern Uttar Pradesh and North Bihar respectively.

Kurukṣetra under the Kurus emerged as an important political and cultural centre. The period was marked by social and political developments, and witnessed transformation in the society with the Brahmins and Kṣatryias forming a united political front against the Śūdras and the aborigines. This entailed their control over a large number of economic activities and thus further deepened the cleavage in the society. At political level the importance of higher nobility had not diminished but they enjoyed a position subordinate to the king. The powers of the king had grown mani-fold and the democratic institutions like the Sabhā had started receding into the background. The Kuru realm, under the great King Parikshit, achieved great heights in all spheres, particularly in the sphere of Vedic texts collection and reformation of rituals. The Ṛgvedic language retained its importance for use in the rituals but it was tempered with the language used locally thus making it intelligible and easy to grasp.

The Kuru-Pāncāla realm rose in prominence, marked by performance of Rājasūya and setting an example of good governance. The Brahmins of the realm were also noted for their scholarship in the Upaniṣads and Vedic rituals. The coronation ceremony assumed an elaborate character with the priest playing a dominant role. The elaboration of some rituals was first seen in Book I of the Ṛgveda dominated by the Viśvāmitras and to some extent in Book III of the Ṛgveda. In the post-Ṛgvedic period, rituals connected with royal consecration became elaborate and complex. Rājasūya,[202] Aindra-Mahabhiseka,[203] Vajāpeya[204] and Aśvamedha[205] were

---

[202] J.C. Heesterman in his monograph, titled, The Ancient Indian Royal Consecration has given a succinct account of rituals connected with '**Rājasūya**' as available from the Atharva-Veda and the Brahmanas. Rājasūya entails performance of ceremonies in sequence, including observance of four monthly sacrifices, performance of unction festival, followed by year-long diksa ceremony and a royal inauguration ceremony.

[203] It involved a complicated ritual and its performance was supposed to bestow on the king various types of sovereignty, such as, Sāmarajya, Mahārajya, Vairājya etc.

[204] It was performed by a Samrāj, a prince of higher position than an ordinary king and also involved participation in a chariot race.

[205] It stands for horse sacrifice. Horse was taken as the symbol of sovereign authority.

different types of rituals with very elaborate and complex paraphernalia in which the Ratnins also participated. These rituals had implications in terms of "material and social benefits" and the sacrifices were performed keeping this factor in view. According to Kumkum Roy[206], these rituals represented "restoration or regeneration of the cosmic order" and their "consequent material and social benefits was worked out through specific components of these rituals".

The elaborate Rājasūya procedure included a game of dice and chariot race. Elucidating the significance of the chariot drive after the king's abisheka (anointment) and the ritual game of dice after he ascended the throne, Heesterman [207]connected this activity with the regeneration of productive forces in the cosmos. R.S Sharma[208], disagreeing with Heesterman, however, maintains that these were intended "to test the sagacity of the chief at the time of election" and "to detect the military qualities of the candidate for the post of the king or the chief of the tribe". Kumkum Roy[209] while succinctly putting across Heesterman's analysis of the rajasuya, maintains that his preoccupation with symbols of cosmic regeneration, makes him miss the social context in which such rituals are performed.

The Rājasūya procedure followed for anointing a king has been described in the Aitareya Brāhmaṇa (Chapter VIII .19).[210] Aitareya Brāhmaṇa emphasizes that if a king is anointed according to the prescribed procedure, the way Indra was anointed, "he wins all victories, finds all worlds, attains the superiority, pre-eminence and supremacy over all kings... having obtained all desires he becomes immortal..." This late Vedic text also refers to emerging kingdoms of the East, viz., Kosala and Videha and enhancement in the status of king who no longer was a mere chieftain but acquired the status of chieftain of chieftains. This served a dual purpose, namely, first a ceremonial purpose and secondly, an occasion to display the growing authority of the King. The presence of

---

206 The Emergence of Monarchy in North India, Kumkum Roy, OUP,1994, P.113

207 The Ancient Indian Royal Consecration, J.C. Histerman, P.133

208 Aspects of Political Ideas and Institutions in Ancient India, R.S. Sharma, PP.164-165, Motilal Banarsidass, Delhi-2009.

209 The Emergence of Monarchy in India, Kumkum Roy, OUP,1994, P.10

210 Harvard Oriental Series, Vol. 25,Edited by C.R. Lanman, Harvard University Pess, Cambridge, MA, 1920

Ratnins such as the 'senānī,' Purohita, Mahishi (Chief queen among the four), the Grāmaṇī, the tax Collector, the Charioteer etc., on such occasions, also provides a clue to the political machinery associated with the king. The transformation [211] of the Rig-Vedic rituals into Śrauta ritual occurred in several stages during the late Rig-Vedic and Mantra period. The period also witnessed diminishing importance of the Ṛgvedic hotṛ priests vis-à-vis the Adhvaryus representing the new Śrauta establishment. The growing stature of the Brahmin class in the body-politic during this phase is exemplified by the crucial role it played in the elaborate and complex coronation ceremony. This becomes apparent in the various passages of Aitareya Brāhmaṇa. There is a warning to the king in AB chapter VIII.20 that he should not play false with a Brahmin[212].

Another important development was that the non-Aryans gained entry into the Vedic fold, but without a right to participate in the Vedic rituals. The Rathakāras, were, perhaps, the only exception, who were allowed to perform Vedic rituals. The process of inclusion of some non-Aryan chiefs in the new Kuru order, also had its impact on the character of the Vedic society. It necessitated certain changes in the ritual practices which became less restrictive but did not guarantee them a right to practice such rituals. The Śrauta rituals were reformed and the modality of their performance was specified categories- wise.[213] This process was further supplemented, as Witzel[214] maintains, by "the development and collection of a large body of ritual texts" and division of "traditional priests into four units: the Ṛgvedic Hotṛ, the Sāmavedic Udgātṛ, the Yajurvedic

---

[211] Inside the Texts Beyond the Texts, Edited by Michael Witzel, P.289,Harvard Oriental Series, Opera Minora, Vol.2, Cambridge, 1997.

[212] This warning is in the background of a story in which Atyarati Janamtapi, a king had uttered falsehood to a Brahmin Vasishtha Satyahavya for which he had to pay the price with his life. Therefore, the message in the Aitareya Brahmana (AB VIII. 24), in the context of the role of the king's Purohita was that "the gods eat not the food of a king without a Purohita." Further, it has been pointed out in this passage that "a king when about to sacrifice should select as Purohita a Brahman (wishing) may the gods eat my food." AB VIII.25 states "The Purohita is Agni Vaicvanara with five missiles; with these he keeps enveloping the king as the ocean the earth. His kingdom perishes not in its youth, life leaves him not before his time, who has for Purohita to guard the kingdom a Brahman."

[213] Staat, W.Rau P.59-60

[214] Inside the Texts-Beyond the Texts, Opera Minora Vol.2, Edited by Michael Witzel, p. 267, Cambridge, MA, 1997.

Adhvaryu and the Atharvavedic Brahman priests." The Kosala-Videha kings continued this trend who invited [215] 'the Kāṇvas and the Tattirīya scholar Bodhāyana' and the 'Aitareyins' respectively for religious duties. The Videha king also invited Brahmins from the western region to act as Śrauta Priests. Further, the Kuru realm became a centre of Brahmanical culture and saw the appearance of post-Vedic Sanskrit.

The stratification of society into four classes was further fine-tuned and the lower order was encouraged to move towards specialization on vocational lines. This was a forerunner of developments in societal sphere seen later in the Indian polity. Ability to extract tributes from the lower rung of the society was an important parameter for determining relationship of higher functionaries with the royal court. Wilhelm Rau[216] touches on various levels of functionaries in the Kuru polity; that included the king at the top, followed by aristocracy, smaller chieftains and the leaders of various clans.

Economically, the society, while retaining a pastoral character, increasingly opted for extensive rice cultivation.

While the Kuru realm remained much in focus as a political and ritual centre during the early post Ṛgvedic period, they could not sustain the leadership of the Kuru-Pañcāla group, probably due to their weakened position in the immediate aftermath of aggression by some other tribes, such as the Sālvas. The scene of political and cultural activities shifted to Pañcāla realm a few centuries after circa 1000 B.C. Kaiśinī was one of their great chieftains who introduced changes in the rituals which is called 'kaiśinī' diksha. This diksha pertains to the consecration ceremony for the soma sacrifice. The other illustrious kings were Kraivya and Satrasaha, who had performed horse sacrifice. The economic and social life was marked by consolidation during this period. A large number of schools following the Taittirīya tradition also came into existence in the Pañcāla domain. The institution of the "Samiti," a special feature of the RV polity which subsequently, had gone into oblivion, reappears in the Pañcāla

---

[215] Ibid, pp.312-13

[216] Ibid

realm where the phrase used is the "Samiti of the Pañcālas."[217] It appears from Bṛhad Āraṇyaka that the Samiti, during the later Vedic period also discussed philosophical issues.[218] Not much detail is available on the Pañcālas exclusively during the early post-Vedic phase since their polity is mostly discussed in conjunction with the Kuru.

b) Kosala-Videha Realm

After the Kuru-Pañcālas, the focus shifts to the land of the Kosala-Videha tribes in eastern Uttar Pradesh and to the north of the Ganges in Bihar respectively. These two areas had settlements of different ethnic backgrounds. Various types and groups of tribes came to inhabit these areas from north-western direction. This mixed nature of settlement gave rise to rivalry among the tribal chieftains to secure the position of great chieftain. Both Kosala and Videha kings favoured the texts and the rituals of the western Brahmins for practice in their region. These regions also witnessed evolution of centralized authority which happened towards the end of the Vedic period. The Brāhmaṇas also mention about one of the Kosala kings, Para Antara Hairanyanabha, having performed the Aśvamedha.The use of iron tools, rice cultivation on a major scale and reorganization of the Brāhmaṇa style texts were carried out during this period. Further, compilation of the Kāṇva ŚB and the Kauṣītaki Brāhmaṇa was also done in Kosala. Witzel[219] observes that "the process of Sanskritization of the newly brahmanized territories of Kosala, Videha and later on, of Magadha, was carried out by the well-tested alliance of the Kṣatriyas and Brahmins."

---

[217] Aspects of Political Ideas and Institutions in Ancient India: R.S. Sharma, p.111, 5th revised edition, Motilal Banarsidass, Delhi, 2005. Dr Sharma maintains that the Samiti is a later development in the early Vedic period since it appears in the latest portion of the Rgveda, that is, Book I and Book X. The Sabhā, in his view, appears in both the earlier as well as the later portions of the Rgveda and is an older institution than the Samiti. The expression 'Samiti of the Panchalas, according to him, denotes that it was a "tribal assembly" which performed civil and political functions.

[218] Ibid p.112.

[219] Inside the Texts-Beyond Texts, Edited by Michael Witzel, pp.333-4, Harvard Oriental Series, Opera Minora, Vol.2, Cambridge, 1997.

Chapter XIII

Features of the Post Ṛgvedic Period

The prominent features of the later Vedic period, to put in nutshell, were:

- The centre of activity moved away from Sarasvati- Drisadvati belt to the eastern part of India, with Kurukṣetra, and later Kosala and Videha capitals becoming the seat of authority.
- It was not the tribal region per se, but the capital cities of the eastern kingdoms signaled the beginning of urbanization process, quite distinct from the rural character of the Ṛgvedic polity.
- The merger and consolidation process among the tribes led to the emergence of super tribes in the eastern region.
- The merger and grouping of tribes resulted in the Kurus-Pañcālas, Kosala-Videhas assuming the position of super-tribes and the important tribes of the Rig-Vedic period, namely, the Bharatas, the Purus, the Turvaśas, the Anus and Druhyus disappeared from the radar.
- In social customs, like marriage, the early post-Vedic period represented a compromise between what Keith[220] describes as a "stage intermediate between the rules of the Sūtras and the laxity of the Ṛgveda."
- The positions of the four classes were formalized with Brahman and kṣatriyas at the upper rung and the vaiśyas at the middle rung and the Śūdras occupying the lowest position in the society.
- There was tremendous growth in the power of the king who had under his control a much larger domain.
- Introduction of elaborate coronation rituals[221] and the presence of big entourage of the king during this occasion reflected the growing importance of the institution of kingship and also an enhancement in the status of the Brahmin who performed the ceremony.

---

220 The Cambridge History of India, Vol. I (Chapter V) P.126, Professor A.B. Keith,The Macmillan Company, New York,1922.

- The growing importance of Brahmin class and the Purohita is reflected in the various passages of Aitareya Brāhmaṇa which point to the harm that may visit an oppressor of the Brahman.
- According to Keith[222], the Grāmaṇi (the village head) "formed the channel through which the royal control was exercised and the royal dues received."
- The Samiti and the Sabhā recede into the background during this period except for a brief mention of the "Samiti of the Panchalas."[223]
- The position regarding judicial administration is vague except stating in general terms that the king as a sovereign wielded authority both in the civil and criminal matters.
- The position of women in the society is reflected in AB VII.13 which shows a certain deterioration.
- Side by side with pastoral pursuits, agriculture received much attention. Extensive rice cultivation was practiced along with cultivation of a few other variety of grains. [224]
- A variety of occupations, such as, ploughers, fisherman, barbers, weavers, carpenters, chariot- makers, potters, smiths, etc. came up during the period. This reflected a trend towards specialization in different trades. The people also possessed knowledge about the use of metals.
- There was an increase in the practice of rituals and more complexity in religious practices. Collection of the Vedic texts and ritual reforms as also growing interest in religion and philosophy were the other features of this period.

We see three important transitions during the span of the Vedic age. Pastoralism was the flavour of the Rgvedic phase and a combination of pastoralism and agriculture became the dominant feature in the post Ṛgvedic phase. Towards the close of the Vedic period, the polity veered

---

[222] Ibid, P.131

[223] See footnote 209.

[224] Wilhelm Rau has cited references from Satpatha Brahmana and Brhadaranyaka Upanishad where the names of ten types of plants have been enumerated. Inside The Texts Beyond The Texts, P.205.

towards agriculture and trade which ushered in an era known as the Second Urbanization.

Chapter XIV

Second Urbanization

The movement of Vedic Aryans from the Northwest region to the Gangetic plain during the post Ṛgvedic period was an event of great political, social and economic significance. The political dimension of this event was reflected in the emergence of a new political order characterized by the merger of tribes and the establishment of territorial kingdoms in the Gangetic plain. The social dimension of this event manifested in acceleration of acculturation process and deepening of class distinction but loosening of the hold of priestly class primarily due to less reliance on complex ritual practices which used to be the main forte of the priestly class. The economic dimension of this event witnessed the rise of cities/towns both as the nerve centres of political and commercial activities along with diversification of occupational activities usually associated with an urban culture and quite distinct from pastoral pursuit which had characterized the early Vedic period. This phase is called the Second Urbanization which, in some respects was distinct from the first urbanization of the Indus Civilization. The features of the second urbanization differed from the first in the matter of city-planning and use of material for construction of dwellings. Another important difference was that the second urbanization flourished in the background of a rural culture as compared to urban culture in the case of the first urbanization. R.S. Sharma [225]holds that urbanization in the mid-gangetic plains occurred in two stages, the first stage beginning with circa 500 BCE and the second stage around 300 BCE. The first stage was characterized by use of 'craft objects, coins, trade, mud buildings...' 'while the second stage was marked by the advent of ring wells, soakpits, brick structures, writing...'.

Patrick Olivelle[226] , however, adducing to the available archaeological and literary data, assigns the second urbanization to the period between the sixth and fourth centuries BCE. The cities, according to him, "functioned as administrative, commercial, and military centres of the kingdoms". By the late Vedic period, there was a change in the political

---

[225] The State and Varna Formation in the Mid-Ganga Plains,An Ethnoarchaeological view, Ramsharan Sharma,P.93, Manohar Publishers,Delhi (Reprinted 2001).

[226] The Early Upaniṣads, Patrick Olivelle, OUP, New York, 1998. P.6.

scene with larger territorial kingdoms replacing smaller tribal outfits. Their capital cities emerged as important urban centres. The polity during this period was dominated by mahajanapadas. The Buddhist texts mention about sixteen such Mahajanapadas , which were entities akin to a state. The prominent ones among them in the Gangetic plain were Aṅga, Magadha, Kaśi, Kosala and Vatsa. Kulke[227] maintains that the imperial phase of Magadha unleashed a process of political and social change and contributed to urbanization in the Ganges valley. Kingdoms during this period represented fixed settlements and the king, as Kulke[228] again observes, 'derived his legitimacy from the ritual investiture by their Brahmin priests' rather from the lineage of the ruling family as was the case during the early Vedic period.

Far-reaching changes took place in the economic sphere to which the indigenous tribes also contributed significantly as they were rated as good artisans and craftsmen specializing in pottery and metal work. Use of iron technology in the clearance of marshland of the middle Gangetic plain and in designing of agricultural implements as also in metal work had a multiplier effect. Not only it substantially improved agricultural production by bringing more arable land into cultivation but also gave a push to non-agricultural activities. Production of agricultural surplus was an important consideration for the growth of urban centres as this was necessary for sustenance of towns which did not produce crops. Thus availability of production surplus became an important factor in the emergence of towns to which political factors also contributed. Some of the settlements in places, such as Rajagriha in Magadha, Shravasti in Kosala, Kausambi in Vatsa, rose in prominence by virtue of being capitals of these kingdoms which was enough to catapult them into important urban centres. The metamorphosis of fixed settlements into towns, and some towns achieving the status of capital cities of territorial kingdoms also helped them to become a centre for exchange of goods. Another important factor for urbanization lay in concentration of artisans, craftsmen in marketplaces (Nigama) which had abundance of raw materials and were easy on access to markets. Such villages had the propensity to develop into commercial urban centres, a place where social interchange was possible and allowed various occupational groups belonging to different social background to thrive. This process was

---

[227] A History of India,4th ed., Hermann Kulke and Dietmar Rothermund, Routledge, 2004, P.58

[228] Ibid, P.44

further facilitated by availability of infrastructure for engaging in trade and commerce. According to Patrick Olivelle[229] "the vast geography known to the Upaniṣads indicates the relative ease of travel and commerce across much of northern India". Excavations carried out in Kausambi, Vaishali, Rajagriha and other places provide evidence of urbanism during the mid-first millennium BC. The evidence of features such as fortification found at Kausambi, layout of urban centres including public buildings, materials used for construction of dwellings, and facilities , such as drains , wells etc. provided in such dwellings and a new type of ceramic (Northern Black Polished ware) discovered during the course of excavations, are clear pointers to fructification of a second urbanization process after the first urbanization of the mature Harappan phase. Patrick Olivelle[230] also refers to "very few agricultural metaphors and images in the Upaniṣads, while examples derived from crafts such as weaving, pottery, and metallurgy are numerous."

Johannes Bronkhorst has discussed the subject of second urbanization from a different perspective. He has drawn attention to the fact that the later Vedic texts do not make any mention of cities while early Buddhist texts mention about cities and towns during the middle of the first millennium BCE. He[231] has sought to explain this dichotomy to 'distaste for city life' which characterized Brahminism. A possible explanation for the absence of any reference to urbanization in Vedic texts, according to Bronkhorst, may have been due to its occurrence 'altogether independent of Vedic society.' Yet another reason could be the penchant on the part of some scholars to assign late Vedic texts to a period preceding urbanization in the Ganges valley. These observations seem quite plausible in the background of the fact that the rural character of the Vedic society did not undergo a change for over a thousand years after the demise of the Harappan urbanite civilization. The Vedic tribes had not totally given up pastoralism even after they descended on the Gangetic plain during the post-Ṛgvedic period. Apart from agricultural pursuit, they also engaged in some subsidiary activities, such as craft and metal work and trade. R.S.

---

[229] The Early Upaniṣads, Patrick Olivelle,OUP,N.Y. 1998, P.7

[230] Ibid. 207

[231] Greater Magadha, Johannes Bronkhorst, Motilal Banarsidass, First Indian edition,2013, P.251

Sharma[232] holds that the diversification of economic activities accounted for more income to the state with corresponding expansion of the state machinery to manage the additional resources and the emergence of a separate class of people who engaged in trade. Michael Witzel[233] also maintains that the late Vedic texts do not mention about cities excepting the occurrence of the word 'nagara' [which implies cities] in very late Brāhmaṇa and Āraṇyaka texts.[234] However, in contrast to Bronkhorst, Witzel, citing evidence from Dīghanikāya II 169.II, further, holds that the earliest Buddhist texts also do not mention cities and that the names of cities, such as "Rājagaha, Sāvatthi, Sāketa, Kosāmbi, Bārānasi" occur only in later Pali texts. The early Buddhist texts, according to him, refer to villages and market places where the Buddha preached sermons. Hence, it is plausible that the Buddha spent the earlier phase of his life in a pre-urban environment while the later phase of his life coincided with the period of Second Urbanization.

During the second urbanization phase, the tribal polity lost its pristine character and what emerged in its place was territorial kingdoms or tribal oligarchies. The social order reflected a strong Brahma-Kṣatriya alliance and an exponential enhancement of their influence in the polity. The vaiśyas and the śūdras also gained in prominence by virtue of their greater role in economic activities but this did not bring about any significant change in their social status as they continued to occupy a lower position in the social order.

A contemporaneous development during the second urbanization phase was the rise of two rational schools of thought, namely, the Buddhism and Jainism which challenged the brahminical dominance and the evil aspects of spiritual practices of the late Vedic period.

---

232 Aspects of Political Ideas and Institutions in Ancient India, R.S. Sharma, Motilal Banarsidass Publishers, Delhi, Reprint 2009, P.364.

233 Moving Targets, Michael Witzel, Indo-Iranian Journal Vol. 52 No. 2-3. 2009, Accessed April 26, 2014 Citable Link http://nrs.harvard.edu/urn-3:HUL.InstRepos:8457940

234 Post-Pāṇinian part of Gopatha Brahmana (I.I.23) and the Puranic –time part of Taittirīya A¯raṇyaka (I.II.7, I.31.2)

Chapter XV

Summary and Conclusions

We have discussed in detail the contents of Vedic texts which throw considerable light on various aspects of Vedic civilization nurtured by Vedic Aryans. We have also dwelt at length the phase of Second Urbanization which characterized the later Vedic period. It is time now to summarize and recapitulate the prominent features of Vedic polity as discussed in the book.

The Vedic Polity encompasses various phases of socio-political development, ranging from the Ṛgvedic to Atharva-Vedic times and that of the other Mantra collections of the Yajur-Veda, the Sāma-Veda and the Ṛgveda Khilas and the period of the early Krishna Yajur-Veda prose.

The two phases of the Vedic period, namely, the Ṛgvedic Saṃhitā period and the Mantra period (during which the Post-Ṛgvedic texts were composed) differ from each other in many respects. Geographically, the Ṛgvedic period flourished in the north and north-west regions including the Sapta-Sindhu areas whereas during the post-Ṛgvedic period, the scene of activities shifted to the Ganga-Yamuna belt, Madhyadesha (Central region) and further towards east and the south. Politically, the early phase was dominated by some major and many smaller Vedic tribes; the Ṛgvedic period is essentially a story of two major tribes, the Pūrus and later the Bharatas, covering a span of some five or six generations of their kings, characterized by intermittent strife. This period was interspersed with the presence of only a few of the other prominent tribes during the early Ṛgvedic period. These were the Yadus-Turvaśas; Anus-Druhyus and later joined by the Pūrus. The duration of the Ṛgvedic period was fairly long, maximally 700 years which was followed by the Mantra period. The duration of the Ṛgvedic period, as many scholars contend drawing support from the various Ṛgvedic hymns, could not have passed without close interaction at different levels between the Aryan and non-Aryan tribes. This interaction was mostly but not always one of acrimony and constant strife but also had a peaceful dividend reflected in the initiation of "multiple processes of cultural, social and linguistic acculturation" on mutual basis between the two. The culmination of these processes resulted in "Aryanization" of local population and "Indianization" of the immigrating Indo-Aryans. This is clearly discernible in the researches of

Kuiper who has established how the language of the Aryan tribes was brought "into harmony with the languages of the indigenous families, in particular Dravidian and Munda".[235] On the political plane too, there are instances of Aryan kings with non-Aryan names, such as Balbutha and Bṛbu.[236] This was something similar to what happened later to Alexander's empire after his demise which broke up into Hellenistic kingdoms each with its own dynasty.[237] While Alexander's campaigns ensured spread of Greek culture, "the Hellenistic kingdoms revealed a two way effects of accommodation and assimilation".

The Vedic polity in the earlier phase was both tribal and pastoral in character. It was not a homogenous entity but consisted of several tribal groupings with different identities, inhabiting different locations. Names of various clans find mention in the Ṛgveda, some representing Indo-Aryan speaking stock while others belonging to indigenous stream. The broad social division consisted of the Vedic tribes and the non-Vedic people. These two categories were differentiated on grounds of colour of their skin or as Romila Thapar[238] describes it as adherence to 'different cultural forms'. The governance structure was fairly simple and so was the ritual practice with exception of rituals connected with Soma sacrifice. The lowest unit in the structure of the Ŕgvedic polity was the family (Kula), following patriarchical norms with grāma (equivalent to a village) as the next higher tier, followed by a group of clans. The Vedic Jana was the highest social unit which represented the whole tribe. The role of protector devolved upon that individual in the tribe who was considered the most capable of protecting the interest of his tribe. Such an individual donned the mantle of chief of the tribe. The chieftain was possessed of military prowess that helped him in leading the tribe over its battles against the indigenous people or other tribes and offer protection to its own people The Ṛgvedic phase also represented a tribal polity driven by a bond of kinship. The political institutions associated with the tribal chief

---

235 The genesis of a Linguistic Area, Kuiper, F.B.J, Text of the Collitz lecture delivered at the summer meeting of the Linguistic Society of America at Ann Arbor, July 30, 1965.

236 Electronic Journal of Vedic Studies, Vol.2, !966

237 Arrian Alexander the Great, The Anabasis and the Indica, Trans. by Martin Hammond, Oxford World's Classics,2013, P.Xii

238 The Penguin History of Early India-From the Origins to AD 1300, Romila Thapar,2002, P.112

were rudimentary in character and limited in the scope of their functionality. These institutions were intended to subserve the ends of a pastoral community, always in strife with each other or against the pre-Aryan population. The existence of the Sabhā and the Samiti, and Ratnins with defined roles depict the political aspect of the tribal polity. The Ratnins performed not just political functions but also very mundane functions. The chariot makers and the carpenter existed during the Rig-Vedic period but we have more information on their role in the society during the post-Rig-Vedic period. There was an increase in the importance of the Rathakāras as is evident from their participation in rituals during the latter period.

A question has sometimes been raised whether an institution of spies had existed during the early Vedic period. In the RV, the word *spas*, denoting a spy, occurs 14 times. For example, the sun or the stars are taken to be the spy of the gods; however, it needs to be clarified that an organized spy system had not yet emerged during the Vedic period. The need for the same, perhaps, did not arise for administering small tribal communities. For the Vedic period, Scharfe[239] also maintains that "the rulers of small tribal communities had sufficient opportunities to run informal checks on their employees and subjects as also to gather information on their neighbors. Even covert operations hardly needed an organizational set up."

A close relationship is seen between the development of Vedic Canon and Vedic polity. On the face of it the Canon reflected a large amount of religious speculation and a certain amount of philosophical speculation. But going deeper, one finds that the Indian mind went far beyond theology and metaphysics. Evolvement of polity went side by side with the development of canon in successive stages. Turn the leaves of the Ṛgveda, Yajur-Veda, the Atharva-Veda and the Brāhmaṇas, and one will come across numerous references to Rāṣṭra, the institution of kingship, the duties of a king and his associates, the description of coronation ceremony, and the role of the priestly class in sacrificial ceremonies and in the affairs of the state. The word Rāṣṭra finds mention in various Vedic texts. RV IV, Hymn 42.1, Book VII, hymn 34.11, 84.2 and Book X hymn 109.3 are eulogy to different gods and portray them as a controller of the universe with ability to impact tribal polity. The occurrence of the term

---

239 The State in Indian Tradition, Hartmut Scharfe, E.J. Brill, Leiden, The Netherlands, 1989, P. 160

Raṣṭra in the Vedic texts does not take us closer to the modern definition of a state. However, the contours of a Rāṣṭra were discernible in the tribal polity of the early Vedic period. It was, however, only in the later Vedic period that the tribal polity evolved to the stage of an emerging state society.

Similarly, the institution of kingship finds mention in different contexts in RV,III, 43.5, RV IX, 92.6, RV,X , 78.1; 97.6; 124.8;; 166; 173 and 191as also in the hymns Atharva Veda, such as AV III, 4.5; AV V, 19, AV VI, 88 and AV VII 12 . There are numerous references about the coronation ceremony and sacrificial rituals in the Śatapatha Brahmaṇa.

The Ṛgvedic text abounds in invocation to different deities, particularly, Indra and Agni and the primary purpose of such invocations was to secure their benediction for success in battles or for welfare of the clan. Without such blessings the stability of kingship or welfare of the clan could never be ensured. The rituals became the medium of such invocations and the king played a dual role as a centerpiece of sacrificial cult and as a protector of the realm. Rituals, which were moderately elaborate during the Ṛgvedic period assumed a detailed and complex character in the later Vedic period. Thus rituals became a prime mover of all social activities and exercised a huge impact on the social order which was further buttressed by the king's association with such rituals. The Vedas show that theology and philosophical speculation engulfed the Vedic Aryans' approach towards life; the king saw in the performance of these rituals as a way to secure the benediction of god for his long rule. The complex character of the rituals required specialized knowledge for their performance. This brought the priests, who were drawn from the Brahmin class and were well-versed in the rituals, closer to the king. This led to the strengthening of the position of the Brahmin class in the society. The king and the priest were mostly together as Brahmakṣatra but they had claims of their own with the priest declaring Soma as their king. Throughout the Vedic period, a close nexus is seen between the king and the priestly class. This relationship further received a boost with complex reorientation of rituals connected with *dasapeya*[240] which required specialized handling by trained Brahmins and virtually excluded the people from participating in the ceremony which used to be the case earlier. This relationship also subsisted on material and metaphysical plane. As regards material plane, they were together in the performance of various rituals, connected with the king's consecration or seeking benediction of gods for adding strength to kingship or his kingdom. However, this relationship was raised to a higher metaphysical plane through performance of different Rājasūya rites that set in motion, as Heesterman[241] observes "cyclical regenerations of the universe" with the king manifesting himself as a "cosmic pillar", "impersonating the cosmic tide of regeneration and decay." This relationship, however, cannot be equated with the types of conflict observed in medieval Europe between the secular and religious powers. The priestly class was endowed with learning and enjoyed special privileges but that did not lead to creation of a separate ecclesiastical set-up on the lines of the Roman Catholic Church or the English Church.

As the Ṛgvedic period passed into post Ṛgvedic phase, the action scene shifted from the northwest region to the Gangetic plain. This change is reflected in all aspects of the polity. The pastoral tribes always on the move became inhabitants of fixed settlements and the merger of tribes during the post Ṛgvedic period led to the emergence of super tribes with larger territories under their control. The consolidation of tribes occurred under the umbrella of two major groups of tribes, namely, the Kuru-Pañcālas and the Kosala-Videha. The diversification of economic activities and enhanced role of the king in the management of larger kingdoms also resulted in the expansion of government machinery for performance of varied tasks. The Kuru-Pañcālas and the Kosla-Videha realm provide good examples in this respect. In the economic sphere, the economy was cattle centered and pastoralism provided the main source of income during the Ṛgvedic period. As the society and the polity evolved further, agricultural

---

240 Ibid, P.176. Dasapeya is a ceremony, connected with the Rājasūya in which the people participated and reflected close bond that existed between the king and the people. However, with the introduction of complexity in the rituals, which the trained priestly class only could claim to handle, the people's role in this ceremony was greatly diminished. This led to a distancing of the king from the people and further strengthening of the bond between the king and the priestly class.

241 The Ancient Indian Royal Consecration, J.C. Heesterman, Mouton & Co. 's-Gravenhage,The Hague, The Netherlands. 1957, P.223-224

pursuit became an important part of the economic activity of Vedic Aryans which also supplemented their cattle business. Thereafter, certain specialized occupations like carpentry, handicrafts, chariot-making etc. also followed suit.

In the social sphere, we find women somewhat better placed during the Ṛgvedic period as compared to deterioration which occurred in this respect during the later Vedic period. Social stratification into four classes in the society was beginning to germinate during the Ṛgvedic period in which the non-Aryans found themselves in the lowest rung of the social order performing a motley of inferior services. Varṇa, which occurs in the last book of the Ṛgveda (Puruṣa hymn) had a seamless journey thereafter, and found a firm footing in the Yajur-Veda. With the Brahmans and the Kṣatriyas having cornered the top two slots in the societal framework, it was left to the Vaiṣyas and the Śūdras to occupy the bottom tier in that order. Birth became a crucial factor in determining a man's station in life and the vocation he was obliged to pursue. The institution of Varṇa was thus morphed into caste system. This had a great impact on Hindu social and religious speculation and persists in some forms till this date, despite efforts made to remove this scourge.

It is pertinent to draw attention here to a series of developments that occurred in political, social and economic spheres towards the end of the late Vedic period. These developments cumulatively are characterized as the Second Urbanization. Patrick Olivelle, as noted earlier, has referred to 'the rise of cities along the Ganges Valley between the sixth and fourth centuries BCE' as an important feature of the Second Urbanization. There was a change in the political scenario and large kingdoms with larger territories replaced smaller tribal outfits. Their capital cities emerged as important urban centres. Excavations carried out in Kausambi, Vaishali, Rajagriha and other places provide evidence of urbanism way back during the mid-first millennium BC.

Lastly, it also needs to be pointed out that even though ritualism predominates the Vedas and the divine hand is conspicuous in the Vedic Aryans' thought process, the Vedic religion retained an ethical orientation that required the state to emphasize morality and the importance of leading a virtuous life. This mindset was reflected in the works of ancient sages which emphasized the over-riding primacy of *ṛta* (cosmic law which only later morphed into Dharma) in the conduct of political activities and regulation of social order. The kingship was not immune to the edicts of Dharma or law. The pre-eminent role of religion and ethics in social speculation and political activities also influenced the development of social and political institutions in subsequent periods and put them on a unique trajectory so different from their western counterpart. Such a legacy had an ennobling influence on the Indian mind and contributed to the development of a peculiarly Indian ethos but at the same time bore seeds of certain distortions which became evident in Indian society at a later stage.

Appendix I

a) Vedic Aryans- Migrants or Indigenous

The question of identity of the Vedic Aryans is extremely important in the context of the study of the various facets of the Vedic civilization ushered in by the Aryans in the Indian subcontinent. The questions that need to be discussed at the outset are who were the Vedic Aryans- were they an indigenous people or migrants and what was the nature of relationship between the Vedic Aryans and the Harappan culture. The scholars view the two issues in different perspectives and a consensus on these issues still belies us.

A large section of the scholars are of the view that the Indo-Aryans were not an indigenous people but came from outside. They have identified the Central Asian region from where they came in successive batches. Such migrations occurred through Baluchistan on the west and Afghanistan on the north-west. Others like Michael Witzel consider Bactria as the staging area from where the migrants moved into the Sapta-Sindhu region and started the process of acculturation of non-Aryans inhabitants. Another noted scholar Asko Parpola[242] is of the view that the first wave of Aryans in Central Asia, came from the Volga steppes towards the end of the third millennium B.C. but later they split into two groups, one moving westward to northern Syria and the second moving eastward to Swat founding there the 'Proto-Rig-Vedic culture'. This provides another evidence of the likely migration of the Aryans from the Central Asian region to the north-west region of the Indian subcontinent. The possibility of migration of Vedic Aryans from Central Asian region also finds some corroboration at the linguistic level. An intimate relationship is seen between languages spoken in Central Asia (BMAC)[243] and that of the Punjab region. Lubotsky[244], examining the structure of the Indo-Iranian

---

242 The Dasas and the Coming of the Aryans in Inside the Texts Beyond the Texts: Edited by Michael Witzel, Harvard Oriental Series, Opera Minora Vol.2, Cambridge, 1997.

243 Bactria- Margiana Archaeological Complex

244 A. Lubotsky ,The Indo-Iranian Substratum, Early Contacts between Uralic and Indo-European linguistic and Archaeological Considerations; Paper presented at University of Helsinki, 8-10,January, 1999.

substratum, has observed that "the phonological and morphological features of Indo-Iranian loan words are strikingly similar to those which are characteristic of Sanskrit loan words" and therefore it follows that the substratum of Indo-Iranian and Indo-Aryans 'represent the same language'. Such loan words occurring in the Rig-Veda is also a pointer to possible immigration of the Aryans from the Central Asian region. Witzel[245] has also drawn attention towards a large body of loan words in the oldest Indian and Iranian texts to substantiate the use of the pre-Indo-Iranian languages by people inhabiting the region of BMAC (Bactria-Margiana Archaeological Complex).

It is believed that the migration was propelled by the attractiveness of the Sapta-Sindhu[246] region for settlement purpose in contrast to the inhospitable terrain of the adjacent regions in Asia which exerted pressure on the population to migrate. There is also a broad consensus among the scholars that the composition of the Rig-Vedic hymns occurred after the arrival of Indo-Aryans in the north-west region. The composition of the ten books of the Rig-Veda is linked to various priestly clans and occurred in stages. This is evident from the names of different Rig-Vedic tribes and their linkages with different priestly clans which occur in the books of the Rig-Veda

There is another school of thought that totally discounts the 'invasion theory' and holds that the Aryans were an indigenous people. B.B. Lal[247],

---

[245] Witzel. M, Linguistic Evidence for Cultural Exchange in Prehistoric Western Central Asia. Philadelphia: Sino-Platonic Papers 129, Dec. 2003 http://www.sino-platonic.org/complete/spp129_prehistoric_central_asia_
linguistics.pdf (accessed on 20 March, 2013, In this paper, Witzel has referred to a large number of loan words pertaining to agriculture, flora and fauna and rituals in the oldest Indian and Iranian texts which were part of the languages spoken in the areas covered by the Bactria-Margiana Archaeological Complex (BMAC). These pre-Indo-Iranian languages later found their way into Iran and Northern India. Also refer Witzel' Early Sources for South Asian Substrate Languages, Mother Tongue Special Issue, Oct. 1999.

[246] The Sapta-Sindhu region is qualified by seven rivers, namely, Kubhā (Kabul), Sindhu (the Indus), Vitastā (Jhelum), Asiknī (Chenab), Paruṣṇī (Ravi), Vipāśā (Beas) and Śutudrī (Sutlej)., Kubha (Kabul river) is in Eastern Afghanistan and the Sapta-Sindhu cover the North and North-Western regions of India up to the Eastern part of Afghanistan.

[247] The Sarasvati flows on –The Continuity of Indian Culture, B.B. Lal, Aryan Books International, New Delhi,2002, pp.70-71.

an archaeologist, is a proponent of this view. He has adduced evidence of the Nadī-stuti hymns[248] of the Rig-Veda to show that the Rig-Vedic river Sarasvatī flowed between Yamuna and Sutlej rivers and on both sides of the banks of Sarasvatī flourished a great civilization in the third millennium BCE which he calls the Indus-Sarasvatī civilization. He maintains that its indigenous character is further attested by excavations at some archaeological sites, namely, Kalibangan, Banawali, Bhirrana etc. on the Indian side which lend credence to his theory that the "authors of the Vedas were indigenous and not 'invaders' or 'immigrant' as held by some scholars"[249].

Such a view also finds support from some Western scholars, such as, J.Muir[250] who discounts the possibility of the Vedic tribes being of foreign origin since none of the Sanskrit books including the most ancient one make any distinct reference to this effect. Edwin Bryant[251] has also questioned the basis of "evidence of a linguistic substratum in Indo-Aryan" as a determining element for the origin of Indo-Aryan.

While there is a broad consensus on the locales where the Vedic texts were composed, there is no meeting point between the views held by the protagonists of migration theory and the nationalist discourse including that of some Western scholars on the question of the origin of Indo-Aryan tribes.

b) Vedic Aryans and the Harappan Culture

The second issue relating to nexus, if any, between the Vedic Aryans and the Harappan culture, is also hotly debated. There are two strands of views on the subject, one view discounts the existence of any connection

---

248 The Sarasvati River is one of the major rivers which finds mention in the Rig-Veda. The Nadistuti hymn (an ode to rivers) in the Rigveda (10.75) mentions that the river Sarasvati flowed between the river Yamuna in the east and the river Sutlej in the west.

249 Vedic River Sarasvati and Hindu Civilization, Ed. S. Kalyanaraman, pp.106-07, Aryan Books International, New Delhi, 2008.

250 Original Sanskrit Texts on the Origin and History of the People of India, their Religion and Institutions, Vol. II: J.Muir, London Trubner & Co., 60, Paternoster Row, 1868.

251 Aryan and Non-Aryan in South Asia, Ed. J. Bronkhorst and M.M Despande, Manohar, 2012,P.80.

between the two and the other view supports the existence of such a relationship. Scholars who negate the possibility of any such relationship, base their argument on the ground of lack of evidence for the use of horses by the Harappan people in the normal course or horse sacrifice on special occasions like the Aśvamedha while this animal is a key feature of the Rig-Vedic period. Further, the urban nature of the Harappan civilization stands in contrast to horse centered, pastoral Vedic society. They hold that the discovery of a tooth of horse at Lothal is not evidence enough to bring the Harappan culture closer to the Vedic Aryans. R.S. Sharma[252], an eminent historian, also discounts the possibility of any linkage between the Vedic Aryans and the Harappan culture. His reasoning is based on the grounds that features of urban culture associated with the Harappan civilization , such as, a well-planned city and evidence of crafts, commerce and store houses – are absent in the Rig-Veda and even "fire altars, a typical Aryan trait, have not been found in Harappa or Mohenjo-daro". Further, the mature Harappan phase does not reflect the practice of cremation followed by theVedic Aryans nor does it show any evidence of use of iron. The Harappan people used bronze and not iron but the Vedic Aryans were familiar with use of iron during battle or hunting and even for clearance of marsh lands for agriculture purposes as the later Vedic texts would seem to suggest.

In the list of scholars who see a nexus between the Indo-Aryans and the Harappan culture, the prominent ones include Walter Fairservis, Michel Danino, F.B.J. Kuiper and B.D. Sharma.

Fairservis[253], adduces to available evidences to show that the 'Harappan world was hardly one in isolation from cultural shifts and changes in regions traditionally assigned to Aryan occupancy.' Further, he describes[254] "the Harappan cultures as an amalgam of pastoral, indigenous and unique traits" that brings it closer to the pastoral society of the Ṛgvedic Aryans. Michel Danino, in his book[255] has drawn attention to the recent excavations of the Harappa sites on the Indian side of the

---

252 Looking for the Aryans, R.S. Sharma, Orient Longman Limited, Hyderabad, 1995

253 The Harappan Civilization and the Rgveda: Walter. Fairservis, in Inside the Texts-Beyond the Texts, Ed.by Michael Witzel, Harvard Oriental Series, Opera Minora Vol.II. Cambridge, 1997,P.61

254 Ibid, P.64

255 The Lost River- On the Trail of the Sarasvati, Michel Danino, Penguin Books, New Delhi, 2010, P.91

Indo-Pakistan border, particularly the India's states of the Punjab, Haryana, Gujarat and northern Rajasthan and links them with the basin of Ghaggar-Hakra[256]. He draws on the observations of Aurel Stein, a reputed Archaeologist, who identified the Vedic Sarasvatī river with the present Sarsuti and Ghaggar. Stein also established the linkage between the sites in the Hakra valley and the Harappan culture.

The recent archaeological evidence, it is claimed, provides some meeting ground between the Vedic tribes and the Harappan culture. Instances of changes in burial practices and in the motifs on the pottery in the late Harappan culture and the absence of writing bring the Harappan people closer to the Vedic culture. The linguistic evidence available from the Vedic texts, shows increased instances of non-Aryan influence on the later Vedic texts following the movement of the Vedic Aryans from the Sapta-Sindhu region to eastwards in the Madhyadesa region (Central region of India). It is also held that interaction between the Aryans and the original settlers, speaking a different language, has influenced the language which the Aryans spoke. F.B. J. Kuiper[257] has carried out a detailed analysis of words of foreign origin in the Ṛgvedic lexemes and concluded that they constitute approximately 4% in the Ṛgvedic lexemes. This figure, he maintains represents a much slower process of Aryanization as compared to western societies where the process of acculturation is much faster. This is primarily because the local population did not have to adjust to the new environment ushered in by the Aryans as they were already 'firmly rooted in their dwelling places and probably were in the majority'. B.D Sharma, another scholar, contests some of the points mentioned by R.S. Sharma, and suggests the existence of linkage between the Harappan culture and the Vedic civilization. He[258] has cited the evidence of fire altars found in Harappa by B.B. Lal, an archaeologist "in his excavations at the third millennium site of

---

[256] Ghaggar today represents the Vedic river Sarasvati and is called Hakra in Bahawalpur which is situated in Pakistan. The Vedic river Sarasvati originated from the confluence of the modern Yamuna and Sutlej near Patiala (a town in the Indian state of the Panjab). It is believed to have flowed through a 6 t 8 km wide channel before drying up and is now known as Ghaggar.(Ref. Vedic River Sarasvati and Hindu Civilization) P.4

[257] Aryans in the Rgveda, F.B.J. Kuiper, Rodopi B.V., Amsterdam-Atlanta, GA 1991, Printed in The Netherlands

[258] B.D. Sharma in Vedic River Sarasvati and Hindu Civilization, Ed. S. Kalyana raman, P.279, , Asian Books International, New Delhi, 2008.

Kalibangan." He has also referred to Lal's finds of terracotta images of the horse found in Mohenjo-daro and Naushero.

Scholars have also attempted to variously interpret the term "Pur" which occurs in the Vedic texts and stands for a 'Fort' to determine the extent of its relevance in establishing relationship, if any, between the Vedic Aryans and the Harappan culture. R.S. Sharma has given a figurative interpretation to the term "Pur" and maintains that the forts occurring in the Rig-Veda do not refer to real forts and mention of this term in the RV (Book X 87.22) is only indicative of the Aryans prayer to Agni "to protect them as a fort would." Sir Mortimer Wheeler identifies the 'Pur' with 'walled cities' of the Indus Valley civilization and attributes their conquest by immigrating Aryans as a possible reason for the downfall of the Indus Valley Civilization. Wilhelm Rau, another noted authority, however, discounts Sir Mortimer's hypothesis and observes that there is no evidence forthcoming from the Vedic texts to identify Vedic 'Purs' with the cities of the Indus civilization. He has focused on the lay-out of the 'Purs' which does not provide any evidence of any typical features of the cities of the Indus Valley civilization, such as, streets, large baths and granaries. According to him, the 'Purs' consisted of 'predominantly circular or oval concentric mud walls fortified with wooden palisades' and were raised quickly in time of war. Rainer Stuhrmann in his article on Rigvedisch pur[259] has, however, questioned Rau's line of investigation on the ground that the poets reflected the imageries of immediate surroundings in their verses as they were not expected to be "chroniclers, authors of tracts on siege methods, nor critics of architecture". He has therefore concluded that the 'Purs' were inhabited by settled artisans, agriculturists and pastoralists who did not adhere to Aryan cult. The 'Purs' served as an extensive front which the Indo-Aryans encountered while trying to take over them by laying siege or through deceit or direct assault. It is said that the Puru[260] and the Bharata Divodāsa[261] took over hundred or so 'Purs' of Sambara[262] located in the mountains west of the Indus.

---

[259] Electronic Journal of Vedic Studies (EJVS) 2008, Vol. 15, Issue 1, p. 1 sqq (c) ISSN 1084-7561 Rainer Stuhrmann

[260] The Pūru represents a group of tribes who along with the Bharatas are prominent in the Ṛgveda and appeared on the scene succeeding earlier groups of migrants such as the Turvaśa and the Yadu. As per the Vedic Index of Names and Subjects, the Pūrus were located in the area along the Sarasvatī[260] and their great kings were Purukutsa and Trasadasyu The Purus were connected with Books V and VI of The Rig-Veda

The foregoing discussions only provide a lead on migration theories and the relationship between the Harappan culture and the Vedic Aryans. A big gap exists between the nationalist discourse and that of some Western scholars and the views of other prominent scholars on the subject. Hence, the issue is still far from any resolution. The decipherment of the Harappan script, which is in the process for the last so many years, may throw some conclusive evidence at a later stage in this regard.

---

261 An important Rig-Vedic tribe with original settlement somewhere in the north-west; around the Indus and then between Sarasvatī and Dṛsadvati; later moved to Ganga-Yamuna belt Daushani was a prominent king of Bharata tribes during the Rig-Vedic period and associated with Books III an VII of the Rig-Veda. Divodasa was, perhaps, the last prominent king of Bharata tribe.

262 According to Macdonell and Keith in Vedic Index Vol.II, the name Sambara finds mention in various books of Rgveda (Bk.i. 51,6; 54,4; 59,6; I0I,2; I03,8; Bk.ii. I2,II; Bk.iv.26,3; 30,I4;Bk.vi.I8,8;26,5; Bk.vii.I8,20; 99,5. He is reckoned as an enemy of Indra.He is supposed to have had a number of forts, variously mentioned in the Rgveda with Divodasa as his great enemy who won victories over him with Indra's aid. Sambara was believed to be an aboriginal tribe, living in the mountains. Divodasa's son Sudas became the famous King of the Bharata who is credited with victory in the "Ten Kings' Battle" on the bank of the river Ravi. Purukutsa, son of Kutsa and probably a contemporary of Sudas, is supposed to have destroyed the seven "old" purs east of the Indus.Thus while Kutsa and Divodasa confronted the purs in the mountain regions, Purukutsa did so in the plains east of the Indus. According to Stuhrmann,"the accounts of conquest of purs contain a concrete nucleus of historical incidents that were immediately embellished poetically". Stuhrmann goes on to claim that though the Ṛgveda does not provide an actual description of the Indus cities but the imagery excerpted from the Rigvedic verses does gel with the cities of the Indus Valley civilization.

Appendix II

A Brief Outline of Vedic Literature

The Vedas are recognized as the repository of the sacred knowledge of ancient India and reckoned as a precious part of its heritage. This sacred knowledge is contained in the hymns of the four Vedic Saṃhitās – the Ṛgveda, the Yajur-Veda, the Sāma-Veda, and the Atharva-Veda – as well as allied Vedic literature. Of these, the Ṛgveda Saṃhitā, is regarded as the most ancient and constitutes the foundation of the Vedic literature. There are divergent views regarding composition of Vedic texts. It is , however, generally held that the composition of most of the Ṛgvedic text seems to have occurred during the time span of 1500 BCE and 1000 BCE and the post Ṛgvedic texts about 1000 BCE or later and the earlier Sūtras between 500 BCE and 200 BCE.

As stated earlier, each of the Vedas has two parts, namely, the Saṃhitās and the Brāhmaṇas. The mantras in the Saṃhitās are constructed in metrical or prose forms and are used for ritual purposes. The Bra¯hmaṇa style texts deal with the application of rituals and the manner in which the various rites of sacrifice are to be performed. The Āraṇyakas, after the Brāhmaṇas, constitute an important portion of the Vedas. These consist of discussions on the Śrauta rituals in the wilderness (as one text says from there you cannot see the roof of any settlement). A.B. Keith, in his book the Aitareya Āraṇyaka (pp.15-16), maintains that the forest (Āraṇya) was used to give secret explanations of some rituals. Only the Ṛgveda and the Sāma-Veda have independent Āraṇyakas, namely, the Aitareya and Kauṣītakī belonging to the Ṛgveda and Jaiminīya Āraṇyaka belonging to the Sāma-Veda. Thus, apart from the four Veda Saṃhita¯s, the Brāhmaṇas, Āraṇyakas and Upaniṣads also come within the definition of the Vedic literature. The Sūtras, whose authorship is traditionally ascribed to human beings, are not in the same class and cannot claim to be a part of the revealed literature. However, they are also closely connected with the Vedas and hence, merit inclusion in the broad definition of the Vedic literature.

1) The Ṛgveda (RV)

The Ṛgvedic Saṃhitā is a collection of 1,028 hymns within its ten books (or Mandalas). The hymns in each of the Mandalas are called Suktas which have individual stanzas. These hymns were composed and handed down orally in different spells separated by hundreds of years. Of these hymns in ten Books, the oldest are contained in Books II-VII; each assigned by tradition mostly to a single clan, in which they were long preserved as a family inheritance. Thus, the composition of the hymns in the Book II is ascribed to Gṛtsamāda, son of Sunahotra of the family of Āṅgiras; Book III toViśvāmitra family; Book IV to the family of Vāmadeva; Book V to the family of Atri; and Books VI and VII to the families of Bhāradvāja and Vasiṣtha, respectively. Book VIII contains hymns (1-66) of the Kaṇva family and the remaining hymns (67-103) are supposed to have been composed by members of Āṅgirasa clan. Book IX is a collection of all the hymns addressed to the Soma which perhaps, originally figured in other books. The Soma enjoys the status of a divinity in the Vedas. The hymns of Book I are supposed to be the work of various poets and Book X is ascribed to various authors such as Atri, Bhāradvāja, Vasiṣtha. The hymns in each of these books, arranged in groups, follow a sequential order as to the gods addressed, such as, first the hymns to Agni, then those to Indra, etc. Inside the groups, the position of the hymns is determined by the number of verses in diminishing order.

Most of the hymns are religious lyric in praise of gods inter-alia, invoking the latter's benediction and a prayer to accept the offerings. A number of hymns are also related to the subjects which cannot be described as purely sacerdotal in character. The blessings sought in these hymns for the most part are of material nature, such as, wealth, food, cattle, protection against enemies, etc. The objective of these prayers seemed to be to secure benefits of a worldly character. A. B. Keith[263] also maintains that a number of hymns deal with matters other than sacerdotal. He has cited hymns in RV Books I.191, X.58, 145, 159,163, 166, 183 in this context. The Rig-Vedic hymns were specially recited by a class of priests called Hotṛis.

Numerous gods, each personifying nature's power, figure in the Ṛgveda. There is a view that the Vedic Indians' perception of the nature manifested

---

[263] The Religion and Philosophy of the Veda and Upanishads, Part I, A.B. Keith, Motilal Banarsi Dass, Delhi, Reprint-2007, P.14

itself in varied forms, such as, rain, thunder, fire, water and wind. These natural phenomena which influenced their daily lives acquired an aura of deities. Among these deities, Indra stands above all the rest and a majority of hymns sing his praise. He is referred to as the God of Thunder and as a slayer of demons. One scholar (Roth) describes him as "protector of human beings and the dispenser of the riches."[264] The other important gods are Agni, Varuṇa, and Uṣas. Next to Indra stands Agni, the God of fire, in the hierarchy and frequently finds mention in the Ṛgveda. The importance of Agni emanates from its central role in all the rites connected with sacrifice. According to Maurer,[265] "Indra is the mighty warrior god, vanquisher of demons . . . Agni, on the other hand, is the arch priest, intermediary between men and gods, the great and omniscient sage, and as the focal point of all sacrifices and provider of warmth and light in the home, closest kinsman to man among the gods." The importance of Indra and Agni in the Ṛgvedic hymns can be gauged from the fact that of one hundred and ninety one hymns contained in the Book I of the Ṛgveda, forty-seven hymns are addressed to Indra and forty-eight to Agni alone or in combination with others. Agni and Indra figure prominently in the hymns contained in RV Books II, III, IV, V, and VI. The hymns in RV Books VII, VIII and X are addressed to various gods. The hymns in RV Book IX are devoted to Soma Pavamana. Varuṇa, another important Ṛgvedic god is portrayed in the hymns as infinitely wise, omnipresent and upholder of truth and ethical values. He also adorns frequently the title of Raja or Samrat and in combination with Mitra is also called the lord of light, one who averts evil and protects cattle. Uṣas is also an important deity who personifies the Dawn and is regarded as a dispeller of darkness and hostility. Other deities mentioned in the Ṛgveda include the Maruts representing storm, thunder and lightning, the Aśvins, the saviour and divine physicians, bringing succor to the distressed; Surya and Savitṛ, solar deities; and Pusan, deity of cattle. Viṣṇu and Rudra (Shiva) do not figure as important deities. They, however, acquired great importance, later, in the Hindu pantheon.

---

[264] This finds mention in the article "Indra in the Rgveda" by E.D. Perry , presented to the American Oriental Society on Oct. 28th, 1880

[265] Pinnacls of India's Past- Selections from the Rgveda, Vol. II, Translated and annotated by Walter H. Maurer, John Benjamings Publishing Company, Philadelphia, 1986.

As commented by scholars, we do observe a marked difference in the quality and style of hymns contained in various books of the Ṛgveda. This, perhaps, can be explained by the gaps in the time-line of the composition of its various books. Books II to VII of RV form its earliest portion while Books I and X are believed to have been later additions. The Ṛgvedic hymns are woven around sacrificial rituals and fire-cult along with an exposition of numerous deities, their respective roles and battles with the demons. The significance, however, of these hymns lies in their speculative nature. These hymns also provide the earliest clue to the development of religious conceptions and understanding of Indian mind. According to Bloomfield,[266] "the paramount importance of the Ṛgveda is after all not as literature, but as a philosophy. Its mythology represents a clearer, even if not always chronologically earlier stage of thought and religious development than is to be found in any parallel literature."

It also needs to be pointed out that some of the hymns which go by the nomenclature "Khilas" do not form a part of the canonical text and were presumably added subsequent to the completion of the Saṃhitā. Moriz Winternitz[267] maintains that eleven Valakhilya hymns found roughly at the middle of Book VIII, but not included in this Book, probably fall in this category. According to Max Muller,[268] some of the Khilas are of considerable antiquity and find mention in the introduction of Śaunaka's (Kātyāyana's predecessor) Anuvaka-Anukramaṇī. He further adds that these Khila hymns were also quoted in the Nirukta.

The Ṛgveda has two important Brāhmaṇas, namely, the Aitareya Brāhmaṇa and the Kauṣītakī Brāhmaṇa. The features of these Brāhmaṇas would be discussed later.

---

266 Religion of the Veda, Bloomfield, Maurice, G P. Putnam's Sons, The Knicker Bocker Press,New York,1908,P.29

267 History of Indian Literature, Vol. I, Moriz Winternitz, Munshiram Manoharlal Publishers Pvt. Ltd., New Delhi , 3rd edition, 1991, P.60

268 Appendix titled "The Khilas of The Rgveda in The Rgveda Samhita, Vol. IV, 2nd edition, ed. F.Max Muller, London, 1892.

2) The Yajur-Veda (YV)

The Ṛgvedic Saṃhitā represents the poetic and ritual aspects of Indian mind reflected in the worship of "personified power of nature,"[269]and in addition deities sustaining the society, such as the Adityas; Varuṇa, Mitra and Aryaman, and Bhaga. The Yajurvedic Saṃhitā is however a collection of prayers, recited by priests during the sacrificial rituals. Composed in prose, the Yajus or formulae are brief and concise and tells us the correct method for performing sacrifices that included preparing "the sacrificial ground, to dress the altar, slay the victims, and pour out the libations". Like the Sāma-Veda, the Yajur-Veda, too, borrows many of its verses from the Ṛgveda. The scene of activities during the period of the Ṛgveda, we have seen, was the Sapta-Sindhu region. This centre, however, shifted during the Yajur-Vedic period, to the land of the Kuru-Pañcālas. The Yajur-Veda has two main divisions, namely, the White Yajur-Veda and the Black Yajur-Veda. The White Yajur-Veda is mainly concerned with sacrificial formulae but does not explain their application in the rituals. It has only one Saṃhitā, namely, Vajasaneyi Saṃhitā with Śatapatha Brāhmaṇa, both representing Kāṇva recension and Mādhyandina recension respectively. The Vājasaneyi Saṃhitā consists of 40 chapters and about 2000 verses. It contains hymns as well as sacrificial formulas in prose. rites The Black Yajur-Veda, on the other hand, provides both the mantras and prose explanation of sacrificial ritual and its Brāhmaṇa texts are integrated in its four Saṃhitās, namely, i) Kaṭhaka Saṃhitā; ii) Maitrāyaṇī Saṃhitā[270]; iii) Kapiṣṭhala-Kaṭha Saṃhitā; and iv) Taittirīya Saṃhitā. These Saṃhitās go by the names of the respective schools, such as Kapiṣṭhala School or Maitrāyaṇī School. It may be seen that Yajus represents a codification of rituals in every detail, the practice of which in rigorous form was assigned to priests who performed specific functions.

---

[269] A Vedic Reader for Students: A.A. Macdonell, Xii, Oxford at the Clarendon Press, 1917

[270] The MS consists of both the mantra and Brahmana portions. The mantra and Brahmana portions pertaining to a ritual are separated but placed in separate prapathakas. In this Saṃhitā, rituals, such as formulas to be employed by Adhvaryu in Darśapaurṇamāsa and formulae relating to preparation of sacrificial rituals have been described. The brāhmaṇa style of prose texts of Maitrāyaṇī Saṃhitā (MS) and Kaṭha Saṃhitā (KS) depict the political and social condition of the period similar to that obtained during the earlier Mantra period.

The recitation of the Yajus formulas (rituals) was assigned to a special class of priest, called Adhvaryus and his assistants.

3) The Sāma-Veda (SV)

The Sāma-Vedic Saṃhitā, are compositions consisting of 1,800 separate verses which are sung at Soma sacrifice by a special priest-class. (Soma sacrifice involves offering of the sap of the Soma plant mixed with milk or barley). These verses are arranged subject-wise unlike in the Ṛgveda where the hymns are arranged according to their authors. Different deities, the Soma, Agni and Indra are invoked in the Sāma verses and their benediction sought for the worshippers. The responsibility of singing the Sāma-Veda verses also devolved on a special class of priest, called *Udgāṭr*. The important Brāhmaṇas attached to Sāma-Veda are: Pañcaviṃśa Brāhmaṇa and Jaiminīya Brāhmaṇa. According to Maurice Phillips,[271] the texts of the Sāma-Veda are "taken almost entirely from the Rig, to be chanted at particular parts of the sacrifice." He refers to Max Muller's[272] observation that "these two Vedas, the Yajur-Veda and the Sāma-Veda, were, in truth, what they are called in the Kauṣītakī Brāhmaṇa, the attendants of the Rgveda." The Chāndogya Upaniṣad belongs to the Sāma-Veda.

4) The Atharva-Veda (AV)

The Atharva-Vedic Saṃhitā in its common Śaunaka version consists of 730 hymns with 6,000 stanzas. Griffith[273] holds that "the Atharva-Veda Sanhita or Collection is divided into twenty Kandas, Books or Sections..." The contents of Books I-XIII are heterogenous in character dealing with all kinds of subjects such as "prayers, formulas and charms for protection against evil spirits..." while the contents in Book XIV- XVIII are systematically arranged on subjects like "marriage ceremony," "the glorification of the Vratya," "funeral rites," etc. Griffith calls it "the Veda of

---

[271] Teaching of the Vedas: Maurice Phillips, Longmans, Green and Co. Newyork,1895

[272] History of Ancient Sanskrit Literature: F. Max Muller, P.457

[273] Translation of the Atharva-Veda: R.T.H. Griffith, Messrs. E.J. Lazarus & Co. , Benares

Prayers, Charms and Spells."[274] Apart from these subjects, the Atharva-Veda also contains a large number of speculative hymns (VIII to XII) and in addition hymns about kings, charms for success in battles, pertaining to marriage and death and references to Brahmins and Kṣatriyas. Bloomfield [275] maintains that the Atharva-Veda like the Ṛgveda represents the 'beginnings of speculative theosophic literature' but with focus on house ceremonies unlike the focus on Soma sacrifices in the preceding three Vedas. He further adds that while the vast armoury of charms, blessings, and curses contained in the Atharva-Veda may be to some extent the result of "the more intimate blending of the Vedic people with the barbarous aborigines of India," he also acknowledges that the "Atharvanic charms are often pervaded by a more genuine Aryan spirit..."

As regards the chronology of the Atharva -Vedic Saṃhitā, we have to distinguish between the time of its composition which is early post Rigvedic and the final redaction which is late 500 BCE. Bloomfield, Griffith, Whitney, Weber and Max M ller, all maintain that its redaction occurred after the Rig, Yajur and the Sāma-Vedas. By the time the redaction of the Atharva-Veda took place, the Varṇa system representing the four levels with the Brahmin at the top of the hierarchy had assumed a proper shape and this is evident from numerous references on this account in the hymns of the Atharva-Veda. Further the geographical data obtainable from this Veda mentions two rivers, Yamuna and Varanavati and the regions of Aṅgas and Magadhas which show how the scene of activity had shifted from the North-West region to further East and south-east. The Atharva-Veda also depicts a total transformation in the daily life of the Vedic Aryans, as compared to the Ṛgvedic Aryans, in matters connected with their various practices and beliefs. The Ṛgvedic deities that occupy a prominent place in this Veda include Indra, Varuṇa, Savitṛ, the Soma, Uṣas, Pusans, Rudra and Maruts. But they do not retain the same character as persona of nature but are invoked to settle scores with the demons. The Gopatha Brāhmaṇa is attached to the Atharva-Veda.

The features of the four Vedas along with data are graphically represented in the table below:

---

[274] Ibid, Preface, pp. I, ii. Abridged

[275] The Atharva Veda: M. Bloomfield, Strassburg Verlag Von Karl J. Trubner, 1899, P.2

Table VIII: The Vedas

Ṛgveda					
Book #	**# of Hymns in the Book**	**# of Hymns to Indra**	**# of Hymns to Agni**	**OtherProminent Ṛgvedic gods and # of hymns (shown in bracket)**	**Important Brāhmaṇas**
Book 1 (Group of Poets)	191	47	48	Agni	Aitareya and Kauṣītakī
Book 2 Gṛtsamāda Clan)	43	12	10	Brahmaṇaspati(4) The Adityas (3)	
Book 3 (Viśvāmitra Clan)	62	24	29	Viśvedeva (4)	
Book 4 (Vāmadeva Clan)	58	17	15	Ṛbhus (5)	
Book 5 (Atri Clan)	87	12	28	Viśvedeva (11) Mitra-Varuṇa(11)	
Book 6 (Bhāradvāja Clan)	75	32	16	Viśvedeva (4)	
Book 7 (Vasiṣtha Clan)	104	16	17	Viśvedeva (22)	
Book 8 + Valakhilya (Kaṇva-Āṅgirasa clan)	103	50	14	Vayu	
Book 9	114			Hymns addressed to Soma	
Book 10 (Various poets)	191	43	29	Viṣṇu, Pusan	
Total	1028	254	206		

Source: Griffiths Trans. Of Rgveda
K.F. Geldner, Der Rigveda,Harvard, 1951, RV Trans.

Yajur-Veda					
Book #	**# of Hymns in the Book**	**# of Hymns to Indra**	**# of Hymns to Agni**	**Prominent Rig-Vedic gods**	**Important Brāhmaṇas**
				This Veda has two major Collections, namely, White and Black Yajur-Veda. White Y.V contains prayers and sacrificial formulae. Black Y. V. contains both the mantras as well as explanation of the various aspects of rituals and/or Sacrificial rites.	In Krishna Y.V., Brāhmaṇas are integrated in the Saṃhitās, e.g., Maitrāyaṇī Kaṭha, Kapiṣthala Kaṭha, Taittirīya Brāhmaṇa
Book 9					

Sāma -Veda					
Book #	**# of Verses in the Book**	**# of Verses to Indra**	**# of verses to Agni**	**Prominent gods**	**Jaiminīya and Pañcaviṃśa**
	1754(Part I+Part II)	189+ Indra with others-153	114		
Part I					
Book 1				Indra	
Book 2				Agni	
Book 3				Mitra-Varuṇa	
Book 4				Soma Pavamana	
Book 5				Aśvins	
Book 6				Aditya; Surya; Savitṛ	
Part II					
Book 1				Pusan	

Book 2	Viśvedevas
Book 3	Maruts
Book 4	Viṣṇu
Book 5	Dawn
Book 6	
Book 7	
Book 8	
Book 9	

Atharva- Veda		
Book #	# of Hymns	Subject
Books 1-7	433	Magical and healing stanzas
8-12	45	Speculative hymns
Book 13	4	glorification of Sun and Royal connection
Book 14	2	On Marriage ceremonies
Book 15	18	Vratya's glorification
Book 16	9	Charms to secure various blessings
Book 17	1	Prayer to Indra for general protection
Book 18	4	Funeral hymns
Book 19	72	Sacrifical formulae, charms, prayers
Book 20	143	Praise of Indra and other deities.
Total	731	

The above table clearly brings out the relative importance of major deities in the four Vedas. The predominance of Indra and Agni is self-evident during the Rig-Vedic period and they also frequently appear in the chants of the Sāma-Veda. While Indra and Agni figure in 254 and 204 hymns of the Ṛgveda respectively; in the Sāma-Veda, too, Agni is invoked in 114 verses and 189 verses are devoted to Indra alone and in approximately 153 verses , Indra is joined by others. The reason for this is not hard to explain. The importance accorded to Agni in the Ṛgveda and the Sāma-Veda, if we go by statistical consideration is primarily due to its central role in the Soma sacrifice which is writ large in the Vedic texts. Likewise Indra's position of primacy is due to his martial prowess reflected in slaying of Vṛtra, and setting the water free as also coming to the aid of gods in their fight against enemies. The Vedic ganas saw in Indra as their saviour in their battle against the aborigines and other Aryan tribes and that was reason enough to put him on a high pedestal. The Rig-Vedic hymns are replete with the heroic acts of Indra and his image as a destroyer of enemies. He is invariably invoked in these hymns as well as in the chants of the Sāma-Veda to bestow his blessings on the seeker. Viṣṇu and Rudra, two important gods of the Hindu pantheon do not figure prominently in the Rgveda and the reason for this, according to Keith[276] is their disconnect with the Soma sacrifice, a central feature of the Ṛgveda. These two deities, however, became very prominent later in the Brāhmaṇas and a number of myths surrounding Viṣṇu further enhanced his stature in the estimation of the priests and the people.

5) The Brāhmaṇas

After the Vedic Saṃhitās, the Brāhmaṇa style texts in the Krishna Yajur-Veda and actual brāhmaṇas of the four Vedas rank next in importance in the Vedic literature, as constituting an essential part of the Vedas. They provide a comprehensive explanation to rituals, inter-alia, linking the sacrificial mantras to the sacrificial rites. The construction of mantras is in metrical or prose forms and they are used for prayer purposes. The Brāhmaṇas, whose antiquity dates to approximately 800 B.C.E, provide detailed exposition of the methodology for performance of various rites of sacrifice. According to Julius Eggeling[277], the Brāhmaṇas "also throw a great deal of light on the earliest metaphysical and linguistic speculations of the Hindus."

Each of the Vedas has its own brāhmaṇas. For example, the Aitareya and Kauṣītakī are the brāhmaṇas attached to the Ṛgveda. The Aitareya Brāhmaṇa (AB) consists of 40 chapters and focuses on the Soma sacrifice. The later portion of this work also deals with the consecration of the king

---

276 The Religion and Philosophy of the Veda and Upanishads, Part I: A.B. Keith, Motilal Banarsidass, Delhi, Reprint 2007, P.109.

277 Satapatha Brahmana Part I (Introduction) Sacred Book of the East 12, Julius Eggeling's English Translation

and the position of the purohita. The Kauṣītakī Brāhmaṇa (KB), which has thirty chapters, also draws upon the Aitareya Brāhmaṇa and has as its subject the Soma and other sacrifices and the rituals connected with it. The Brāhmaṇas also contain myths and legends. Similarly, the Taittirīya Brāhmaṇa (TB) is connected with Black Yajur-Veda and the Śatpatha Brāhmaṇa (SB) with White Yajur-Veda. Among other things, the TB deals with Rājasūya[278] (Conferment of kingship or overlordship on "lesser kings") and Agnihotra (fire-offering). The SB is associated with Vājasaneyi Saṃhitā and discusses a wide range of subjects including legends relating to the occurrence of Great Flood, building of ceremonial sites for the Soma sacrifice, new and full moon sacrifices, fire altars, creation of universe, recitation of myths associated with the period etc. It occurs in two recensions, the Kāṇva and Mādhyandina. From the Śatapatha Brāhmaṇa, we derive the knowledge about the spread of Brahminical culture to Kosala and Bihar. Apart from the land of Kuru-Pañcālas which was a seat of Brahminical culture, there was further spread of this culture to the east of Madhyadesa and covered Kosala and Videha.

Tandya or Pañchaviṃśa and Jaiminīya Brāhmaṇas (JB) are connected to the Sāma-Veda. Both deal with explanations of Samans[279] and legends connected with them. The Gopatha-Brāhmaṇa is attached to the Atharva-Veda and borrows in parts from other texts, particularly, from the AB, the KB, the SB and Taittirīya saṃhitā. This Brāhmaṇa glorifies the Atharva-Veda and also bears the stamp of Vaitana Sūtra. Santucci [280] ascribes the difference among the Brāhmaṇas to "the duties of a particular priest associated with that particular Saṃhitā." For example, the duties of Hotṛ, the invoker, (one who recites the mantras during sacrificial rite) are specified in the Brāhmaṇas of the Ṛgveda whereas the duties of Udgātṛ

---

[278] The Religion and Philosophy of the Veda and Upanishads, Pt. II, P.340: A.B. Keith, Reprint 2007, Motilal Banarsidass Publishers Pvt. Ltd. Delhi. The royal consecration, i.e., Rajasuya, as described in the Satpatha Brahmana, involves performance of lengthy rituals, including the king's visit to the houses of twelve Ratnins with sacrificial offerings. Performance of Ra¯jasu¯ya was a display of royal authority and endowed the king with charisma and over-riding authority over other kings.

[279] Sāmans are melodious notes of religious nature in the Sama-Veda . These Sāmans are sung by Udgatṛs (priest).

[280] An Outline of Vedic Literature: James A. Santucci, Scholars Press, Missoula, Montana.USA, 1976

(singer of Sama chants) are prescribed in the Brāhmaṇas of the Sāma-Veda. In this way the Hotṛ of the Ṛgvedic Brāhmaṇa recites sacrificial mantras; the Udgātṛ of the Sāma Brāhmaṇa sings the Sāma chants.

6) The Āraṇyakas

The Āraṇyakas, after the Brāhmaṇas constitute an important portion of the Vedas. These consist of instructions imparted in the wilderness outside the settlement, and explain the metaphysics and symbolism of sacrifice. A.B. Keith in his book the Aitareya Āraṇyaka (pp.15-16) maintains that the forest (Aranya) was used to give secret explanations of the rituals. Among the important Āraṇyakas are the Aitareya and Kauṣītakī belonging to the Ṛgveda and Taittirīya and Kaṭha Āraṇyakas to the Black Yajur-Veda and are a continuation of the Taittirīya Brāhmaṇa. Āraṇyaka of White Yajur-Veda is contained in SB XIV, sections i - iii. Aitareya Āraṇyaka consists of eighteen chapters. It deals with a variety of subjects ranging from rituals of the Soma sacrifice to theosophical matters of Upaniṣadic variant. Kauṣītakī Āraṇyaka consists of fifteen chapters. It draws heavily from the Aitareya Āraṇyaka and the Kauṣītakī Upaniṣad. The Taittirīya Āraṇyaka consists of ten chapters of which the last four are Upaniṣads[281] and the rest are Āraṇyakas. This Āraṇyaka deals with Pravargya rituals, processes relating to cremation and burial of the dead, duties of a widow, origin of sacrifice, brahmanic education and a series of cosmogonic questions.

7) The Upaniṣads

Chronologically, the Upanisads come at the end of the Vedas; hence, they are also called Vedanta. We do not have any definitive material regarding the authorship of various Upaniṣads and possible period of their composition. All we know from internal evidence is the names of various scholars, such as Yajñavalkya, Uddālka, Śāṇḍilya, Saṭyākama Jabala and others whose teachings formed the basis of the Upaniṣadic doctrines. Similarly no precise dates can be given regarding the composition of the Upaniṣads, which seem to have taken place around 800-500 BCE. The scholars have, however, identified Bṛhad Āraṇyaka, Jaiminīya Upaniṣad

---

[281] The Tattiriya Aranyaka of the Black Yajur-Veda, Edited , by R.L. Mitra C.B. Lewis at the Baptist Mission Press, Calcutta, 1872, P. 7 .

Brāhmaṇa and Chāndogya as the earliest three Upaniṣads, followed by Taittirīya, Aitareya and Kauṣītakī. These Upaniṣads are believed to have been composed in the areas where the brahminical order dominated. As such, the geographical area of their composition would lie between the Himalayas in the north and the Vindhyas in the south and the Punjab in the west and Bihar in the east. The Upaniṣads stand on a different footing as compared to the Brāhmaṇas. The Upaniṣads are deemed as a continuation of the Brāhmaṇas, but their essence lies in philosophical speculation whereas ritualistic doctrines predominate the Brāhmaṇas.[282], [283] .MacDonnell[284] holds that the conceptions, Brahma and Atman "are commonly treated as synonymous in the Upanishads." Explaining this he states that the Brahma represents 'the cosmic principle' pervading the universe whereas the Atman is "the psychical principle manifested in man." According to Santucci,[285] "the Vedic Upaniṣads are, for the most part, discussions or dialogues on the true nature of reality, called either Brahmana or Atman which underlie both the psycho-physical microcosm and the macrocosm." Brian Black[286] has emphasized the social dimensions embedded in the narratives of the Upaniṣads which, according to him are reflected in "i) instructions passed from teachers to students; ii) debates between rival brahmins; 3) discussions between Brahmins and kings, and 4) conversations between Brahmins and women". The concept of *ātman* (the Self) is central to these narratives which not only reflect deep philosophical insight but also as a practical guide for conduct of one's life.

---

[282] According to S.Radhakrishnan, an eminent Philosopher, "the Upanishads give in some detail the path of the inner ascent, the inward journey by which the individual souls get at the Ultimate Reality. Elucidating further, he adds that the Upanishads do not advocate "any one set of dogmas, rites or codes" rather their focus is on "spiritual experience and psychological discipline."

[283] Sri Chinmoy draws attention to the Upanishadic view of the god, the soul and the world. The Upanishads describe Brahman as the God, Atman as the soul, and the Jagat as the world. According to him, meditating on them leads to "inner immortalization."

[284] A History of Sanskrit Literature: A.A. Macdonell, Munshiram Manoharlal, New Delhi, 3rd Edition, P.221

[285] An Outline of Vedic Literature: James A. Santucci, Scholars Press, Missoula, Montana, USA, 1976

[286] The Character of the Self in Ancient India, Brian Black, State University of New York, 2007. P.169.

There are differing views regarding the number of the Upaniṣads. Patrick Olivelle[287] puts 108 as the common number of the Upaniṣads in the South, and 52 in the north. Views also differ regarding the number of principal Upaniṣads. According to the standard opinion the number of principal Upaniṣads is eighteen. The prominent principal Upaniṣads include Bṛhad-Āraṇyaka (BU), Chāndogya(CU), Aitareya (AU), Taittirīya (TU), Īśa (Isa), Kaṭhaka (Kaṭha), Kena (Kena), Mundaka (MU), Māṇḍukya (Ma.U) , Kauṣītakī Brāhmaṇa Upaniṣad and Jaiminīya Upaniṣad Brāhmaṇa which is similar to Chāndogya Upaniṣad. The salient features of these Upaniṣads are discussed below.

- **Bṛhad-Āraṇyaka Upaniṣad.** It is regarded as the oldest and most important of the Upaniṣads. It is a part of the Śatapatha Brāhmaṇa, (Sections 14.4 to 9) and focuses, amongst other things, on the doctrines of transmigration of souls and Karman (action). It also deals with modes of worship.

- **Chāndogya Upaniṣad and Jaiminīya Brāhmaṇa Upaniṣad** are linked to the Sama-Veda and deals with sacrifices and forms of worship. It focuses on the genesis and importance of *AUM*, which symbolizes the Supreme.

- **Aitareya Upaniṣad.** It belongs to the Ṛgveda and is a part of Aitareya Āraṇyaka. It explains the various facets of Atman (Brahma), Atman as a creator of the world where the man is its highest manifestation. It describes the three places where the Atman resides in man, i.e., in his senses, mind and heart. This can be experienced when a man is in a state of walking, dreaming or in deep slumber. It also maintains that the Atman traverses three phases after death and treats salvation as the end of transmigration. It also deals with 'the nature of the Atman'[288] and treats consciousness as Brahma.

- **Taittirīya Upaniṣad.** It is linked to the Taittirīya school of the Yajur-Veda and has a section on Dharma. This Upaniṣad deals with pronunciations and provides lessons on pronunciation. It focuses on contemplation of Brahma and describes the five-fold nature of the world and the individual.

---

287 Upanishads, Patrick Olivelle, Oxford University Press, New York, 1996, P. xxxiii

288 A History of Sanskrit Literature, A.A. Macdonell, Munishiram Manoharlal, New Delhi. 1972 P.229.

- **Ísa Upaniṣad.** It is a middle level Upaniṣad associated with Vajasaneyi school of the Yajur-Veda. It stresses the need for cleansing souls for reaching high level of contemplation but side by side also emphasizes the importance of leading an active life.

- **Kaṭhaka Upaniṣad.** It is a middle level Upaniṣad and belongs to Kaṭha school of the Yajur-Veda. It consists of two chapters, each having three sections. It deals with the question of life after death through the legend of Nachiketas. In this legend, the Yama[289] in answer to Nachiketas third question relating to life after death, revealed that "life after death... are only different phases of development. True knowledge, which consists in recognizing the identity of the individual soul with the world soul, raises its possessor beyond the reach of death."

- **Kena Upaniṣad.** It belongs to the Jaiminīya school of the Sama-Veda and is a part of the Jaiminīya Upaniṣad Brāhmaṇa. It focuses on the question of Mukti (deliverance) through obtaining the knowledge of the Absolute. This is possible only by developing the higher wisdom through cultivation of a sense of total detachment from the worldly objects.

- **Mundaka Upaniṣad.** It is a later Upaniṣad and belongs to the Atharva-Veda. It deals with the concept of Brahma knowledge, which was imparted by the creator to Atharvan[290]. According to this Upaniṣad, there are two kinds of knowledge: the higher knowledge of the Supreme Brahman and the lower worldly knowledge. The higher knowledge results in higher wisdom which opens the door for approximating the Brahman. It maintains that craving for worldly objects and entertaining desire lead to re-birth. The wise men that are free from desire attain liberation. It opposes Vedic ritualism.

- **Mandukya Upaniṣad.** It is also a middle level Upaniṣad and belongs to the Atharva-Veda. It expounds the meaning of AUM. According to Dr Radhakrishnan[291], "the syllable aum, which is the symbol of Brahman

---

[289] Ibid., P.227

[290] Atharvan here refers to the head of a semi-divine family of mythical priests. (Vedic Index, Vol.I , P.17

[291] The Principal Upanishads: S. Radhakrishnan, Harper Collins Publishers, 23rd impression, 2012, P.695

stands for the manifested world, the past, present and the future, as well as the unmanifested Absolute."

- **Kauṣītakī Brāhmaṇa Upaniṣad.** It is one of the earlier Upaniṣads and belongs to the Rgveda. It explains the path the soul traverses after death in pursuit of transmigration. It also shows the way to the palace of Brahma.

8) The Sūtras (Approx. 500-200 B.C.)

Another important strand of the Vedic literature is called the Sūtras, which come after the Brāhmaṇas, the Āraṇyakas and the Upaniṣads. The Sūtras are concise rules and designed to fulfill practical needs. They represent the first attempt towards systematizing Brahmanic rituals and the Upaniṣads. According to Keith[292] one of the key differences between the Brāhmaṇas and Sūtras is that 'the Sūtras often give optional forms of procedures' for performance of certain rites, whereas 'the Brāhmaṇas contain no hint' in this regard. The composition of these Sūtras is believed to have taken place between 500 BCE-200 BCE, It is, however, difficult to assign any particular date.

The Sūtras have been divided into three parts, namely, i) Śrauta Sūtra; ii) Gṛhya Sūtras; and iii) Dharmasūtras. The Śrautasūtra[293] explains observance of rituals in performance of solemn ceremonies/sacrifices with the assistance of the priests. Winternitz[294] says that Śrauta Sūtras provide direction "for three sacred sacrificial fires, for the fire sacrifice and the new and full moon sacrifices, the sacrifices of the seasons, the animal sacrifices and especially for the Soma sacrifice with its numerous variations". The practice of Śrauta rituals, involving raising an altar of

---

292 The Religion and Philosophy of the Veda and Upanishad, Part I: A.B. Keith, Motilal Banarsidass Publishers PVT. LTD., Reprint, 2007 p.26

293 The Śrauta rituals, according to J.C. Heesterman, "represents a highly refined and systematized code of basic elements(manipulations, formulas, liturgical performances, gifts to the officiants), which are composed into uniform patterns which by means of altering, replacing or adding one or more elements can be adapted to circumstances." J.C. Heesterman's The Ancient Indian Royal Consecration. P.3. The Ancient Indian Royal Consecration, J.C. Heesterman, De GruyterMouton.

294 History of Indian Literature, Vol.I: Moriz Winternitz, Munshiram Manoharlal Pvt. Publishers, Third Edition, 1991, P.272

three fires introduced complexity in fire sacrifice which earlier was a simple affair meant to propitiate gods for obtaining material gains. This further signified growing importance of Agni, the god of fire in the divine hierarchy, and the priestly class who alone were professionally qualified to recite mantras to suit the occasion and to perform complex fire rituals. This also lent an elitist character to the priestly class. Concurrently, the Kṣatriyas, perceived as providers of materials for complex and elaborate Śrauta rituals, also gained in importance and there developed a bond between the priestly class and the kṣatriyas in mutual self-interest.

Like the Brāhmaṇas, Āraṇyakas and the Upaniṣads, the Sūtras also have linkages with one of the four Vedas. Śrauta manuals of the two Sūtra schools, namely, the Śāṅkhāyanas and the Āśvalāyanas, belong to the Ṛgveda. Both these Sūtras describe rituals connected with royal consecration but the Śāṅkhāyana Śrauta Sūtra presents a more detailed and pompous version of royal sacrifices. The Śrauta-Sūtra of Āśvalāyanas is linked to the Aitareya Brāhmaṇa. Similarly there are five Śrauta Sūtras – Ārṣeyakalpa, Ksudrakalpa, Latyayana, Drahyayana and Jaiminīya – that belong to the Sāma-Veda. Śrauta Sūtra of Kātyāyana belongs to the White Yajur-Veda. Kātyāyana Śrauta-Sūtra brings out the difference between Rajya and Samrajya and follows Śatapatha Brāhmaṇa.The prominent Śrauta Sūtra connected to Black Yajur-Veda is that of Baudhāyana and Āpastamba. The Śrauta Sūtra of the Atharva-Veda is called the Vaitana Sūtra. For performance of Śrauta rituals, three sacrificial fires, as mentioned above, are required.

Alongside, Śrauta Sūtra are the Gṛhya sutras which lay down rules for ceremonies connected to the domestic life of an individual and his family from the time he takes birth until his demise. Gṛhya Sūtras deal with division of society into four main classes, their occupations, obligations, duties and privileges in religious and temporal matters. They also deal with the privileges and duties of the three higher classes. Like Śrauta Sūtras, Gṛhya Sūtras are also linked to the Vedas. For example, the Ṛgveda's Śāṅkhāyana Gṛhya Sūtra; the Sāma-Veda's Gobhila Gṛhya Sūtra; White Yajur-Veda's Paraskara Gṛhya Sūtra; Black Yajur-Veda's Gṛhya Sụtra of Āpastamba; and the Atharva-Veda's Kauṣīka Gṛhya Sūtra. Gṛhya Sūtra rituals can be performed by using single domestic fire.

The Dharmasūtras are based on tradition and contain instructions on spiritual and secular aspects affecting daily life of the people belonging to four classes. They deal with customs, beliefs and daily life issues. They are the earliest law books and emphasize that the government should ensure enforcement of duties assigned to the four castes. The important Dharmasūtras include the schools of Gautama, Baudhāyana, Āpastamba and Vasiṣtha. Gautama Dharmasūtras deal with his theory on government, administration of justice by the king, his precepts on taxation and certain miscellaneous responsibilities of the state. Although he does not favour the higher classes opting for lower occupations earmarked for the Śūdras but he does not exclude such a possibility in emergent cases where the exigencies of the situation preclude any other alternative. Gautama virtually reduces the Śūdra class to the status of a serf, in the matter of his physical survival and prescribes severe punishments for participation or showing interest in Vedic studies. In Gautama's scheme of things, Brahmins are accorded a position of high status and privilege and he even places them outside the purview of the king. He favours exemption for the Brahmins from punishment, confinement or exile. Elaborating his concept of administration of justice by the king, he sees nothing wrong in groups and associations having their own rules limited to their spheres of activities.

Baudhāyana deals with multifarious issues, such as various kinds of sacrifice, duties of religious orders and kings, the position of women, law of inheritance, criminal justice system etc. He adopts a differential approach in prescribing the quantum of punishment for committing crimes of a similar nature and in this approach the Śūdras find themselves as heavily discriminated. In the matter of administration of justice, he outlines in details various stages to be observed before arriving at a final decision in a particular matter. He favours a percentage of gross produce, one-sixth, one-eighth or one-tenth as land tax. Āpastamba deals with law of marriage, duties of householder, kingly duties, local government and taxation issues, civil and criminal laws etc. He casts a duty on the king in the matter of planning of a city and his palace. He evinces considerable interest in the running of local government and injuncts that the field of selection for manning local government jobs should be limited to the Brahmin, Kṣatriya and Vaiṣya classes. He, however, shows special consideration for Brahmins, women, disabled and the Śūdras and seeks exemption from taxation for these categories. In the legal sphere also, he prescribes scales of punishment for different categories of crime.

Vasiṣtha Dharmasūtra is important for his precepts for the king and fiscal measures. He obligates the king to enforce performance of duties assigned to the four classes but also favours due deference to local laws / practices.

He casts a duty on the king regarding the administration of property held by widows and minors. He expands the usual scope of taxation by including artisans in the category of tax payers. He also favours certain more categories, such as unmarried girls, servants of the king, widows, old men etc., to be exempted from the liability to pay tax. He also advocates that in the matter of a property dispute, reliance should be placed on evidence emanating from documents, actual possession and witnesses.

Bibliography

Acharya, Shiva, *Nation, Nationalism and Social Structure in Ancient India*, Decent Books, Najafgarh Road, New Delhi, 2005.

Altekar, A.S, *State and Government in Ancient India*, Motilal Banarsidass, Delhi, Motilal Banarsidass, Reprint 2009.

Altekar, A.S., *The Position of Women in Hindu Civilization*, Motilal Banarsidass, Delhi. 2nd edition, Reprint, 1987.

Anderson, B., *Imagined Communities: Reflections on the Origin and Spread of Nationalism*, Revised Edition, Verso, London, 1991.

Arrian, *Alexander the Great, The Anabasis and the Indica*, Trans. by Martin Hammond, Oxford World's Classics, 2013.

Barth. A., *The Religions of India*, Routledge & Kegan Paul, London, 1882.

Basham, A.L., *Aspects of Ancient Indian Culture*, Asia Publishing House, New York, 1970. The Wonder that was India, Sidgwick & Jackson, London, 1954.

Bhargava, P.L., *India in the Vedic Age*, The Upper India Publishing House, Lucknow, 1956

Bhattacharya, B.B., *Sama-Veda Samhita with Sayana's Bhasya*, Calcutta, 1936

Bloomfield, M., *Hymns of the Atharva-Veda*, Greenwood Press, New York, 1969.

Bloomfield, M., *Atharva-Veda and the Gopatha Brahmana*, Strassburg : Karl J. Trubner, 1899.

Bloomfield, Maurice, *Vedic Concordance*, Cambridge, Mass., Harvard Oriental Series, 1906.

Blunt, E., *The Caste System of Northern India*, Reprint 2010 by Isha Books, Delhi 110009.

Brian B., *The Character of the Self in Ancient India*, State University of New York Press, 2007.

Bronkhorst, J., *Greater Magadha-Studies in the Cultures of Early India*, 1st edition, Motilal Banarsidass, Delhi, 2013.

Bryant, E.F. an Patton, L.L. (eds), *The Indo-Aryan Controversy*, Routledge, London and New York, 2005.

Bryant, E., *The Quest for the Origins of Vedic Culture: the Indo-Aryan Migration Debate*. Oxford University Press, New York, 2001.

Chakrabarti, Dilip K.& Saini, Sukhdev, *The Problem of the Sarasvati River and Notes on the Archaeological Geography of Haryana and Indian Panjab*, Aryan Books International, New Delhi, 2009.

Chakrabarti, Dilip K. Nation First, *Essays in the Politics of Ancient Indian Studies*, Aryan Books International, New Delhi, 2014.

Chanda, Ratna, *Caste System, its evolution through Ages*, Sanskrit Pustak Bhandar, Kolkata, 2009

Chattopadhyaya, Sudhakar, *Racial Affinities of Early North Indian Tribes*, Munshiram Manoharlal Publishers, New Delhi. 1973.

Choubey, B.B., *Treatment of Nature in the Rgveda*, Vedic Sahitya Sadan, Hoshiarpur, 1970.

Choudhury, M., *Tribes of Ancient India*, Indian Museum, Calcutta, 1977.

Dandekar, R.N., *Vedic Bibliography, 3 Vols. Vol I*, Karnataka Publishing House, Mumbai Vol II- University of Pune, 1946 Vol III- Bhandarkar Oriental Research Institute, Pune,1961.

Danino, M., *Indian Culture and India's Future*, DK Printworld, New Delhi, 2011.

Danino, M., *The Lost River- On the Trail of the Sarasvati*, Penguin Books, New Delhi, 2010.

Deshpande, Madhav, *Rig-vedic retroflexion, Aryans and Non-Aryans in India*, ed. by Madhav Deshpande and P.E. Hook, Ann Arbor, 1979.

Dharmadhikari, T.N, *The Maitrayani Samhita: its rituals*, Adarsha Sanskrit Shodha Samstha, Pune, India.

Eggeling, J., *The Satapatha Brahmana, according to the Text of the Madhyandina School*, Clarendon Press, Oxford, 1882.

Erdosy, G. (ed.), *The Indo-Aryans of Ancient South Asia,* Walter de Gruyter, Berlin- New York, 1995.

Fairservis, W. "The Harappan Civilization and the Rgveda", in *Inside the Texts-Beyond the Texts,* Edited by Witzel, M., Harvard Oriental Series, Opera Minora Vol.II. Cambridge, 1997

Falk, H., "The Purpose of Vedic Ritual", in Witzel, M., (Ed.) *Inside the Texts Beyond the Texts,* Harvard Oriental Series, Cambridge, 1997.

Frawley, D., *Gods, Sages and Kings,* Passage Press, Salt Lake City, Utah, 1991.

Frazer, R.W. *A Literary History of India,* New York, Scribner, 1898.

Geldner, K.F., *Der Rigveda,* Harvard, 1951, RV Trans. Harvard Oriental Studies, numbers 33, 34, and 35.

Geldner, K.F., *Vedische Studien,* Vol.2, Nabu Press, 2012

Gellner, E., *Nations and Nationalism,* Blackwell Publishing House, Oxford, 2006.

Ghoshal, U.N., *History of Indian Political Ideas,* Oxford University Press, Bombay, 1959.

Gilbert, P., *The Philosophy of Nationalism,* Boulder, CO: Westview Press, 1998.

Gonda, J., *A History of Indian Literature,* Harrassowitz, Wiesbaden, 1975.

Gonda, J., *Ancient Indian Kingship from Religious Points of View,* E.J. Brill, Leiden, 1969.

Gonda. J, *Mantra Interpretation in the Satapatha-Brahmana,* E.J. Brill, Leiden, 1988.

Gopal, R., *India of the Vedic Age,* Delhi, 1959.

Griffith, R.T.H., *Translation of the Atharva-Veda,* Messrs. E.J. Lazarus & Co., Benares, 1916.

Griffith, R.T.H., *The Hymns of the Rgveda,* 4th Edition, Calcutta, Reprint 1963

Griffith, R.T.H., *The Hymns of the Sama-Veda*, 4th edition, Varanasi, 1963.

Griffith, R.T.H., *The Texts of the White Yajur-Veda*, 3rd edition, Reprint, Benares, 1957.

Griffith, R.T.H., *The Hymns of the Atharva-Veda, Two Vols.* Varanasi, 1968.

Griswold, H.D., *The Religion of the Rgveda*, Motilal Banarsidass, Delhi, Reprint, 1999.

Grosby, S., *Nationalism-a very short introduction*, Oxford University Press, New York, 2005.

Hayes, C.J.H., *The Historic Evolution of Modern Nationalism*, Macmillan, New York, 1931.

Hearn, J., *Rethinking Nationalism*, Palgrave Macmillan, New York, 2006.

Heesterman, J.C., *The Ancient Indian Royal Consecration*, Mouton &Co.'s-Gravenhage, 1957.

Hume, R.E., *The Thirteen Principal Upanishads*, 2nd ed., Oxfor University Press, Oxford, 1931.

Jamison, W. S., *Sacrificed Wife and Sacrificer's Wife, Women, Ritual and Hospitality in Ancient India*, Oxford University Press,New York, 1996.

Jayaswal, K.P., *Hindu Polity*, 2nd ed., Bangalore, 1943.

Kane, P.V., *History of Dharmasastra*, Bhandarkar Oriental Research Institute, Poona, 1941

Kalyanaraman, S. (Ed), *Vedic River Sarasvati and Hindu Civilization*, Aryan Books International, New Delhi, 2008.

Keith, A.B., *Aitareya and Kausitaki Brahmanas*, Trans., Harvard, 1920.

Keith, A.B., *The Veda of the Black Yajus School*, 2Vols., Motilal Banarsidass, Delhi, 1967.

Keith, A.B. *Religion and Philosophy of the Veda and Upanishads*, 2Vols., Reprint, 2007, Motilal Banarsidass, Delhi.

Keith, A.B, *Rigveda Brahmanas: The Aitareya and Kausitaki Brahmanas of the Rigveda*, Cambridge, Mass.: Harvard Oriental Series, 1920.

Keith, A.B. , *The Aitareya Aranyaka*, Clarendon Press, Oxford, 1909.

Kenoyer, J.M., 1998, Ancient Cities of the Indus Valley Civilization, OUP.

Klaus, Bruhn (ed.), *The Predicament of Women in Ancient India*, Geerdes Midimusic, Berlin 2008.

Kohn, H., *The Idea of Nationalism: A Study of its Origin and Background*, Macmillan, New York, 1951.

Kosambi, D.D., *Ancient India: a History of its Culture and Civilizations*, World Pub. Co. New York, 1969.

Kosambi, D.D. *An Introduction to the Study of Indian History*, Bombay, 1956.

Kuiper, F.B. J., *Aryans in the Rigveda*, Amsterdam-Atlanta, GA 1991

Kuiper, F.B.J, *The genesis of a Linguistic Area*, Kuiper, F.B.J, Text of the Collitz lecture delivered at the summer meeting of the Linguistic Society of America at Ann Arbor, July 30, 1965.

Kulke, H. and Rothermund D., *A history of India*, 4th Edition, Routledge, London-New York, 2004.

Laitin, D.D, *Nation, States and Violence*, Oxford University Press, Oxford, 2007.

Lal, B.B., *The Sarasvati Flows on – The Continuity of Indian Culture*, Aryan Book International, New Delhi, 2002.

Lanman, C.R. (Ed.), *Rigveda Brahmanas*, Harvard Oriental Series, Vol. 25, Harvard University Press, Cambridge, MA, 1920

Law, B.C., *Tribes in Ancient India*, Bhandarkar Oriental Research Institute, Poona, 1943.

Law, B.C. *Some Kshatriya Tribes of Ancient India*, Bhartiya Pub. House, Varanasi, 1924.

Law, N.N., *Aspects of Ancient Indian Polity*, Orient Longman, Bombay, 1921.

Leone, B., *The Isms: Modern Doctrines and Movements*, Nationalism Opposing View Points, Revised 2nd edition, 1986, Greenhaven Press,Minnesota.

Lopez, C.A., *Atharvaveda-Paippalada*, Harvard Oriental Series, Opera Minora Vol.6, Cambridge, 2010.

Lubotsky A., "The Indo-Iranian Substratum", Early Contacts between Uralic and Indo-European linguistic and Archaeological Considerations; Paper presented at University of Helsinki, 8-10,January, 1999.

Macdonell, A.A and Keith, A.B., *Vedic Index of Names and Subjects, Vol. II*, 1st ed. London, 1912.

Macdonell, A.A and Keith, A.B., *Vedic Index of Names and Subjects, Vols. I&II*, Motilal Banarsi Dass, Bunglow Road, Delhi, 1982.

Macdonell, A.A, *Hymns from the Rgveda*, Heritage, Calcutta-London, 1922.

Macdonell, A.A, *A Vedic Reader for Students*, Oxford at Clarendon Press, 1917.

Macdonell, A.A., *A History of Sanskrit Literature*, Munshiram Manoharlal, 3rd edition, Delhi, 1972.

Macdonell, A.A. and Keith, A.B., *Vedic Index of Names and Subjects*, 2 Vols., Motilal Banarsidass, Delhi, Reprint, 2007.

Majumdar, R.C., *Readings in Political History of India, Ancient, Medieval and Modern*, B.R. Publishing Corporation, 1976.

Maurer, W.H., *Pinnacles of India's Past*, John Benjamings Publishing Co., Philadelphia, 1986.

Mcrindle, J.W., *Ancient India as described by Megasthenese*, Trubner&Co. London, 1877

Mehta, Rohit, *The Call of the Upanishads*, Motilal Banarsidass, Delhi, 1970.

Minkowski ,C., "Rathakara's Eligibility to Sacrifice", *Indo-Iranian Journal*, Vol.32 No.3 July 1989, Kluwer Academic Publishers, Boston-London .

Mitra, R.L, (ed.), *The Tattiriya Aranyaka of the Black Yajur-Veda,* Baptist Mission Press, Calcutta, 1872.

Muir, J., *Original Sanskrit Texts on the Origin and History of the People of India, 4 Vols.*, 2nd ed., London, 1872.

Muller M., (ed.) Appendix titled "The Khilas of The Rgveda in The Rgveda Samhita", Vol. IV, 2nd edition, London, 1892.

Muller M., T*he Hymns of the Rgveda with Sayana's Commentary,* Reprinted by the Chowkhamba Sanskrit series Office, Varanasi, 1966.

Muller M., *A history of Sanskrit Literature,* Allahabad, 1917.

O'Flaherty, W.D., *The Rig Veda, An Anthology,* Penguin Books, Harmondsworth, Middlesex, 1981.

Oldenberg, H., *The Religion of the Veda,* Trans. Into English by S.B. Shrotri, Motilal Banarsidass, Delhi, First Edition, 1988.

Oldenberg, H., *Buddha, His life, doctrine, his order,* W. Hoey (trans.), Williams and Norgate, London, 1882.

Olivelle, P., *The Early Upaniṣads,* Oxford University Press, New York, 1998.

Osada Toshiki (ed.), *Occasional Paper 1 Linguistics, Archaeology and Human Past,* Indus Project, Research Institute for Humanity and Nature, Kyoto, Japan, 2005.

Pande, G.C. (ed.) *The Dawn of Indian Civilization up to 600 BC,* Vol.I, Part I, Centre for Studies in Civilizations, New Delhi,1999.

Panikkar, K.M. *Origin and Evolution of Kingship in India,* Baroda, 1938.

Parasher, Aloka, *Mlecchas in Early India,* Munshiram Manoharlal Publishers, New Delhi, 1991.

Pargitter, F.E., *Ancient Indian Historical Tradition,* Oxford University Press, London, 1922.

Parpola, A. "The Dasas and the Coming of the Aryans" in Witzel, M., (Ed.) *Inside the Texts Beyond the Texts,* Harvard Oriental Series, Cambridge, 1997.

Patton L.L. (ed.), *Authority, Anxiety and Canon, Essays in Vedic Interpretation,* State University of New York Press, Albany, 1994.

Perry, E.D. *"Indra in the Rgveda",* presented to the American Oriental Society on Oct. 28th, 1880

Peterson, P., *Hymns from the Rgveda,* Edited by H.D. Valenkar, Pune, 1959.

Philips, C.H. (ed.), *Politics and Society in India,* George Allen and Unwin, London, 1963.

Phillips, A., *War, Religion and Empire - The Transformation of international orders,* Cambridge University press, New York, 2011.

Phillips, M., *Teaching of the Vedas,* Longmans Green and Co., New York, 1895.

Prasad, B., *Theory of Government in Ancient India,* The Indian Press Ltd., Allahabad, 1928.

Prasad, B., *The State in Ancient India,* The Indian Press, Allahabad, 1928.

Proferes, N. T., *Vedic Ideals of Sovereignty and the Poetics of Power,* American Oriental Society, New Haven, Connecticut, 2007.

Radhakrishnan,S., *The Principal Upanishads,* Harper Collins, 23rd Impression,Noida, 2012.

RaghuVira and L.Chandra, *Jaiminiya Brahmana of the Sama-Veda,* Nagpur, 1954.

Ramamurty, A., *The Central Philosophy of Rgveda,* Ajanta Publications, Delhi, 1991.

Rapson, E.J., *The Cambridge History of India,* Ancient India, Vol.I, Macmillan Co. New York, 1922.

Rau, W., *Staat Und GesellSchaft In Alten Indien,* Wiesbaden, 1957.

Rau, W., "Permanent Vedic Settlements" in Witzel, M., (Ed.) *Inside the Texts Beyond the Texts,* Harvard Oriental Series, Cambridge, 1997.

Rau, W. "The Meaning of pur in Vedic Literature," Abhandlungen der Marburger Gelehrten Gesellschaft III/1, München: W. Finck., 1976.

Raychaudhuri, H.C., *Political History of Ancient India,* 7th edition, University of Calcutta, 1972.

Renou, L., *Religions of Ancient India,* The Athlone Press, London, 1953.

Rhys Davids T.W, *Buddhist India,* Montana, Kessinger Publishing, 2004.

Romm, J. (ed.) *The Landmark Arrian: The Campaigns of Alexander,* Pantheon Books. New York, 2010.

Rose, H.A., *A Glossary of the Tribes and Castes of the Punjab and North-West Frontier Province, Vol.I,* Nirmal Publishers and Distributors, New Delhi, 1997.

Roy, Kumkum, *The Emergence of Monarchy in North India,* Oxford University Press, Delhi, 1994.

Royal Institute of Internationla Affairs, *Nationalism, A Report by a Study Group of Members of the RIIA,* Oxford University Press, London, 1939.

Samasrami, P.S., *The Aitareya Brahmana of the Rgveda with commentary of Sayana Acharya, 4 Vols.,* Asiatic Society of Bengal Calcutta, 1906.

Santucci, J.A., *An Outline of Vedic Literature,* Scholars Press, Montana, 1976.

Sarao, K.T.S., *Urban Centres and Urbanisation,* Third Revised Edition, Munshiram Manoharlal, New Delhi, 2010.

Satavalekar, S.D., Yajur-Veda Kathaka Samhita ed. Aundh, Svadhyaya Mandala, 1943. Maitrayaniya Samhita, Aundh, Svadhyaya Mandala, 1943 Sukla Yajur-Veda Kanva Samhita, 1940

Scharfe, H. *The State in Indian Tradition,* E.J. Brill, Leiden-New York, 1989.

Schmidt, H.P., "Notes on gveda 7.18.5-10. Indica", *Organ of the Heras Institute of Indian History and Culture, Bombay,* 17, 41-47, 1980.

Schmidt, H.-P., *Some Women's Rites and Rights in the Veda,* Bhandarkar Oriental Research Institute, Poona, India, 1987.

Seton-Watson, H., *Nation and States: An Enquiry into the Origins of Nations and the Politics of Nationalism,* Metheun, London, 1977.

Sharma, J.P., "The Question of Vidhata in Ancient India", JRAS, 1965

Sharma, R.S., *Aspects of Political Ideas and Institutions in Ancient India*, 5th Revised edition 2005, Motilal Banarsidass Publishers Pvt. Ltd., Delhi.

Sharma, R.S., *Origin of the State in India*, University of Bombay Publication, 1989.

Sharma, R.S., *Sudras in Ancient India*, 3rd ed., Motilal Banarsidass, Delhi, 1990.

Sharma, R.S., *Looking for the Aryans*, Orient Longman, Hyderabad, 1995.

Sharma, B.R. (ed.), *Kanva Samhita, Vol. I.*, T.N. Dharmadhikari & Mrs N.M. Dhadphale, Vaidika Samsodhana Mandala, Pune-37, 1988.

Sinha, H.N., *The Development of Indian Polity*, Asia Publishing House, N.Y. 1962.

Singh,Upinder, *A History of Ancient and Early Medieval India-From the Stone Age to the 12th Century*, Pearson Education, a Division of Dorling Kindersley (India) Pvt. Ltd., Delhi, 2009.

Smith, A.D., *Nationalism in the Twentieth Century*, Martin Robertson, Oxford, 1979.

Snyder, L.L., *The Dynamics of Nationalism: Readings in its meaning and development*, Princeton, N.J. 1964.

Spellman, J.W., *Political Theory of Ancient India*, Clarendon Press, Oxford, 1964.

Sri Aurobindo, *The Secret of the Veda*, Sri Aurobindo Ashram, Pondicherry, 2004.

Stuhrmann, R., "The roots of the interpretation of dreams in India and Greece – a comparative investigation", *Electronic Journal of Vedic Studies*, Vol. 15, 1, 2008.

Summers, J., *Peoples and International: How Nationalism and Self-Determination Shape a Contemporary Law of Nations*, Koninklijke Brill NV, Leiden, The Netherlands. Eric Castren Institute Monographs on International Law and Human Rights. Vol.8, Martinus Nijhoff Publishers, 2007.

Thadani,N.V, *The Mahabharata*, Bhartiya Kala Prakashan, Delhi, 2013.

Thapar, R, *Ancient Indian Social History*, Orient Longman, Delhi, 1978.

Thapar, R., *From Lineage to State,* Oxford University Press, New Delhi, 1990.

Thurston, E., *Castes and Tribes of Southern India, Vol. VI,* Government Press, Madras, 1909.

Trikha J.K., *Rgveda-A Scientific and Intellectual Analysis of the Hymns,* Somaiya, Publications Pvt. Limited, Bombay, 1981.

Varma, V.P., *Studies in Hindu Political Thought and its Metaphysical Foundations,* Motilal Banarsidass, Delhi, 1974.

Vata.S, and Mudgal.S, (Ed.) *Women and Society in Ancient India,* Om Publications, Faridabad, 1999.

Vira Raghu, *Kapisthala Katha Samhita,* Meharchand Lachhman Das, Delhi, 1968.

Wallis, H.W., *The Cosmogony of the Rgveda,* London, 1887

Weber, A, Taittiriya Samhita (ed.), *Indische Indien,* Trans, Keith, A.B., Harvard, 1914.

Whitney, D.D, *Atharva-Veda Samhita,* Motilal Banarsidass, Delhi, 1968.

Whitaker, J.L , *Strong Arms and Drinking Strength,* Oxford University Press, 2011.

Williams, M., *Religious Thought and Life in India,* London, 1883.

Wilson, H.H, *Rgveda Samhita (First Book), Translated from the original Sanskrit,* Allen &Co., London, 1850.

Winternitz, M., *History of Indian Literature,* Vol.I, 3rd edition, Munshiram Manoharlal Pvt. Publishers, 1991.

Witzel, M., "Early Indian History: Linguistic and Textual Parameters", in *The Indo-Aryans of Ancient South Asia,* (ed.) by G. Erdosy, de Gruyter, Berlin-New York, 1995.

Witzel, M., "Early Sanskritization", *Electronic Journal of Vedic Studies,* Vol.1, Issue 4, December, 1995.

Witzel, M., "Early Sanskritization, Origins and Development of the Kuru State" in B. Kolver (ed.) *The State, the Law and Administration in Classical India,* Munchen, 1997.

Witzel, M., (Ed.) *Inside the Texts Beyond the Texts,* Harvard Oriental Series, Cambridge, 1997.

Witzel, M., *Linguistic Evidence for Cultural Exchange in Prehistoric Western Central Asia.* Philadelphia: Sino-Platonic Papers 129, Dec. 2003

Witzel, M., "On the localization of Vedic texts and Schools, India and the Ancient World", in G. Pollet (ed.) *History, Trade and Culture, before A.D 650.* P.H.L Eggermont Jubilee Volume, Leuven, 1987.

Witzel, M., "Rgvedic History: Poets, Chieftains and Polities", in G. Erdosy (ed.), *The Indo-Aryans of Ancient South Asia,* de Gruyter, Berlin New York, 1995.

Witzel, M., *The Development of the Vedic Canon and its Schools: The Social and Political Milieu in Inside the Texts Beyond the Texts,* Harvard Oriental Series, Opera Minora, Vol.II, Cambridge, 1997.

Witzel, M., *The Realm of the Kurus: Origins and Development of the First State in India,* Summaries of the Congress of the Japanese Association for South Asian Studies, Kyoto, 1989.

Witzel,M., "Moving Targets? Texts, language, archaeology and history in the Late Vedic and early Buddhist periods", *Indo-Iranian Journal* Vol. 52 No. 2-3. 2009.

Yamazaki, G., *The Structure of Ancient Indian Society: Theory and Reality of the Varna System,* Toyo Bunko, Tokyo, 2005.

Glossary

Agni — A fire god, next in importance to Indra; enjoys a crucial position in every sacrifice.

Aditya — A secondary god; represents a diversified form of the Sun.

Adhvaryu — Priest assigned the duties of reciting Yajur-Vedic formulas

Aitareya Brāhmaṇa — A Brahmana attached to Ṛgveda deals with sacrifices and rituals.

Akṣāvāpa — The keeper of dice; one of the Ratnins of the king in the Vedic period.

Āpastamba — An ancient sage; a writer of sutras and law.

Aryan — A race which migrated from Central Asia and initially settled in the Sapta-Sindhu region.

Asura — Demon.

Aśvamedha — Horse sacrifice.

Aśvins — Twin gods in the Vedas, divine physicians who help the distressed.

Bhagádugha — Distributor of portions.

Bhūpati — Represents lordship of earth.

Brahma — A supreme god, later a member of triad along with Viṣṇu and Shiva.

Brāhmaṇa — Work attached to the Vedas; deals with explanation of rituals.

Bṛhad Āraṇyaka Upaniṣad — One of the oldest Upaniṣads; known for its philosophical speculation and commentary on Puruṣa Sukta

Dāśarājña — The 'Battle of Ten Kings' in the Ṛgveda

Dharma — Righteous conduct; morality; social order;

Dharmaśāstra — Text dealing with law and conduct.

Dharmasūtra — Concise rules on law and custom.

Gaṇa — A tribal community.

Gautama — An author of Dharmaśāstra.

Grāma — A group of people inhabiting a place; villages as permanent settlements in later Brāhmaṇas

Grāmaṇī — Head of a village.

Gṛhapati — householder

Hotṛ — a special priestly class for reciting Rig-Vedic hymns

Indra — Powerful god of thunder and lightning in the Vedas.

Kṣatra — Represents a dominion.

Kṣatriya — One of the four varṇas (classes) whose principal function was to protect the society from external onslaughts and maintain internal order.

Mahārāja — A great monarch.

Mahājanapada — large territorial state

Maruts — A group of deities symbolizing storm, thunder, lightning, wind and rain.

Mantra — A Vedic hymn.

Nirukta — A later Vedic text authored by Yaska; provides etymological explanation of words, and mantras.

Pariṣad — A council; functioned as advisor to the king.

Parjanya — A Vedic rain god.

Prajāpati — Supreme lord of men; assumed great importance in the later Vedic period.

Prithvī — The earth.

Puṣan — worshipped as a pastoral god. Represents another aspect of Sun god.

Purohita — A family priest of the king in the Vedic period.

Rāja, Rājan — A king.

Rājasūya— A great sacrifice performed at King's coronation confirming his title.

Rāṣṭra — A kingdom or a group of small states.

Ratnins — The Jewel-bearers in the King's court during the Vedic period. It was a heterogeneous body comprising persons of different denominations.

Ṛgveda — A collection of hymns in praise of various gods. The oldest of the Vedas.

Ṛta — The cosmic laws; concerned with regulation of political and social order

Rudra — A Vedic god; later became Shiva.

The Sabhā — A clan assembly, later evolved into an elite body.

Sāma-Veda — A Veda of chants at Soma ceremonies and in praise of various gods.

Saṃgrahītṛ — One of the king's Ratnins with the responsibility of tax collection; treasurer.

Saṃgrāma- tribal units

Saṃhitās — Understood in the sense of collection of hymns of a Veda.

Samiti — Folk assembly. Some scholars view it as an important institution during the Vedic period used for consultation on important matters.

Sapta-Sindhu — The standard list of rivers included under the expression Sapta-Sindhu fluctuates. It is common to identify this expression with seven rivers, namely, Kubhā(Kabul), Sindhu(the Indus), Vitastā (Jhelum), Asiknī(Chenab), Paruṣṇī (Ravi), Vipāś (Beas) and Śutudrī (Sutlej). These rivers along with rivers Sarasvati and Gomal (Gomati) find mention in the Book X hymn 75 of the Rig-Veda but the river Vipās (Beas) does not find a mention.

Sarasvatī — A goddess associated with learning; one of the most celebrated Ṛgvedic River.

Śatapatha Brāhmaṇa — deals with the philosophy, mythology and magical practices of Vedic period.

Senānī-- commander

Shiva — An important god in the later Vedic period; also finds mention in the Ṛgveda

Smṛti — Literally means "that which is remembered" ; refers to Brahminical texts dealing with civil and religious laws-presents codified customary laws of the Hindus. The texts falling in this category are supposed to have been composed by personal authors.

Soma — Fermented juice of Soma plants given in libations to the gods. Soma sacrifice involves offering of the sap of the Soma plant mixed with milk or barley. Soma enjoys the status of a divinity in the Vedas.

Śrauta Sūtra- are manuals to guide performance of solemn sacrificial rites during the Vedic period.

Śruti — Sacred knowledge orally transmitted, believed to be of divine origin, deals with canons of Hinduism; It stands for the Vedic texts that was heard by inspired seers.

Śūdra — In the four-fold Varṇa system, occupies the lowest position and engages in services of lower order

Sūrya — Represents the Sun god; personifies the disc of the Sun.

Sūta — messenger

Taittirīya Brāhmaṇa — Explains sacrificial ritual; a later Vedic text.

Takṣan — Carpenter

Uṣas — Personifies the Dawn; an important goddess in the Ṛgveda

Udgātṛ — Priest assigned the function of reciting Sāma-Veda formulas

Viṣṇu — Not a prominent god in the Ṛgveda; later becomes prominent with Shiva and Brahma.

Vaiśya — Occupies third place in Varṇa system; engages in agriculture and trade.

Varṇa — contemplation regarding four classes in the Puruṣa-Sukta (RV 10. 90.12)

Varuṇa — A superior Vedic god, often clubbed with Mitra.

Vasiṣtha — An important Vedic rishi.

Vedic Corpus- The four Vedas, Brāhmaṇas, Āraṇyakas, Upaniṣads and earlier Sūtras constitute theVedic corpus

Viś — It would imply the people in general (in Vedic context)/and: and a (temporal) settlement.

Viśaḥ — It means an accumulation of settlements (settlements of Vedic tribes).

Vṛtra- cosmic serpent, snake without hands, feet.

Vairājya — non-monarchical state

Index

A

A.A. Macdonell, 15, 65, 68, 71, 73, 117, 167, 176, 177
A.B. Keith, 15, 45, 68, 71, 73, 99, 139, 163, 164, 173, 174, 175, 179
A.S. Altekar, 16, 122
Adhvaryu, 130, 137, 167, 195
Aditya, 171, 195
Agni, 101, 102, 104, 110, 111, 117, 136, 160, 164, 165, 168, 170, 171, 172, 180, 195
Aindra-Mahabhiseka, 134
Aitareya Aranyaka, 163, 175, 177, 187
Aitareya A¯raṇyaka, 13
Aitareya Brahmana, 51, 74, 75, 80, 88, 99, 133, 135, 136, 140, 166, 173, 180, 191, 195
Aitareya -Brahmana, 13
Aitareya Upaniṣad, 177
Aitareyins, 137
Aja, 73, 87
Ajatashatru, 87
Aksavapa, 61, 108, 113, 195
Alexander, 20, 23, 148, 183
Alina, 73
Alinas, 65, 67, 80
Allchin F.R, 19
Altekar, 122, 183
Anderson, 183
Ánga, 144
Angas, 74, 88, 133, 169
Angiras, 68, 69, 72, 164
Ān˙girasa, 36, 73, 86, 170
Anus, 26, 65, 66, 68, 69, 77, 101, 139, 147
Anus-Druhyus, 26, 66, 147
Apastamba, 61, 63, 180, 181, 195
Aranyakas, 24, 41, 45, 163, 175, 179, 180
Āraṇyakas, 24
Arjikiyas, 65
Ārṣeyakalpa, 180
Aryan, 18, 21, 22, 32, 59, 66, 67, 75, 93, 117, 119, 123, 128, 136, 147, 155, 156, 158, 160, 169, 184, 187, 195
Aryans, 17, 18, 21, 23, 24, 25, 31, 35, 36, 41, 64, 74, 75, 93, 118, 119, 127, 129, 136, 147, 150, 152, 155, 157, 158, 159, 160, 169, 173, 184, 185, 187, 189, 192, 193, 194
Ascendancy, 133
Asikni, 65, 66, 69, 70, 75, 80
Asko Parpola, 155
Asura, 195
A¯śvala¯yanas, 180
Asvamedha, 130, 134, 138, 158, 195
Āsvamedha, 51
Asvins, 165, 171, 195
Atharva Veda, 24, 102, 169
Atharva-Veda, 13, 15, 37, 45, 61, 62, 102, 105, 108, 110, 112, 115, 122, 134, 149, 163, 168, 169, 174, 178, 180, 183, 185, 186, 193
Atri, 36, 69, 70, 72, 73, 78, 86, 164, 170
Aurel Stein, 159

Ayus, 73

B

B.B. Lal, 156
B.C. Law, 74, 79
Baden-Powell, 107
Bal Gangadhar Tilak, 16
Balbutha, 23, 148
Balhika Pratipiya, 88
Balhikas, 65, 76
Battle of Ten Kings, 44, 67, 68, 69, 70, 73, 74, 195
Baudhayana, 13, 50, 74, 181
Baudhayana-Srauta Sutra, 13
Baudhayana-Dharmasutra, 13
Benedict, 183
Beni Prasad, 16, 124, 126, 128
Bhagadugha, 108, 113, 195
Bhalanas, 65, 67, 74, 80
Bharadvaja, 36, 72, 73, 74, 77, 80, 82, 86, 164, 170
Bhāradvāja, 77, 86, 164
Bharata, 31, 66, 68, 74, 79, 81, 160, 161
Bharata Divodasa, 160
Bharatas, 26, 48, 65, 67, 68, 70, 71, 72, 74, 81, 134, 139, 147, 160
Bhupati, 195
Black Yajur-Veda, 167, 180
Bloomfield, 111, 127, 166, 169, 183
BMAC, 34, 156
Bodha¯yana, 137
Brahma, 100, 120, 132, 150, 176, 177, 178, 179, 195, 198
Brahman, 49, 100, 111, 114, 115, 124, 136, 137, 139, 140, 150, 169, 176, 178
Brahmana, 15, 50, 68, 70, 71, 75, 87, 88, 100, 101, 111, 125, 133, 135, 138, 140, 163, 166, 167, 168, 169, 171, 173, 174, 176, 177, 178, 179, 183, 185, 190, 195
Brahmanas, 24, 25, 41, 45, 60, 99, 104, 105, 108, 112, 113, 114, 117, 134, 138, 147, 149, 150, 163, 166, 168, 170, 171, 173, 174, 175, 176, 179, 180, 186, 187
Brāhmaṇas, 24
Brbu, 23, 123, 148
Brhad Aranyaka Upanishad, 195
Brhad-Aranyaka Upanishad, 177
Brhadaranyaka-Upanishad, 13
Brian Black, 25, 51, 176, 183
Brian K. Smith, 131
Bruno Leone, 53
Buddhism, 146

C

C.R. Lanman, 135
Caidya, 101
Cedis, 74, 133
Chandogya, 13, 109, 168, 176, 177
Chandogya-Upanishad, 13
Characteristics of the Post Rig-Vedic Period, 139
Christopher Minkowski, 16, 112
Cult of Sacrifice, 128

D

D.R. Bhandarkar, 74
Daivavata, 80, 82, 101
Dakṣiṇa, 131
dasapeya, 151

Daśapeya, 56
Dasarajana, 195
Dasyus, 79, 93, 117, 128
Dayanand, 16
Deposition of a King, 104
Devas, 95
Dharma, 24, 39, 152, 177, 195
Dharmasashtra, 195, 196
Dharmasutra, 13, 128, 181, 195
Dharmasutras, 179, 180
Dhvasan Dvaitavana, 76
Dietmar Rothermund, 114, 115, 124, 126, 144
Drahyayana, 180
Drghatamas, 74
Drsadvati, 66, 74, 161
Druhyus, 65, 67, 68, 69, 70, 77, 101, 139

E

E.J. Rapson, 51, 52
E.W. Hopkins, 35
Edward Washburn Hopkins, 35
Edwin Bryant, 16, 34, 157

F

F.B. J. Kuiper, 23, 159
Fairservis, 158, 185
five tribes, 67, 68, 69, 72, 77

G

Gana, 196
Gandharis, 65, 74, 76
Gargi, 122
Gārhapatiya, 131
Gaudar tribes, 120
Gautama, 181, 196
Geldner, 15, 81, 103, 170, 185
Gomal, 36, 156
Gopatha-Brahmana, 13
Go-vyacha, 113
Grama, 46, 59, 61, 196
Gramani, 60, 61, 108, 113, 136, 140, 196
Grāmaṇi, 46, 60, 112, 113
Gramya-vadin, 112
Grhya Sutras, 39, 179, 180
Grhyasutra, 61, 128
Gṛhyasūtra, 63
Grtsamada, 36, 86, 164, 170
Gutama-Dharmasutra, 13

H

H.Falk, 21, 119
H.H. Wilson, 119
H.N. Sinha, 16, 59, 127
H.N.Sinha, 60
Hairanyanabha, 87, 138
Hanns-Peter Schmidt, 121, 123
Harry Falk, 16, 119
Hartmut Scharfe, 16, 27, 95, 96, 100, 101, 112, 135, 149
Henry Thomas Colebrooke, 15
Hermann Kulke, 16, 114, 115, 124, 126, 144
Hermann Oldenberg, 15, 127, 130
Hotr, 174, 195, 196, 197, 198, 199
Hotṛ, 50, 128, 130, 136, 175
H-P. Schmidt, 67
Hrtsvasaya, 88

I

Ikṣvāku, 75
Indra, 21, 22, 31, 63, 67, 70, 77, 78, 95, 99, 100, 101, 102, 104, 110, 111, 113, 135, 161, 164,

165, 168, 169, 170, 171, 172, 190, 195, 196
Institution of Varṇa, 123
Ísa Upaniṣad, 178

J

J. Bronkhorst and M.M Despande, 34, 157
J.B.S. Kuiper, 16
J.C. Heesterman, 16, 105, 134, 151, 179
J.Muir, 157
Jaiminiya, 13, 68, 70, 75, 163, 168, 171, 175, 177, 178, 180, 190
Jaiminiya-Brahmana, 13
Jaiminīya Brāhmaṇa, 168
Jaiminiya Upanishad Brahmana, 177
Jainism, 146
James Santucci, 16
Janak, 87
Johannes Bronkhorst, 145
John Muir's, 15
John Spellman, 16
John W. Spellman, 101
Journal of American Oriental Society, 13
Journal of the Royal Asiatic Society, 13
Julius Eggeling, 173

K

K.P. Jayaswal, 63, 110
K.P.Jayaswal, 16, 110
Kaisini, 87, 137
Kambojas, 65, 87
Kanva, 50, 63, 71, 72, 73, 74, 75, 77, 78, 79, 138, 164, 167, 170, 174, 191, 192
Kaṇvas, 36, 68, 69, 70, 77, 86, 137
Kapishthala-Katha Samhita, 167
Kasi, 87, 144
Kasu, 74, 101
Kathaka- Samhita, 13
Kạthaka Saṃhita¯, 167
Kạthaka Upaniṣad, 178
Katyayana-Srautasutra, 13
Kaurama, 78
Kausambi, 144, 152
Kaushitaki Brahmana, 138, 168
Kausitaki, 13, 76, 81, 82, 163, 166, 176, 186, 187
Kauṣītakī Āraṇyaka, 175
Kauṣītakī Brāhmaṇa, 179
Kausitaki-Upanishad, 13
Kausitaki-Brahmana, 13
Keith, 15, 22, 45, 59, 62, 65, 99, 118, 139, 140, 161, 164, 173, 179, 186, 187, 188, 193
Kekayas, 65
Kena Upaniṣad, 178
Khilas, 24, 147, 166, 189
Kikatas, 75
King's Consecration, 105
King's Duties, 106
kingship, 17, 61, 63, 96, 97, 99, 100, 101, 102, 103, 114, 139, 149, 150, 151, 152, 174
Kiratas, 87
Kosala, 17, 27, 75, 133, 134, 135, 137, 138, 139, 144, 151, 174
Kosalas, 87, 133
Kraivya, 75, 87, 137
Krishna Yajur-Veda, 24, 147
Krivis, 66, 75
Krumu, 36, 156

kṣatra, 63, 96, 120, 132
Kṣatradhṛti, 56
Ksattr, 108, 113
Kshatra, 62, 100, 150, 196
Kshatriya, 49, 118, 125, 181, 187, 196
Kshatriyas, 17, 49, 60, 107, 120, 125, 132, 138, 152, 169, 180
Ksudrakalpa, 180
Kubha, 36, 74, 156
Kuiper,F.B.J, 23, 148, 187
Kuru, 13, 17, 27, 37, 41, 50, 60, 75, 78, 81, 114, 133, 134, 136, 137, 138, 151, 167, 174, 193
Kurukṣetra, 60, 75, 78, 114, 133, 134, 139
Kuru-Panchala, 27, 50, 133, 134, 137, 151
Kuru-Panchalas, 17, 50, 138, 167, 174
Kurus, 32, 37, 44, 50, 75, 80, 81, 82, 114, 133, 134, 139, 194
Kuruśravana, 75

L

Latyayana, 180
Lubotsky, 33, 155, 188

M

Macdonell and Keith, 59
MacDonnell, 59, 65, 118, 176
Madhuchchandas, 68, 69
Madhyadesa, 21, 23, 75, 76, 80, 81, 82, 87, 159, 174
Madhyadesha, 25, 41, 82, 87, 147
Mādhyandina, 167, 174
Magadha, 75, 87, 138, 144, 145
Mahajanapadas, 144
Maharaja, 196
Mahārajya, 134
Mahavrsa, 88
Mahavrsas, 65, 76
Mahishi, 136
Mahisi, 113
Maitrayani Samhita, 13, 37, 105, 167, 184
Maitreyi, 122
Maitriyani Saṁhitā, 63
Mamata Choudhury, 78
Mandukya Upaniṣad, 178
Mantra, 24, 48, 136, 147, 167, 185, 196
Manu Smriti, 40
Maruts, 69, 101, 165, 169, 172, 196
Matsyas, 66, 67, 74, 76, 82, 133
Matsyaya doctrine, 101
Maurer, 165, 188
Maurice Bloomfield, 15
Maurice Phillips, 168
Max Muller, 15, 25, 32, 40, 124, 166, 168, 169, 189
Methodology, 40
Michael Witzel, 16, 37, 66, 119, 136, 138, 155, 158, 185
Michel Danino, 158
Mitra, 31, 112, 127, 165, 167, 170, 171, 175, 189, 198
Moriz Winternitz, 166, 179
Mūjavant, 76
Mujavants, 74
Mundaka Upaniṣad, 178

N

N.C. Bandyopadhaya, 16, 109
Nahusa, 76
Nami Sapya, 87
Narada Smriti, 40
Nasatya, 31

Nasatya (Ásvin), 31
nationalism, 18, 53
Nirukta, 75, 166, 196
Northern Black Polished ware, 145

O

Oldenberg, 81, 129, 189
Origin of Kingship, 99
Other Political Institutions, 107

P

P.V. Kane, 16
Paippalada Samhita, 13
Pakthas, 65, 67, 77
Palagala, 108, 113
Pancajanah, 77
Pañcaviṃśa Brāhmaṇa, 77, 104, 168
Pancavimsa-Brahmana, 13
Panchalas, 41, 50, 71, 82, 87, 114, 133, 138, 139, 140
Panchavimsa, 174
Para Antara, 87, 138
Paravatas, 66
Parikshit, 75, 134
Parishad, 196
Parivṛkti, 113
Parjanya, 196
Parsus, 78
Parusni, 44, 65, 66, 67, 68, 69, 70, 71, 72, 76, 86
Parvata, 77
Patrick Olivelle, 16, 131, 132, 143, 145, 152, 177
Position of Women, 120, 122, 183
Pragiter, 81
Prajapati, 99, 109, 196
Prithvi, 196
Pulindas, 87, 88
Pundras, 88
Pur, 66, 160
Purohita, 17, 61, 105, 108, 111, 113, 114, 136, 140, 196
Puru, 31, 44, 67, 68, 70, 71, 86, 99, 160
Purus, 26, 65, 66, 67, 69, 70, 71, 72, 75, 77, 101, 139, 147
Purusa-Sukta, 124, 198
Pusan, 119, 165, 170, 171, 196

R

R.C. Mozumdar, 16
R.G. Bhandarkar, 16
R.L. Mitra, 175
R.S. Sharma, 16, 116, 119, 138, 158
R.T. H. Griffith, 15, 79
R.T.H. Griffiths, 69
Rainer Stuhrmann, 16, 160
Raja, Rajan, 196
Rajagriha, 144, 152
Rajan, 45, 61, 95, 110
Rajanya, 95, 96, 99, 112, 113, 124
Rajasuya, 99, 100, 105, 113, 114, 134, 151, 174, 196
Raja-suya, 105
Rājasūya, 51, 56, 134
Rashtra, 64, 149, 150, 197
Rastra, 46, 61, 62, 63, 112
Ratha-kara, 60, 108
Rathakaras, 61, 107, 112, 136, 149
Ratnins, 61, 100, 107, 113, 135, 149, 174, 195, 197
Rgveda, 15, 18, 23, 35, 45, 51, 66, 67, 68, 69, 70, 71, 72, 73, 75, 78, 80, 81, 86, 99, 102, 110, 113,

119, 121, 122, 124, 129, 138, 139, 149, 152, 156, 158, 159, 160, 161, 163, 164, 165, 166, 167, 168, 169, 170, 172, 173, 174, 175, 177, 179, 180, 184, 185, 186,188, 189, 190, 191, 193, 195, 197, 198
Ṛgveda, 22, 24, 26, 32, 33, 35, 36, 37, 40, 41, 43, 44, 45, 46, 59, 61, 63, 67, 70, 100, 104, 106, 121, 122, 123, 147, 148, 156, 180, 197
Rig-Vedic, 17, 24, 25, 26, 31, 35, 36, 40, 41, 44, 48, 50, 51, 63, 64, 65, 66, 68, 71, 72, 73, 75, 86, 91, 97, 100, 105, 111, 114, 117, 122, 124, 125, 126, 127, 133, 134, 136, 137, 139, 147, 149, 156, 158, 164, 165, 166, 167, 169, 170, 171, 172, 175, 196, 197
Rnamcaya, 78
Romila Thapar, 26, 54, 60, 118, 148
Roth, 15, 46, 111, 165
royal consecration, 100, 105, 114, 134, 174, 180
Royal Institute of International Affairs, 53
Rta, 24, 25, 95, 127, 197
Rudra, 100, 165, 169, 173, 197
Rusama, 78

S

S.B. Shrotri, 127, 130, 189
S.Radhakrishnan, 176
Saibya, 80
Salvas, 66, 87, 137
Sāmarajya, 134
Sama-Veda, 14, 24, 44, 147, 163, 167, 168, 172, 174, 177, 178, 180, 183, 186, 190, 197, 198
Sambara, 22, 160, 161
Samgrahitr, 61, 108, 113, 197
Sam-grahitṛ, 112
Sam-grama, 110, 112
Saṃhitā, 45, 49, 61, 63, 67, 163, 164, 166, 167, 168, 169, 174
Samhitas, 24, 32, 37, 39, 104, 112, 113, 163, 167, 171, 173, 197
Samiti, 17, 46, 61, 102, 104, 107, 109, 110, 137, 138, 140, 149, 197
Sandilya, 175
Sankhayana-Grhyasutra, 13
Śāṅkhāyanas, 180
Sanskritization, 138, 193
Santucci, 174, 176, 191
Sapta-Sindhu, 21, 23, 25, 27, 32, 35, 36, 41, 86, 87, 93, 114, 147, 155, 156, 159, 167, 195
Sarasvatas, 78, 79
Sarasvati, 21, 36, 44, 66, 68, 69, 70, 71, 72, 74, 76, 77, 78, 79, 86, 139, 156, 158, 159, 160, 161, 184, 187, 197
Sarasvatī, 36, 66, 71, 72
Sarayu, 36, 86, 156
Satapatha Brahmana, 13, 50, 61, 123, 150, 167, 173, 174, 177, 180, 184, 197
Śatpatha Brāhmaṇa, 174
Satrasaha, 87, 137
Satvants, 79
Satyakama Jabala, 175
Savaras, 88
Savitr, 165
Sayana, 15, 183, 189, 191

Schmidts, 67
Second Urbanization, 60, 143, 152
Selection or Election of a King, 99
senani, 61, 136
Senani, 107, 108, 113
Shiva, 165, 183, 195, 197, 198
Shravasti, 144
Sigrus, 79
Simyus, 79
Sir Mortimer Wheeler, 160
Sivas, 65, 67, 80
Smriti, 198
Social Characteristics, 117
Social Contract, 100
Soma, 24, 46, 50, 56, 76, 86, 95, 105, 110, 128, 134, 150, 164, 165, 168, 169, 170, 171, 173, 175, 179, 197, 198
Soma Pavamana, 165
Sovereignty and Raṣṭra – The Vedic View, 55
Sovikarta, 108
spas, 26, 149
Spellman, 101, 115, 192
spy system, 26, 27, 149
Srauta ritual, 49, 136
Srauta Sutra, 13, 74, 179, 180
Sri Chinmoy, 176
Sṛñjaya, 80, 82
Sruti, 39, 198
Stridhana, 123
Sudaksina, 87
Sudäs, 67
Sudhakar Chattopadhyaya, 78
Sudra, 49, 124, 181, 198
Surya, 165, 171, 198
Suta, 108, 113
Sutlej, 20, 27, 66, 156, 197
Sutras, 24, 41, 51, 139, 163, 179, 180
Sutudri, 66
Sva, 96

T

Taittirīya Āraṇyaka, 175
Taittiriya Brahmana, 14, 174, 175, 198
Taittiriya Samhita, 63, 167, 193
Taittiriya- Samhita, 14
Taittiri¯ya Upaniṣad, 177
Taittiriya-Aranyaka, 14
Taksan, 108
Taksa-Rathakarau, 113
the Ganges, 19, 36, 54, 66, 86, 88, 114, 133, 138, 143, 144, 145, 152
The Sabha, 108, 109, 138, 197
Theodore N. Proferes, 28, 56, 63, 190
Tribal Kingdoms, 133
Trtsus, 66, 67, 80, 81, 82
Turvasas, 65, 71, 72, 77, 80, 101, 139

U

U.N. Ghoshal, 16
Uddalka, 175
Udgatr, 168, 174, 198
Udgāṭṛ, 136, 175
Upaniṣads, 24, 25, 34, 39, 45, 51, 131, 145, 175, 177, 179, 198
Upanishad, 50, 76, 81, 82, 99, 109, 122, 134, 140, 168, 175, 177, 178, 179
Upanishads, 24, 41, 45, 51, 66, 99, 133, 163, 164, 173, 174,

175, 176, 177, 178, 179, 180, 186, 190, 195
Upinder Singh, 16
Ushas, 165, 169, 198
Uśīnarani, 81
Usinaras, 66, 80, 81, 82, 133
Uttara Madra, 65
Uttara-Kuru, 133
Uttara-Kurus, 65
Uttara-Madras, 133

V

V.P. Varma, 63, 109
Vahikas, 88
Vairājya, 134
Vaishali, 145, 152
Vaishya, 112, 118, 181, 198
Vaishyagramani, 113
Vaishyas, 120, 132, 152
vaiṣyas, 118
Vaitana Sūtra, 174, 180
Vajapeya, 134
Vajasaneyi Samhita, 167, 174
Vajasaneyi-Samhita, 14
Vamadeva, 36, 69, 70, 73, 86, 164, 170
Vāmadeva, 72, 80
Varna, 17, 123, 125, 126, 152, 169, 194, 198
Varo-Susa man, 123
Varuna, 31, 63, 95, 99, 100, 102, 110, 112, 127, 165, 167, 169, 170, 171, 198
Vasas, 66, 76, 81, 82
Vasishtha, 36, 69, 70, 74, 76, 79, 86, 136, 164
Vasistha, 14, 67, 68, 73, 79, 80, 81, 82, 86, 170, 181, 198
Vasiṣtha, 68, 69, 70, 71, 73, 74, 77, 164
Vasistha- Dharmasutra, 14
Vatsa, 144
Vāvātā, 113
Vayu, 69, 79, 170
Vedas, 15, 16, 24, 32, 34, 39, 40, 41, 43, 45, 95, 117, 125, 150, 152, 163, 164, 168, 169, 172, 173, 175, 180, 190, 195, 196, 197, 198
Vedic canon, 17, 44, 45, 48, 52
Vedic Canon, 49, 194
Vedic grid, 17
Vedic Grid, 67, 83
Vedic King, 101
Vedic Literature, 66, 174, 176, 190, 191
Vedic Polity, 24, 147
Vedic Rāṣṭra, 59
Vedic society, 101, 117, 120, 121, 129, 136, 158
Vidarbha, 133
Videha, 27, 66, 87, 133, 134, 135, 137, 138, 139, 174
Vidhata, 46, 55, 111, 191
Vipas, 66
Vis, 46, 103, 198
Viś, 198, See
Viśaḥ, 47, 199
Visanins, 65, 67, 80, 82
Vishnu, 165, 172, 195, 198
Viśvāmitra, 36, 67, 68, 69, 73, 74, 75, 78, 86, 170
Visvedeva, 170
Visvedevas, 63, 172
Vitasta, 65, 66, 69, 70
Vrcivants, 65, 80, 82
Vrtra, 21, 104, 173
Vṛtra, 21

W

Walter . Fairservis, 158
Walter S. Fairservis, 16
Whitaker, J.L, 22
White Yajur-Veda, 167, 174, 175
Wilhelm Rau, 16, 59, 61, 96, 106, 108, 112, 114, 119, 137, 140, 160
Wilhelm Rau's, 59, 61

Y

Yadus, 26, 65, 66, 67, 68, 72, 77, 101, 147
Yadus-Turvasas, 26, 66, 147
yajna, 125, 127
Yajnavalkya Smriti, 40
Yajur-Veda, 14, 24, 44, 46, 112, 147, 149, 152, 163, 167, 168, 171, 173, 174, 175, 177, 178, 180, 186, 189, 191
Yamuna, 25, 36, 41, 66, 68, 72, 73, 74, 77, 79, 133, 147, 161, 169
Yasuhiro Tsuchiyama, 62
Yaugandhari, 87

Z

Zimmer, 74, 77, 78, 103, 108

www.ingramcontent.com/pod-product-compliance
Lightning Source LLC
Chambersburg PA
CBHW052115300426
44116CB00010B/1670
* 9 7 8 1 6 2 2 7 3 0 3 6 0 *